THE VOICES IN MY

MW00586848

Charles is born into the American Catholic Dream. Father is cruel to be kind ("Charles was good this week. Charles was bad this week."), pitting him against his sister in the battle for affection. Momma, in her native Italian language, calls him *piccolo Gesù* (Little Jesus).

In his personal battle of good versus evil, Charles turns to daydreams. Can he be saved? Seeking redemption requires more than good intentions. It requires luck too, the kind that places the exact right person in the exact right time and place. It requires love that has nothing to do with money and everything to do with finding a soul that has been petrified by lifelong emotional rejection.

A woman to the rescue? Or is the voice of a saint that does the trick? Or maybe it's the voice of young political activist, or is it the voice of the Archangel Metatron?

Little Jesus tells his tale in the second person voice of "You" … just one of the many voices in his head.

Charlie Stella Bibliography

Eddie's World (December 2001, Carroll & Graf)
Jimmy Bench-Press (December 2002, Carroll & Graf)
Charlie Opera (December 2003, Carroll & Graf)
Cheapskates (March 2005, Carroll & Graf)
　Shakedown (June 2006, Pegasus)
Mafiya (January 2008, Pegasus)
Johnny Porno (April 2010, Stark House)
Rough Riders (July 2012, Stark House)
Dogfella: How an Abandoned Dog Named Bruno
　Turned This Mobster's Life Around—A Memoir
　(May 2015, Da Capo Lifelong Books)
Tommy Red (September 2016, Stark House)

The Voices
in My Head:
A FICTIONAL MEMOIR

Charlie Stella

STARK
HOUSE

Stark House Press • Eureka California

THE VOICES IN MY HEAD

Published by Stark House Press
1315 H Street
Eureka, CA 95501
griffinskye3@sbcglobal.net
www.starkhousepress.com

ISBN: 978-1-951473-50-1

Book design by Mark Shepard, shepgraphics.com
Cover illustration by Anthony Caliendo

First Stark House Press Edition: November 2021

Thanks to the following people for their guidance and encouragement with this thing:

This fictional memoir was started more than eight years ago in an MFA class at Southern New Hampshire University. Back then it was my thesis for graduation. It has been sliced and diced, written and re-written, several times since. Confronting one's demons precludes ignoring the demon one becomes. Nor can one avoid the daily prosecution of one's conscience.

This project began with the guidance of Richard Adams Carey, Diane Les Becquet, Merle Drown, and a host of readers, including Gonazalo Baeza, Peter Rizofsky, Don Kirkandall, Ann Cucci-Stella, and especially the one who finally convinced me to send it to my publisher, my cugino, Jason Pierantoni.

This fictional memoir is dedicated to our grandchildren, Evelyn, Eleanor and Luca ... their parents (Charles, Leslie, Dustin and Madalynn) and their Aunt and Uncle (Nicole and Anthony).

And, as always, Dave Gresham, who put the writing needle in my arm some 45 years ago in Minot, North Dakota.

A special thanks to Greg Shepard for his encouragement and support, and the memory of Ed Gorman. Outside of writing some very kind reviews of my novels, I'd never met Ed, nor did he know me except for my crime novels and whacky blog posts. When he learned I was seeking a new publisher back in 2009, when I was close to the crime writing abyss, Ed asked to read *Johnny Porno*, and then suggested Greg Shepard of Stark House Press also take a look-see. Until 2010, Stark House Press had published reprints of classic noir novels. Greg liked *Johnny Porno* enough to take it on as Stark House's first original crime novel. Ed is a legend in the industry and was one of the kindest people in the business. He was also first and foremost a humanitarian. I remain forever in his debt.

Table of Chapters

PART I

*"Beloved, now are we the sons of God, and it doth not yet
appear what we shall be: but we know that, when he shall
appear, we shall be like him; for we shall see him as he is."*

1 John 3:2

In the beginning ...

You arrive at 6:04 a.m. on June 1, 1956, the second child, although
technically you're number three, number two didn't make it, of Speranza
Stephanie Marie and Thomas Rocco Stella. You entered the world
silent, a blue baby, resurrected with a slap. It isn't an easy birth. You
ripped your mother's insides out. She nearly dies from internal
hemorrhaging within two days of the holy event. Her uterus is removed,
sealing your fate as the baby of the family, not to mention the last male
carrying your surname.

What happened inside her womb remains a frustration you can't
express. Your brain was fully developed within three months of
conception. All senses alive and well by six months, but you couldn't and
can't speak, at least not yet. You were an adult trapped in the body of
a developing fetus. Now you're an adult trapped in the body of an infant.
Frustration will fuel your temper over time. It will also fuel cognitive
dissonance and distort a world view often antithetical to the better
angels of your nature.

You saw your sister's mark scratched on the walls of your mother's
womb: Adelaide was here. You saw another name, your brother who
didn't make it, but the name was crossed out: ~~Carmelo was here~~.
Advanced knowledge of the name you'd be getting caused you to try and
remove the scratch from the name, but instead you tore the womb and
were the cause of your mother's internal bleeding. You tell her you're
sorry, but she can't hear you. Nobody can.

You're moved from Manhattan General Hospital on 17th Street and
Second Avenue to your parents' apartment at 112 East 2nd Street, a
fifth-floor, one-bedroom walkup, where they live rent free because your
paternal grandfather, your namesake, Carmelo, owns the building.
Both sets of grandparents and aunts will share split shifts taking care
of the new baby while your mother recovers from her near-death

experience.

The apartment on Second Street has a big kitchen with red wallpaper, and a kitchen set your mother's father bought them as a wedding present when he hit the Italian lottery two days before their big day, or there would've been a card with ten dollars inside, all they could've afforded.

A walled-off bathroom without a sink is off to the right of the kitchen. The bedroom is straight back beyond the bathroom. Showers and baths require a five-floor trek to the first floor apartment where your grandfather Carmelo lives, so sponge baths at the kitchen sink are the preferred method of bathing. The bedroom has windows looking down at a small playground and the backs of the buildings on East 3rd Street. This is 1956 Manhattan, and the streets below are spotted with produce carts and occasional big-ass cars like the Buick Roadmaster, Plymouth Belvedere, Chevrolet Bel Air and Checker Taxis, like the taxi that brought you home.

There's also a windowless, narrow room, first used for storage until your sister was born three years earlier. It's too narrow to share, so your crib is in the master bedroom alongside your parents' bed, causing much angst for your sibling.

Although later in life you'll never remember your parents being happily married, they've already been living in the Second Street apartment for three years. A conversation you hear while they stand over your crib goes like this:

"Thank you for giving me a son, Hope."

"He should be our second."

"You have to forget that."

"I can't forget it."

"Come on, what's dead is dead."

"Please don't say it like that, Tommy."

"What's dead is dead."

Another time, when your mother is cleaning dishes at the kitchen sink, your father leans over and asks her if the kids are asleep.

"Finally, yes," she says. "Thank God."

"Good." He lifts the back of her housedress and grabs her ass.

"Tommy, stop. What are you doing?"

"Let's make another one."

"You're crazy. I can't have another one."

"Come on, let's fuck."

She's crazy in love with this man, your father, so she giggles at first, and then lets him have his way.

Your adult brain thinks: *Why not? They seem happy enough.*

Dibadibadiba: An Age of Innocence ...

"Dibadibadiba," you say.

"No diba now," your mother says. She's been home more than a year since you nearly killed her. She's on the couch with you on her knees facing her. Your sister is taking a nap in her tiny bedroom and your mother is using the alone time to get you to say Momma before you say Dadda. You want your pacifier, what you've come to call Dibadibadibadib.

"Say Ma-ma."

"Dibadibadibadib."

"Come on, Charlie, say it for Mommy."

I can't say it, you're thinking. *Just give me the fucking pacifier.*

"Dibadibadibadib," you say.

"No, not now. Come on, little boy, say it for Mommy. Say Ma-mma. Ma-mma. Come on, little *Gesù*, say Momma. Momma, Little *Gesù*."

"Dibadibadibadib."

You will undergo a few name changes in the apartment on Second Street. Your official name on the birth certificate is Carmelo, but you're called Charlie because your parents fear their son being considered an immigrant. Your mother is an overprotective woman, especially when it comes to her kids, and extra especially when it comes to you. Not only does she treat you as if you were the second coming, she continues to call you her baby *Gesù*, which is Jesus in Italian.

And when she tickles your chin and you smile, it's as if the sun just came out.

"Oh, look at that smile! *Che bello, figlio mio. Come è bello, piccolo Gesù.*"

When your sister is asked if she wants to say hello to her brother, she responds, "That's my brudthy?"

"Yes, he's your brudthy."

"Hi, brudthy."

"Can you say his name? It's Charlie."

"No, he's my brudthy."

"You want to call him brudthy?"

"Yes. He's my brudthy."

"You like your brudthy?"

"I love my brudthy."

Not for long. It's only a matter of time before your addition to the family upsets the applecart at casa Stella. A few months later, during another of your mother's attempts to get you to say the magic word,

Mamma, your sister and father are there and neither is too happy about the attention you're getting.

"Why does she always pick him up?" your sister asks your father.

"Because he's a baby, honey," your mother says. "Mommy did the same thing for you when you cried."

You're sucking on your pacifier, but then it drops from your mouth and you ask for it. "Dibadibadibadibadib."

"Alright, Mommy has it."

As she goes to wash it in the sink, you continue singing the diba song, much to your father's angst.

"What the hell is that anyway? Dibadiba. There something wrong with him?"

"No," your mother says, annoyed at the suggestion. "He's learning how to talk."

"I don't like him," your sister says. "He's always crying."

"Don't say that," your mother says. "He's your brudthy."

"He's a big baby. You're always picking him up."

Your sister turns to your father for support and he winks at her. She sighs and lays her head on his lap.

"She's maybe got a point," he says. "About picking him up all the time."

Your mother ignores the jealous commentary and continues to overcompensate your duress. Your sister and father remain unhappy about it. They cling to one another in a common bond. The enemy of their enemy is their friend.

You may have been born innocent, Little Jesus, but your salad days are over.

The obvious solution is to buy a house where the kids can have their own bedrooms. Fortunately, living rent free has permitted them to save some coin. By year five on Second Street, the five-floor walkup has become too much of a struggle anyway. Toting two chunky kids up and down five flights of stairs a few times a day is no picnic, not to mention your sister is about to start kindergarten. The family eyes a home in the blue collar, Italian-Jewish, community in Brooklyn called Canarsie.

"It's a good neighborhood," Grandpa Carmelo tells them. "Lots of Jews."

It is something you'll notice down the road regarding Grandpa Carmelo. He uses a lot of Yiddish language when he speaks. You often wonder why, but you like the sound of that language and pick it up yourself over time.

Canarsie was an early fishing village until pollution killed off most of the edible catch. Southern Italian immigrants and Jews settled into Canarsie during the 1920s and will remain there until the white flight of the 1980s and 90s. You will live there through the height of the racial tensions of the late 1960s and early 1970s. Canarsie will become, however briefly, what its original *Lenape* language suggested, a fort or fenced-in land, where whites will desperately attempt to keep minorities outside the perimeter. Real estate agencies that sell to blacks will be firebombed. School buses bringing minority children into Canarsie public schools will be met with protestors wielding baseball bats. Race riots, small and big, will break out at the high school all four years you attend, and there will be studies published on the overzealous protectionism of a community determined to remain segregated.

Some more financial help from Grandpa Carmelo allows them to buy a two-family home in the heart of blue-collar Canarsie. It will be home base for the next ten years, where you will be raised amidst the smells of Madaglia D'oro black coffee, onion-based sauce everyone in your family refers to as gravy, and chain-smoked Marlboros. In later years it will be the past you remember best, when your family was still whole, when you were too young and self-absorbed to understand the internal crumbling of its infrastructure.

Money will be tight on your father's lithographer salary, even with the overtime he does on weekends, but they'll make ends meet by cooking pasta five nights a week and not eating meat on Fridays, compliments of the Catholic Church.

Your adult brain does not see into the future, so welcome to the American dream, little Carmelo, and enjoy it while you can.

The Lost Years/The Bunning Rule ...

The lost years for the first Jesus were estimated to be between the ages of 12 and 30. For you, they're closer to your birth and not nearly as long, ages 2-6.

It is when your adult brain begins its relationship with speech. You have the words and can read and pronounce them. Problems arise the few times you do use them, because you draw weird stares from those around you. Like the day you overhear two of your uncles discussing a game pitched the night before by Jim Bunning of the Philadelphia Phillies. Someone left the newspaper open to the sports page on the table while you were making a mess of your oatmeal by eating with your hands instead of the perfectly good spoon on your tray, but the newspaper was close enough for you to read an article about the game Bunning pitched against the Mets. An hour or so later, you're outside on the back porch watching your uncles smoking their cigarettes while they discuss last night's game and try to keep an eye on you.

"They hardly touched Bunning," your Uncle Lou says. "You know how he throws, that sidearm bullshit he uses. Mets couldn't hit him again."

"Sidearm?" Uncle Joe says.

"His throwing arm perpendicular to the ground," you say in forced baby speak.

Both your uncles didn't see you speaking, but they sure heard you. They turn to you wide-eyed, until Uncle Lou turns to Uncle Joe and says, "The fuck he say?"

"I don't know," Uncle Joe says, "but it just scared the shit out of me."

"Say it again, Charlie," Uncle Lou says.

"Dibadiba," you say.

You realize speaking to them was a mistake and immediately clam up. It is the episode that sparks your Bunning rule, an attempt to never speak above your physical appearance again. When it comes to conversations and word usage, at least for now, you're a ringer, Little Gesù, and the last thing adults want, especially real adults, is a little smart-ass making them feel foolish.

This will become a problem moving forward, but especially while you're still locked in a 3, 4, 5 and 6 year old body; the frustrations of having an adult brain locked down, so to speak, feeds your temper, which is already rocketing towards epic and at times warp speed.

Like the time you spy a candy bar on the table but can't reach it from your high chair. A flood of some your father's most often repeated curse words fills your head and then spews from your mouth.

"Damn it" turns to "Goddamn it" turns to "God fucking damn it" turns to "cocksucker!"

The things kids sometimes think … and then say.

Fortunately for you, your mother stepped outside to get the laundry off the line and your father is already out of the house. Your sister heard something but isn't sure what it was. She steps out of her room and looks at you.

"What?" you say.

Her eyes open wide and you realize you shouldn't have spoken.

Soon as she's gone, you think, "Damn it, Charlie," but what you say is, "The fuck is your problem?"

Her head pops out of her room again, except this time she's pissed off. "I'm telling daddy you cursed," she said.

"Dibadiba," you say.

You will be brought up Catholic, so forgiveness is always at the end of a road made rougher by your own doing, even if you're not really Little Jesus. Outside of religious ceremonial obligations, your paternal side of the family wanted nothing to do with the Catholic Church. Your mother's side of the family is another story. Maternal references to the son of God will not only enhance an overzealous imagination, they will squeeze a lifetime of guilt from the core of your soul.

Jesus knows when you say bad words. Jesus cries when you don't listen to your mother. Jesus knows if you don't pray. Jesus knows if you don't wash your hands before dinner, and so on, but Jesus loves you and you have to be a good boy, or Jesus will send you to hell.

Down the road you will question why Jesus would waste his valuable time watching whether or not you washed your hands, but earlier on it is ingrained into your head that He not only sees and hears and knows all, He died to save you and everybody else, so you best not disappoint or piss Him off. The consequence, burning in hell, is some serious shit.

Your maternal grandmother, Nani, will constantly remind you that you must be good or you'll make Jesus cry. Her brother is a priest in Italy, and she probably should've been a nun, but she was your grandmother instead, and she will commend your better behavior with constant references to the Lamb of God. *"Questo è un buon piccolo Gesù. Buono, piccolo Gesù. Bellissimo piccolo Gesù."*

The convergence of Nani, the Catholic Church, and your mother's over protectiveness will have you wondering at an early age whether or not you, little Carmelo, are actually Him, Little Jesus, on a second world tour. Although you won't be turning water into wine anytime soon, nor taking away the sins of the world, your mother is so sure you'll require extra protection and prayer the rest of your life, she invites her parents to move in so there will always be an extra set of attentive, loving eyes to keep you from drinking carpet cleaner, Lysol, and all other household products that might cause irreversible harm.

You're oblivious to your surroundings, but your father is okay with you the first few years. You are, after all, his first and only son. Not to mention the damage you did to your mother's womb to preclude the birth of any future Stella. Reality sinks in with the move to the house, and boy does the worm turn. In fact, it isn't long after the move to Canarsie before he resents the attention his wife and everybody else is giving Little Jesus and not him. The boatloads of emotional warts from his relationship with his father are played out between the two of you, and unfortunately for you, his issues with his father will shape much of his angst with the new kid on the block. Pragmatism will rule, and since you aren't able to perform any miracles, he'll spend much of his and your life reminding you of it.

"You think you're something special, Mister?" he says to you on your fifth birthday, immediately after you drop some of your birthday cake on the living room rug. "You couldn't eat in the kitchen like everybody else?"

He's standing over you in a white V-neck T-shirt and workpants. The smoke from his Marlboro streams from his nose. You focus on the Stella eyebrows that pinch close together right before he frowns. You're afraid to answer; the chance you're going to upset him further precludes your speaking. You shrug instead.

"You don't know?" he says. "Well, you're not."

You swallow hard in anticipation of a slap he often delivers when you least expect it, but that day it's even worse than an unexpected slap. He leaves you standing in limbo. You weren't even worth the effort it would take to make you cry.

Somewhat offsetting the obvious disappointment he feels for his only son is his actual firstborn, your sister, who by now isn't as demanding all fucking day and night. She's also Daddy's little girl, and let's face it, your sister isn't the reason the in-laws have moved in.

You don't remember much from your earliest years, so you can only go by the stories you've been told over and over: You were a happy, chubby-faced baby, who became excited whenever he saw Grandpa Carmelo's 1956 Chrysler New Yorker and yelled: "Poppa car! Poppa car!"

You pronounced the word smoke like the word fuck and caught a smack for it, the first of so many more, the day you were told to ask Poppa car Carmelo if he wanted a smoke, except you forgot the Bunning rule and said, "Poppa want a fuck?"

The crying you do from getting smacked or yelled at is most often put on for the sake of avoiding the weird looks you get when you slip and say something no kid your age should say. Like the time your mother couldn't figure out how to adjust a kitchen cabinet drawer that had derailed. You saw your father fix it the night before, but the draw has come derailed again, and your patience is running thin watching your mother struggle.

"Take the fucking thing out first," you say.

It is exactly what happened the night before when your father took the job from your mother because he too couldn't handle watching her struggle.

"What did you say?" your mother says, her eyes opened wide in terror.

This time Dibadiba isn't going to cut it and you get smacked on the can, because your mother would stab herself before smacking you in the face.

The only way she doesn't tell your father is if you cry long and hard, which is what you do, because adult brain or not, your father can make you see stars when he's pissed off. Your adult brain has already figured out that the last thing he wants to deal with after a long day of working as a lithographer is hearing about his smart-ass son cursing his mother, especially when said son's vocabulary should be a lot more limited.

When he does slap you, your crying won't make a difference. You'll get one in the face and two on the ass, and if you cry too loud or too long, a few more slaps in the same order, face first, then your ass, will follow.

So on your first day of school, when a tiny redhead covered in freckles chases you all over the PS 115 schoolyard while yelling your name and screaming how much she loves you, you restrain the urge to tell her to fuck off already. Bad enough you're already mortified, you're also forced to circle the schoolyard two times before the freckled girl's mother finally stops her. You almost tell the woman to put a leash on her kid, but fortunately you remember the Bunning rule and clam up.

The problem is it happens the same way the next day, and a few of the first, second, and third grade bullies are fed up with your schoolyard celebrity, so you receive your first official ass whipping. The upside to that experience is that after being punched and kicked while on the floor, you never really get hurt. What you get is angry instead, and all that does is fuel the rage you can barely restrain. So when you and one of your tormentors are alone in a school stairway one day, you pin him to the wall, show your teeth, and knee him in the nuts.

You expect a battle the next day, but nothing comes of it. Either he was too humiliated to tell anybody, or he was too afraid you'd go after him again. The result is not only a lesson, it's something your father could be proud of. At least you think so.

Your hope for fatherly approval is strengthened the day your mother is trying to relax while on vacation upstate in Whaley Lake, New York, and you're being a general pain in the ass by not staying in one place longer than it takes to check or see a raise at the card table. Uncle Lou suggests tying a rope around a tree and your waist and they do it. You don't care because you know Mom is just a few feet away and they gave you a piece of orange to eat. Later, when your father arrives, he's incensed at seeing his son tied to a tree, and he tells them you're no dog and he releases you from bondage.

Your adult brain thinks: *Now we're talking.*

But there's a devil on your shoulder, or maybe it's an angel, and it warns you not to get excited, Little Jesus, because he's not done with you yet, boyo. Sometimes persecutions are a lifelong game.

A Jazz Singer ...

At age seven, after watching *The Jazz Singer*, starring Al Jolson, five days in a row on channel nine's *Million Dollar Movie*, you discover you have a knack for imitating voices. You practice Jolson's voice whenever you're alone, and eventually you're overhead by your parents, and you go from performing solo in your room to standing-room only shows in the living room.

You're a hit. Even your father enjoys the shows, especially watching you mimic Al Jolson's melodrama where he goes down on one knee and sings/talks the lyrics to "Mammy".

Mammy. My little mammy.

The sun shines east. The sun shines west. I know where, the sun shines best.

You see your father smile and it makes you want to keep singing. Things are looking up. Your father enjoys it so much he makes you perform it in front of his father, your namesake, and then your paternal cousins. He's so cute, your relatives say, but you're starting to feel the embarrassment of being their entertainment. You wish you had the blackface to wear, the way Jolson did in the movies. At least then you could make believe you're hiding.

In the background to one of your holiday performances your sister is rolling her eyes and the sibling rivalry you're unaware of has begun in earnest.

You, Little Jesus, are in for some payback.

The rivalry is thrust into full throttle when you're forced to perform an Al Jolson rendition of "April Showers". The theatrics that begin after the lyrics *"keep on looking for a bluebird and listening for its song"* brings on the kind of ridicule that can destroy a young boy growing up in Brooklyn. Your sister recognizes the opportunity for what it is and the first of the really nasty names are hurled your way.

Your adult brain hasn't been confronted with the word faggot yet, but you know it's a bad enough word for your father to tell her to stop calling you one, and it is that single recrimination from him that pushes her over the edge. She is the smarter of the family siblings by far. You are a daydreamer by comparison, or why else would you imitate Al Jolson? She goes from calling you names your adult brain is familiar with (*stupid, idiot, sissy, faggot, jerk,* etc.) to following your father's lead and his mastery of the subtle put-down. It is a genetic gift passed from one generation of Stellas to another, perfected by degrees, gleaned with education and sharpened by self-loathing, and in your sister's case, a hatred born of the basest form of parental rejection, when a father becomes disappointed that his daughter isn't as pretty as she is smart. Born chunky, she will remain that way her entire life.

Lay that kind of shit on a young woman and you can almost guarantee she'll take it out on the closest, most vulnerable creature within her reach.

That's you, Little Jesus.

"I told the kids up the block what a faggot you are with your stupid singing," she says.

"Dad makes me do that."

"Yeah, right. And what about your Army soldiers, or throwing that stupid ball against the garage? I heard you talking to yourself out there one day."

Embarrassed she might have heard you broadcasting a World Series game you were pitching in your head, you try to deny it. "What are you talking about?"

"I heard you, so don't lie. Dad's right, you're a daydreamer."

"When did he say that?"

"You better grow up."

It is no surprise some forty-eight years later that her double doses of put-downs last until a few hours before her death, when she finally apologizes through a morphine-addled babbling.

"I'm so charry, sarlie," she tells you hours before she passes.

You're fifty-two at the time of her death, and nowhere Jesus enough to forgive her.

At the end of 1962 your singing days end on a sour note. The Jolson in you cowers. Growing up in Canarsie will require change, and misdirection will be the key to that change. It will come in a few more years, but you will suffer hundreds more humiliations before you learn to punch back.

Not to worry, Little Jesus. Over time you'll be a natural at punching back both verbally and physically.

You adult brain thinks: It must be difficult being a parent, or an older sibling.

Welcome to Calvary ...

"Why'd Santa go downstairs, Mommy?" you ask.

"Maybe he had something big to bring," she says.

"But the tree is up here."

"Just go downstairs," your father says.

It is Christmas Eve, 1963, and your father has created a surprise train board. There are lights and houses and factories, with lights inside the houses and factories. There are streets and lawns and trees and little people and cars populating the village. There is a mountain made of plaster and covered with latex paint, model railroad trees and fake snow. It has two levels of tunnels that the HO-gauge, steam-spewing, Pennsylvania Railroad locomotive will pass through on its route around the train board. It is in the basement you're terrified to enter without an adult, but this Christmas Eve, because Santa was confused and left the goods downstairs instead of under the fake tree in the living room, you're told to go downstairs.

The basement is pitch-black as you take a terrified step at a time until you reach the cold cement floor. The unfinished basement odor is unmistakable: dampness, wood, and something that smells like an overloaded electric outlet about to burn. You try not to look to the right, where the boiler is walled off on the far side of the basement. It is the most terrifying of all the rooms in the house. It is where your father stores most of his tools in an old dresser that stands against the wall two feet to the right of the boiler itself, two feet you never dare navigate without someone standing behind you.

On the stairs you listen for your mother's voice. She says, "Please, Tommy, do it now. He's scared down there."

"In a minute, Hope," he says.

You don't know what's going to happen in one minute, but you're terrified that the Santa Claus you and your sister were forced to take a picture with in Macy's the week before will suddenly jump out and give you a heart attack.

"Tommy!" your mother says.

"Okay, already. Go ahead. Jesus Christ, you're gonna make him a girl someday."

There's a flash of lights and a buzzing sound. You turn away from the stairs and see what seem like hundreds of little lights, but one that is moving. You step back in an attempt to gather it all in. The smell you couldn't identify earlier might be what's in front of you, puffs of smoke moving left to right. Your eyes finally adjust, and then open wide as the realization of the miracle is processed in your Little Jesus brain.

It is a fantasy come true, your own little world. You want to run to it, but your legs aren't working. You're not sure what to do. You hear your mother's footsteps on the stairs behind you and she yells, "Merry Christmas! Look what Santa brought!"

"Holy shit," you say.

"Hey!" your father yells.

"Sorry," you say, but then you see him smiling at your mother and you know he got a kick out your adult brain response to a child's fantasy come true.

It is the greatest moment of your young life, but it isn't going to last very long. Once you're standing in front of the controls, afraid to touch them, your father reminds you it's still his world.

"Just make sure you don't break anything, Mister."

You feel the adrenaline of the moment turn to poison. A lecture follows. You learn this *isn't* a toy. This took *a lot of work*. Those trains *cost money*. Don't ever let him catch you *crashing them*, or *letting your friends play with them, or putting your soldiers on the mountains or anywhere else on the train board*. By the time he's finished, all you want to do is go upstairs to bed. Christmas has gone from great to depressing in the time it took your sister to play one of her new 45 Shangri-Las records.

You will never forget that night, for both good and bad reasons. Not ever. It is the first of many more Calvary moments to come.

You're adult brain wonders why he forsakes you?

Daydream Believer ...

You won't try to hide "'neath the wings of a bluebird as it sings," but you will seek shelter from the storm that is brewing around you. It's still three years from when The Monkeys will record "Daydream Believer", but you'll live the lyrics.

By the start of the fall classic, your adult brain develops a defense mechanism to escape uncomfortable surroundings such as school. You run home to watch the World Series and let your imagination run wild. As soon as the game is over, instead of doing your homework, you're out in the back yard pitching the game all over again.

"Koufax checks the runner on first, grips the ball a little tighter inside his glove, takes the sign, winds up and ... Steeeeerike three, Tresh is out'a there!"

It's the call you make in your Little Jesus head after tossing a sponge ball at the square strike zone box you've drawn on the side of the garage with chalk you've stolen from school. You're an adult inside the noggin, but you're also still a kid and you're determined to take advantage of both sides of the coin. The imaginary pitching mound is a half-step from the rosebush your grandmother planted along the fence. One day you're Sandy Koufax. Another day you're Whitey Ford. The call of the game often leaves your head and is expressed verbally.

"That's five straight strikeouts by Koufax," you say.

When you're not tossing the ball against the garage, there's the lot beyond your backyard that splits 95th and 96th Streets, where trolley tracks had once served the community between the Canarsie train station and the pier on Jamaica Bay. The lot can be a jungle for playing war, or a baseball stadium with a home run fence, because many of the Italian families on the block have fenced off their yards behind their homes to plant vegetables. One of the fences features an advertisement for *Coca-Cola*, and if that doesn't give it a real feel, the flag pole on the opposite side of the lot behind another home serves as a foul pole.

In your Little Jesus imagination, you're able to daydream that lot into whatever you need whenever you need it, baseball stadium or war jungle. Over time your ability to daydream will be diagnosed as Maladaptive, a psychological defense mechanism used to deflect emotional abuse. Over time, it will save you. An epic daydream can last but a few seconds and cover a lifetime.

Your adult brain thinks: *Now I got this*, but then one day your report card needs signing and there's no avoiding handing it over to your mother. You can tell she wants to hide it from your father, but she's too concerned about that F you managed to secure for the second straight semester for bad behavior. Her son's achievement for being a class clown isn't something to ignore.

When your father sees the report card, which aside from the F in behavior, is a bunch of C's and D's, he glares at you and says, "Explain yourself, mister."

You haven't read Philip Roth's *Portnoy's Complaint* yet, but you sure have an inkling of a response floating around your Little Jesus, somewhat overdeveloped, noggin.

"Explain myself, Dad? Okay, here goes: I FUCKING HATE SCHOOL! Hate it like you hate butter. Hate it like you hate fish. Hate it like you apparently hate me. Look, I am the epic daydreamer you'll label me. It's true. I sit there in that fucking classroom and wish I were anywhere else, except maybe a dentist's office. The teacher writes on the blackboard, breaking up sentences, and I'm at Shea Stadium taking batting practice for the Mets. I'm on a battlefield in Europe fighting the Nazis who were defeated some 16, 17, 18 years ago. I'm so out of touch, I don't even know that that war is over yet. America may be sending kids off to die in Vietnam, but to me the enemy is still wearing those obnoxious Nazi helmets and jackboots, and deserving of machine gun fire from my Mattel "Tommy Burst" machine gun. I have no fucking clue what I'm supposed to do in school. What do I care about English grammar? I can

speak the mother tongue well enough for the neighborhood we live in. I
can even give it some flavor, the same flavor I hear you and your friends
spice it up with. Who needs to know what a split infinitive is? Is that
really necessary? Isn't it better I know how to throw sidearm or switch
hit? It's not like I want to teach that bullshit someday. Split infinitives?
Split this!"

Of course none of that comes out of your mouth. Your balls are still way too small to confront your father. You shrug instead, and then comes the slap.

Explain yourself? You'd rather catch that slap and a few dozen more first. In a few years you'll explain it to him in a barrage of insults that would make Al Capone blush (before he killed you), but you still won't know what the fuck a split infinitive is. And guess what? You won't give a shit any more now than you did then. You'll also make a lot more money than him, legally and illegally, so how about he explains *himself*? How about he tells you why and how he fucked up and couldn't pay the freight on the divorce settlement he wrangled out of your all too trusting mother.

And, oh, by the way, guess who picks up the slack for that, you slap happy motherfucker?

Your adult brain rethinks the situation: *Now I got this?*

The Poor Christmas ...

By the time Christmas 1965 rolls around, there isn't much money, not enough for anything near the presents Santa brought last year, and your parents apologize for it. There's a portable record player for your sister and a boxed Civil War soldier set for you. That's it, but you and your sister feel terribly guilty, and you both wish there was something you could do besides telling them it's the best Christmas ever one more time.

Your parents are upstairs having a Christmas drink with their tenant. The two of you are in the living room watching *Miracle on 34th Street* until your sister turns the television off just before your favorite part, when Kris Kringle nails Mr. Sawyer on the noggin with his umbrella.

"Hey!" you say.

She rolls her eyes, looks to the fake Christmas tree, at the empty candy dish on the coffee table, and then sighs dramatically.

"I feel bad for them," she says.

"Me, too," you say.

"I hate to see Daddy like this. I hate when he feels bad."

"Mommy too."

"Daddy more."

You don't understand why she feels that way, but you have noticed your father is more tight-lipped than usual the last few days.

"I'm glad nobody came over this year," you say.

"Yeah, me too," she says. "There's nothing in the house."

"You think we're poor?"

"Feels like it."

Neither of you have a clue what it is to be poor, but this clearly isn't a normal Christmas. There isn't a party atmosphere. No yucky smell of the traditional Sicilian fish dishes, no stacks of wrapped presents under the tree, nor is there much in the way of refreshments. There's the dinner your mother cooked, a few leftover meatballs and pasta. Even the house doesn't smell like Christmas this year. Not having company means there won't be any pastries, and you've both already taken the few peppermint candy canes off the fake tree.

"It's not fair," your sister says. "Daddy works so hard."

There's no doubt about that. Your father is the epitome of a hard working blue collar American. He'll always be a hard-working man, but his motives for doing so will change of a sudden. It's a life change you're adult brain will have to learn to handle, like it or not.

You nod at what your sister said, but you're still more concerned about your mother and the shame she must feel for being what you think is being poor. It's your mother who has to live in the house all day. Your father gets to leave for work or whenever he wants. Your mother is always home.

"I wish they'd find money," you say.

"Me, too," she says, then gets up and inexplicably hugs and kisses you. "Good night, brudthy," she says, "Merry Christmas."

You almost cry for how good she makes you feel.

You eventually crawl down to the foot of the Christmas tree where the field of cotton doubling as snow surrounds the base. The Nativity statue gives you goose bumps. Even inside your living room with the heat cranking, it looks cold on that field of cotton.

You've been fully indoctrinated by the Catholic Church, and although you will one day turn your back on it, for now you live in fear of offending the real Jesus, his Dad, and the Holy Ghost. You've been told they are everywhere and can see everything, and you're paranoid because of it.

You lean your head on the soft cotton and daydream you're in Bethlehem, and you swear you can see a smile on the face of the Jesus statue. You won't question why a Middle Eastern family is white for another 30 years, but it is irrelevant then.

THE VOICES IN MY HEAD

You want to help. You can see the animals surrounding the baby and imagine their breath is keeping him warm the way it happens in Christmas movies. You get close to the statue with the straw and you're sure Jesus is smiling at you. It is an infectious smile you return tenfold because of the sudden relief you experience.

If He's smiling, then everything will be okay. If He's smiling, it's because you and your sister felt guilty and weren't selfish. The real Jesus loves you for not being selfish.

Some 40 years later, you'll read the book, *Zealot*, by Reza Aslan, about the real Jesus. You'll come to realize that not only was the real Jesus a socialist, it's the only reason he was crucified, and that it had nothing to do with taking away the sins of the world.

Back in your living room with your head pressed to the cotton while staring at the statue of the baby Jesus, you don't hear your parents return until they're in the kitchen and your father says, "The hell are you doing, Mister?"

Startled by his voice, you spin onto your side, terrified, eyes opened wide. "Playing with Jesus," you say.

Your father turns to your mother. "See?"

You don't know what he's referring to, but you know it isn't good.

"Get out from under there and go to bed," he says. "It's late now. Play with something else tomorrow, not that stuff under the tree. Understand? We bought that stupid Civil War shit, so use it."

You look to your mother. She's struggling to smile and lessen the blow.

"Understand?" your father says, louder this time.

"Yes," you say.

"Alright, then. Go to bed. Come on, let's go."

You stand up and move toward him for a kiss good night, but he's already stepping inside the bathroom. You kiss your mother instead and she wishes you a Merry Christmas. You go to bed wondering why your father didn't kiss you good night.

It's a heavy thought to consider, especially after the mostly good feelings you've recently had with the old man. Your adult brain thinks: *Maybe he's having a bad day.*

Father Demo Square ...

As tired as you should be the night of the poor Christmas, you aren't sleeping anytime soon. Instead, you remember how your maternal grandparents won't be around for another week. They are the ones who shower the most love on you and your sister, but they are living on the other side of the world with *Zia* Fran in New Jersey. You miss them terribly because you notice how your father isn't half as angry when Grandpa Pete, your favorite, lives with you.

It is simple math even you can compute: *Nonno*, Grandpa Pete, will lie for you. *Nonno* will sneak you coin for candy and ice cream. *Nonno* will take you to Manhattan by train and let you stand in the first car so you can look out the window and stare at the tracks as if you're the engineer. *Nonno* will smile with pride when he speaks Italian to his friends in Greenwich Village where he buys you a slice of brick-oven pizza on Carmen Street. *Nonno* will buy you Manhattan Special soda and let you feed the pigeons breadcrumbs in Father Demo Square, which becomes your favorite place in the city, and where you want your ashes spread, assuming, of course, there isn't a second resurrection.

Nonno will watch wrestling with you and translate what Bruno Sammartino says when he speaks Italian after he's been jumped by one of the bad guys during his interview with Ray Morgan every Saturday morning. *Nonno* will even let you get away with cursing. He'll occasionally threaten to tell your father, but he never will. There will never be any confusion with *Nonno*. He will be your protector. He is love.

So the night of the poor Christmas, while you're missing *Nonno*, you finally fall asleep assured by the first baby Jesus' smile that there will be money for your parents soon, and because of how terrible you felt for them earlier, you make a vow, no matter what, to be a giver and not a taker. You will try to remain this way, although you do fuck it up for a few years, but that night you thank the first baby Jesus as you close your eyes intent to dream of better days to come.

You think this, adult brain and all, because sometimes dreams do come true. You know this from watching *Walt Disney's Wonderful World of Color* every Sunday night. You can even sing it because the last lyrics of the Pinocchio theme song tell you so.

When you wish upon a star
Your dreams come true

That song chokes you up as a kid and continues to do so for the rest of your life.

As it turns out, better times in the form of coin are around the first corner. It's what's around the second corner that you, Little Jesus, never see coming.

Until then, even your adult brain finds relief in the ignorance that is indeed bliss.

Marlboro Man ...

It's silly stuff, especially for an adult brain, but you're in heaven one morning as you play with your WWII soldiers instead of the "stupid Civil War shit" in the living room, and your sister is singing along with the Shangri-Las in front of the mirror in her bedroom, the 45's spinning on her portable Victrola. Sometimes the battles that rage on the rug in your living room keep you safe. There is tension in the house and it's between your mother and father.

That morning your mother is cooking breakfast while your father remains in bed. The house smells of bacon and eggs and pancakes and coffee, but you can't pull yourself away from the battle raging on the living room rug. Your favorite soldiers from the television show, *Combat*, are fighting off an ambush. Sergeant Saunders is trying to save Kirby and Caje, who are dragging a wounded Littlejohn after he was shot in the leg. Your soldiers, though they walk through the valley of the shadow of death, remain brave, heroes one and all.

Doc and Lt. Hanley are pinned down by a German machine gun. The battle has been fierce, with many well done sound effects, and it is close to finished when your mother says, "Let's go before your father wakes up."

"One more minute," you say, with just enough attitude so your father hears it.

"Now, Mister!" he yells.

You rush into the kitchen, eat as fast as you can, then return to the battle a few minutes before your father takes your place at the kitchen table. He appears to be particularly angry about something you can't understand, something you won't understand until you're unhappy with your own life several years down the road. He isn't a breakfast-type of father and only sips his coffee while smoking his Marlboros. Eventually he brings his coffee and cigarettes into the living room. He wants to watch a movie, but much to his angst you've got the floor covered with your soldiers. He tells you to keep it down, but you forget yourself and make war sounds just like the ones on *Combat*, the television show from where you gave your toy soldiers their names.

Rifle shots and their reverbs fill the air.

"Da-dush, da-dush, da-dush."

"Goddamnit!" he yells, and then heads back into the kitchen.

His outburst startles you. You gather your troops and put them back inside the shoebox you store them in. You sit on the couch and watch as your father frowns at the kitchen table as if everything in his world is wrong. He crushes out a cigarette, grinding the ashes over and over until they become a fine dust. You already know the frown, but the crushing of his cigarette ashes becomes his trademark. He does it when he's pissed off, and it will always seem he's pissed off when you're around.

A few minutes later you hear your parents arguing. Apparently the battles you recreate in the living room are fueling an overabundance of daydreaming that your father insists will keep you from growing up. "Life isn't fun and games," he says. "They won't pay him to play with toys."

Your mother tries to defend you by stating and restating your age, but somehow that only upsets your father even more. "He won't be a kid the rest of his life," he says. "He's a world-class daydreamer is what he is."

You can hear his angry tone, but desperate for optimism your adult brain thinks what it wants to think. World-class has to be something good, and it sets you off to daydreaming all over again. You're a celebrity of sorts, a boy able to epic daydream on cue, but then your father says, "It's about time he gets rid of that crap and starts acting like a man."

You're only nine years old, and although you have that adult brain in your noggin, you've no idea how a nine year old can act like a man. Why did he buy you a Civil War soldier set if playing with them was a problem? You're purposely playing with WWII soldiers because he already made a comment about your early interest in the Civil War, what you pronounce "Silver War."

You want to be a man. You want to make him proud. You don't want him to feel disgusted with you, as he obviously feels when he crushes his cigarette ashes into a fine dust over and over, and you're always around when that happens.

Not quite yet, but in another year or so, with the help of your sister, you will bury most of the Civil War soldiers in the backyard in staged funerals for the war dead. It will be one of the better moments between the two of you. You will dig the holes and she will say the prayers, and both of you will make the sign of the cross and say, "Amen" before you cover the dead with dirt. Once the soldiers have been buried, you will never speak of them again. Not speaking of the dead is a Stella family code you're practicing, but will never be able to replicate. Once something was dead, it stayed dead for your father and his father, but not for you, Little Jesus.

Not no way, not no how.

Until your miracle rebirth, resurrections were out of the question, even in discussion form, which is why you won't learn about your uncle Frank until you're an adult, because after he was killed during World War II, his name was never brought up again.

Death will knock on your family's door soon enough. Nani, your mother's mother, will suffer a stroke and die after a six-week coma. It is the first family death you experience and it will rock your world. You will have nightmares placing you alone with your dead grandmother in the funeral parlor on Bleecker Street. You will smell the floral arrangements as if they surround you. The horrible bleeding heart made of red roses will remain in your head forever. They're positioned to the left of her coffin, where Nani, dressed in a hooded religious robe, suddenly sits up in the coffin and turns her head to look at you. Or the other version, when the coffin is in your backyard at the foot of the metal clothesline ladder and the casket opens as you stare at it from the back door of your house. The blood pulsing in your ears becomes her footsteps as she makes her way across the yard. It will be years before the nightmares end, but you will remember them forever.

You will miss Nani terribly, yet also fear her, and it all has to do with guilt. Shortly after you had heard your father say something bad about President Kennedy, you opted to back your father and hope for something terrible to happen to the President.

"*I hope somebody shoots him already,*" is what you say, and when somebody does shoot the President, you believe it has to do with the tit for tat bargain you made with God for your father's hope, and the tradeoff was your grandmother.

Anything for the Marlboro Man, but you never meant it to be Nani.

Your adult brain welcomes you to a life of guilt, Little Jesus.

Choo-Choo Charlie ...

"Don't play with your food, Mister," your father says.

It's a slice of meatloaf you stood up and turned into a wall that German soldiers were hiding behind. You'd cracked off a piece and must have whispered a bomb sound like "Ba-kwah." You're embarrassed at being caught.

"I'm not playing," you say.

Smack!

"Tommy!" your mother says.

"What?"

"Don't hit him like that."

"Mind your business."

"He is my business," she says.

And her retort encourages you. "I don't like meatloaf," you say.
Smack!
"Damn it, Tommy!"
"Don't hit him," your sister says, surprising everyone at the table.
"Don't hit my brother."
It is both an awkward and amazing moment. Your sister coming to your defense, especially to your father, was not to be expected. You're still recovering from the shock of that last smack, it was a hard one, but now there's a different kind of tension at the table, a tension totally foreign to your father. He looks at your sister, then your mother, and finally at you.
"Fine," he says, then gets up and leaves.
"You okay?" your sister asks.
You're still in shock, except now it's from her defense of you. You can't speak. You nod instead. When you look up at your mother, you can see her eyes are wet, and that she's staring at your sister. You wish you knew what the hell was going on, but you don't know. You only know that you love your sister. You can almost hear her say what you loved most as an infant, *"I love my brudthy."*
Half an hour later, you're down in your basement, your head tilted to one side as you lean your face against the train board to watch the Pennsylvania Railroad locomotive exit a tunnel or execute a curve after a switch track. It's as if your eyes are a camera recording the event. You breathe in the fumes of the electric transformer and the oil-smoke puffs coming from the engine. You are fascinated with how real you can make it all seem. You can scale yourself down to HO size and see the locomotive and the train board as a world unto itself. You imagine your family living on the train board amidst the trees and mountains. You imagine everyone getting along.
You become somewhat obsessed with trains. Your adult brain brings the fantasy out of the basement onto the street in the form of riding your bike. You ride around the block over and over, recreating a subway ride like the ones your grandfather takes you on when traveling to and from Greenwich Village in Manhattan. You're the Canarsie line L train heading out of the Rockaway Parkway station. You focus on the sidewalk in front of you as you pedal up to speed. The gaps in the sidewalk are the joints in the rails as the bike's tires roll over them and hammer home the steady beat the same as a real train. You need to stay within the rails as your bike makes its way around the block. First is the long stretch of 95th Street before a left turn at Avenue N, then a short ride before another left on 96th Street, and the last long stretch before the next Left on Avenue M. Round and round you go.

THE VOICES IN MY HEAD

You think like an engineer and slow down when making the sharp curves, and speed up again on the long stretches of straight track. You are lost in your world of trains. It is yet another escape valve Little Jesus has epic daydreamed to avoid what has become an uncomfortable world, like getting slapped at dinner for playing with your food.

And when some marital discord becomes apparent, even you, Little Jesus, can't help but notice it.

"Where are you going now?" your mother asks your father.

"I don't know. What do you care? You're gonna play cards again anyway."

"You can play with us for a change."

"I'd rather shoot myself."

"I can call the game off, if you want to do something together."

"No, you play. I'll go out. I won't be late."

Your mother steps closer to him and sniffs his cologne. "English Leather?"

"Don't break them, Hope. I'll see you later."

That night you notice your mother is watching the time. She even ends the game earlier than usual, then waits up until your father comes home. The next morning you hear them arguing behind closed doors, and when your father uses the kitchen telephone, your mother goes up on her toes to watch the numbers he dials. You're not sure why, but you know it's sneaky, and you wish to hell she wouldn't do it.

And when she does, you grab your bike again and escape what makes you uncomfortable to witness. You're back on your bike rounding the block over and over.

If it's one thing your adult brain has figured out, Little Jesus, it's how to daydream your way out of a shit situation.

The Sunshine State ...

You're ten years old, so Vietnam is just an annoyance on the evening news you wish you didn't have to watch. You'll miss getting your legs blown off or killed by a single year after the draft officially ends in 1973. Before the summer of 1966 is over, your father takes the family to Miami, Florida, on vacation instead of buying a pool. It was the choice he gave you and your sister, a pool or Florida.

You're psyched. You don't know anybody in your neighborhood that has been on a jet. You've seen them flying overhead on their approaches to and departures from JFK, but that's as close as you've ever been to one until you're Miami bound.

Day one at the Eden Rock hotel your mother gets serious sunstroke and is bedridden for the rest of the week. This gives your father a green light to go out each night and try to nail as many women as he can within the next six days. You're adult brain doesn't actually know that yet, but it wasn't hard to figure out soon thereafter.

Fortunately for your father, a cousin of his is currently living in Miami on other people's money. Later in life you're told his cousin was bipolar with manic delusions of grandeur, but because his brother was the president of a bank back in New Jersey, he was able to live the life of a playboy until he pissed up the wrong tree and ran afoul of the Mob, which caused his banker brother to embezzle funds to keep the dreamer alive. That week the cousins spend their nights chasing local Miami tail. Your father will take you and your sister to a few of the dopey tourist attractions during the day, but come evening, he and his cousin are playboys after dark.

The first of the daytime attractions is an aquarium with a long canal in which the sharks are fed. People line up all along the fiberglass fence to observe the frenzy. Your father puts you up on his shoulders to better see the monsters tearing at the chunks of fish left dangling from ropes. It is a bloody, frightening scene as the sharks bite and shake their heads back and forth until the semi-circle of meat is ripped from the fish they're eating. Then, as your father steps nearer to the fence, a thought crosses your mind and you begin to panic.

Is my father about to drop me into the canal?

Can a father really forsake a son this way? Can he throw you to the sharks? Is this an Abraham-like test for him? Is it an Isaac-like one for you? Will a voice suddenly appear from the blue stating: *"Stop! Do not hurt your son. You have proven your faith and shown how much you love Me by willing to sacrifice your son for Me. Therefore, I shall bless you and your family, and through you, I shall bless all the nations on earth."*

It was a story from religious instruction that troubled you deeply. Upon first hearing it, you had many questions no one answered. They all told you that you have to have faith. Upon hearing that God also provided a lamb for the sacrifice, even after scaring the shit out of both Abraham and his son, you thought, *"What a mean bastard!"*

Fortunately, you're not dropped into the shark canal. You're still in one piece when a stranger has to pry you off your father's shoulders.

"What's wrong with you?" your father asks.

You're still too upset to answer, so your sister answers for you.

"He was afraid," she says, once again defending and shocking you at the same instant.

Your father ignores her and asks you why you didn't take his hand.

"He was afraid," she repeats, louder this time, and it works. Your father notices other people are watching, and he becomes much more pleasant. He smiles before he tussles your hair.

Later, while the three of you are eating lunch at one of the aquarium cafeterias, your father and a woman are trading smiles. Your sister notices first and says, "Who's she?"

"What?" your father says.

"Who's she?" your sister asks again.

"Nobody," he says, then takes a dollar bill from his wallet and tells her to go get an ice cream pop for "you and your brother."

After your sister heads to the ice cream kiosk, your father turns to you and says, "She was a pretty one, huh?"

It's an awkward moment. You feel disloyal for agreeing. Your mother is back in the hotel room sick with sunstroke, and you're pretty sure your father isn't supposed to say other women are pretty.

You see the other woman offer one last smile before she gathers two kids and heads for one of the outdoor exhibits. Your father is watching her walk away.

"Dad?" you say.

"What?" he says without looking at you.

"When are we going back to the hotel?"

"Would you look at the ass on that?" he says.

"Her ass?"

He looks at you all confused. "Huh? Oh. What about the hotel?"

"When are we—"

"Soon enough. Don't be a pain."

And just like that, you feel as if you've ruined everything all over again.

Back in the room you can't help but notice how your mother seems stressed come the morning. Your father is sleeping in late when she orders breakfast for you and your sister. You see her going through his dirty clothes while he's still sleeping. You're not sure what she's looking for, but then she goes through his wallet and you assume it has to do with money.

You're in your twenties when you learn how your mother never suspected your father of cheating until the money started rolling in from the swag in the basement. Once there was cash, he was chasing women at every opportunity. Your mother will claim he was never involved beyond lustful conquests, including the woman whose name she learned was Sheila (*"You think I don't know you have a girlfriend? You think I don't know who it is?"*), because your father was cocky enough to shit close to where he ate.

It isn't until he's moving Chivas Regal for a wiseguy when he falls for somebody the way it happens when families turn to shit, but that's not for another few years. Back in Florida, the last few days are spent around the pool. Even after your father forces you to learn how to swim, you will not go back into the water for the rest of the week, not in the ocean or in any of the hotel pools. Sharks will haunt your dreams the rest of your life, and it doesn't help any a few years later when you go to the movies to see *Jaws*.

In the end, your family vacation in the Sunshine State ends as one big bust. Outside of an Eastern Airlines pin in the shape of angel wings one of the stewardesses gives you on the return flight to JFK, there's nothing good you can remember. On that return flight to New York you're sitting in a window seat alongside your father. Your mother and sister are directly ahead of you. The stewardess is another pretty lady, and after she puts the pin on your shirt, you see her smile at your father after he winks at her.

He sees you were watching, and he winks at you too, and you think it's the greatest thing in the world that your father winked at you. Who cares about Florida? Maybe he does like you.

And there it is, proof positive how easily adult brains can be manipulated and/or fucked with.

No soldier, you ...

It's a bright summer day. The smell of a fresh cut lawn somewhere on 96th Street lingers as day-dreaming consumes you. Will your parents let you have a fish tank? If they do, you'll want to have the black shipwreck model you've seen in the pet store on the bottom of a tank jammed into blue-green gravel. Angelfish, Nanofish, Frogfish, Butterflyfish, Gobies, Eels and other species of tropical fish swim in and out of the wreck the way you imagine they'd do in the ocean. Your adult brain creates documentaries about how the ship was sunk, either a casualty of war or some raging storm. The films run through your mind as the imaginary aquarium your parents haven't permitted yet is construed somewhere in your noggin, and because you're self-absorbed, you don't notice what's going on just ahead of you until you're almost on top of it.

One block from the pet store you finally notice the struggle going on between a younger kid from your block and a slightly older black kid. Joe Fanello is holding fast to his bicycle by the seat and rear wheel, the black kid has the handle bars and is pulling hard.

"Let go!" the black kid says.

"You let go!" Joe yells.

The black kid clenches his teeth and yanks hard. "Let go!"

Joe is starting to lose his grip and yells for help.

A black kid in Canarsie outside of the Seaview projects isn't normal. Although you don't understand racial dividing lines yet, you've never seen a black kid anywhere near where you live.

"Gimme the bike!" the black kid yells.

"Help!" Joe yells.

An older man wearing a white T-shirt steps out of his house and yells at the black kid. "Hey, get the hell out of here!"

The black kid looks up, sees the man at the exact same time Joe sees you, except the man is coming down the stoop and you're standing there frozen with fear. The black kid lets go and runs toward Rockaway Parkway. Joe thanks the man, gives you a look of disdain, hops on his bike and pedals back toward home.

No red badge of courage for you. There was no dark in which to hide your cowardice. The struggle for the bike took place in the clear brightness of a sunny summer day. You were seen and so you cannot deny. You head back home in shame you've never experienced before, wishing you'd never stepped outside your house.

Freezing that day triggers a craving for a purple heart of redemption, a need for a do-over that will consume you. Freezing that day will launch you into fights and other crazy shit for most of the rest of your life, turning almost everything into challenges, both real and imaginary. Pride becomes something your adult brain has little to no control over and it will haunt you for a long time to come.

At dinner the same night your sister is no longer protecting you. She brings up the episode as soon as your father sits at the table.

"Joe up the block almost had his bike robbed today and he didn't do anything," she's pointing at you when she says it.

"What are you talking about?" your mother asks.

"On Avenue N. Some kid tried to steal Joe's bike and Charlie saw it and didn't help."

"That true, Mister?" your father asks.

Shamed into silence, you resort to a shrug, and can see your father's frown without looking. You turn and see your sister is smiling. You feel rage. Rage for her and yourself.

Your father crushes the ashes of another Marlboro, frowns so you can see it, says he'll eat later, and then leaves the table.

A few days later, in a feeble attempt to regain some of your lost pride, you start your first official fight. Sean Ryan, one of a bunch of Ryan children living in a house on the same street as you, is a year older. Sean is good with his hands and has some moves for a fat kid, and he pins you before you know what happened. He's sitting on your chest and has your arms pinned beneath his knees. You're fair game, but Sean doesn't light you up. Instead, he looks down at you, more bored than angry. You look up at him, still expecting to get popped, but he lets you up and that's the end of it.

The fight occurred on Avenue N, across the street from Sean's house, but word spreads quickly enough for your sister to hear of it and report the incident over dinner again, and again your father leaves the table. He's ashamed of you.

You're ashamed of yourself.

A week or so later there's a return match over a Spalding rubber ball Sean finds in the street in front of your house, but you claim it's yours, and it's not. Still determined to redeem yourself, you issue a loud challenge, and just before the pushing begins, you notice your father standing in the doorway. Your chest swells with newfound bravado as you quickly put Sean in a headlock just like Bruno Sammartino does to the bad guys on the Saturday morning wrestling shows. A moment later your father turns his back and shuts the front door, and your bravado leaves as fast as it surged. Down you go. Once again Sean sits on your chest. Once again he takes pity on your pathetic ass and doesn't batter your face. He looks down at you until you signal for him to get off.

There's no need for your sister to report this one. That night your father doesn't even stay home for dinner. You go to bed early but can't sleep for trying to figure out what happened, how you were in command one second and on your back the next.

No soldier, you, Little Jesus. Not yet, but you know you need to redeem yourself soon, and with your fists, because your adult brain hasn't figured out how to do your fighting for you.

Not yet.

Sex Education 101 ...

Before you launch yourself into fights for the sake of Purple Heart redemption, you do your best not to leave the safety of your backyard where you can make believe you're one of the hero WWII toy soldiers attacking Nazi machine gun nests in rosebushes once planted by Nani. One day when you're playing with your WWII Army soldiers you imagine yourself to be the figure holding the Thompson .45 machine gun, Sergeant Saunders from *Combat*. The set is complete with Germans (gray), Japanese (yellow), British (blue) and American (green) figures, all in various battle poses. You're creating a battlefield on the edge of the grass close to your grandmother's rosebush, where the grass ends and the dirt begins is a trench for the Americans to assault. You're just beginning the battle when Mark Santo yells down to you to from his bedroom window in the apartment building next door to your house. He's sixteen years old, already in high school, but he's played catch with you a few times out in the street. He's even showed you how to field ground balls and how to grip a bat.

He tells you to come upstairs. He has army soldiers from when he was young he wants to show you. You're more impressed with him asking you upstairs than you are about the soldiers. Mark is someone most of the kids your age look up to because he's a good baseball player and he's in high school. Most of the parents on your block say he's smart, because he goes to Brooklyn Tech High School, one of the better high schools.

You've never been inside the apartment building next to your house, a brick three-family with a narrow driveway. Inside the front door is a vestibule with a glass door at the top of four marble steps. You can see the stairway from behind the glass door. You reach for the doorknob and a buzzer sounds. You take the stairs to the second, then third floor. Mark is waiting for you just inside the apartment; he's holding the door open.

Once inside you notice how clean the apartment is—immaculately clean. There is a smell you can't identify, but it reminds you of church. Incense maybe? Your hands and clothes are still dirty from setting the soldier figures in the dirt under the rosebush. You stand very still while Mark explains how he has some toys he needs to get rid of because they take up too much room. He says he might give you his soldiers, the ones he's not saving for his own kid someday.

You're very shy and are afraid to ask any questions or say the wrong thing. You're also afraid to touch anything for fear of getting it dirty. You've never been in someone else's apartment or house without their parents. Mark's parents both work. His father is a construction worker. His mother works part-time at the church rectory. Mark has the run of the apartment to himself on days when his mother works, at least from the time he gets home from school until she gets home from the rectory.

Mark's room is as neat as the rest of the apartment. Nothing is out of place. There are model airplanes hanging on strings from the ceiling and model warships on the window sills. There are baseball cards glued into picture frames hanging on the walls. His room is like a museum and you can't help but stare at everything.

He takes out a brown paper A&P grocery bag filled with army soldiers from a trunk near his desk. He says he hasn't played with them in a long time and you can probably have them once he decides which ones he wants to keep. Your eyes get big. There are tanks and jeeps and other trucks in the bag, plus what looks to be at least one hundred soldiers. He has everything you have, plus ten times more. He even has Nazi artillery with swastikas on each tank and truck. You're already dreaming of setting up battlefields in your living room and playing out the war movies you've watched with your father on television.

Mark says, "Go ahead and set them up. I'll be right back."

You're still uncomfortable in this neatest of apartments. Your house isn't half as clean. There's always a mess of some kind and there are always people around. Your family isn't big, but they're always there. If not your parents, sister or grandparents, friends of your mother often stop in and spend an hour or two having coffee and cake. Every Friday and Saturday night there's a card game in the basement, six of your mother's friends playing through the night into the early morning. It seems you're never alone.

Your room is nothing like Mark's room. You cheat when you put together models and never use all the pieces. Then when you play with the models you always break them. Even when you're punished and told to clean your room, it never looks half as neat as Mark's room.

You set the soldiers up and are into the battle you've created before you know it. You make war sounds and can see the explosions of battle in your head. You mimic the soldiers' pain like an actor shot in a war movie. You grimace and arch your back when one of the soldiers is bayoneted. Some American soldiers are killed from a German artillery barrage, the same way you'll one day learn your father's brother was killed in the Ardennes forest during the Battle of the Bulge. You're moving a Nazi tank across the battlefield when Mark asks if you want something to drink.

You turn around and are confused at what you see. Mark is standing in the bedroom doorway in his underwear. He holds a glass of milk in one hand. His other hand is inside the front of his underwear. There is a bulge in his underwear. You try not to stare.

"We have chocolate chips and Oreos, if you want," he says.

You follow him to the kitchen, but you don't ask him why he took his pants off. You don't ask about the bulge in his underwear either. You take a chocolate chip instead while he pours you a glass of milk. You notice his right hand is back inside his underwear. As soon as you finish eating one cookie, he pulls down the front of his underwear and says, "Ever see one this big?"

He's smiling, so you smile. You're still too shy and naïve to know what's going on. You know what he's doing is bad, but there's nobody there for either of you to get into trouble. And it's not like you're doing it.

"Have you?" he says.

You giggle and say, "No."

"Not even your Dad's?"

"I don't think so. I don't think I saw his."

"You can make it bigger. Yours, I mean."

You're embarrassed and giggle again, more nervously this time.

"I mean it," he says. "You can make yours bigger. I'll show you. Watch, take it out."

Your adult brain is figuring shit out now, but it has yet to be confronted with sex, so you're more curious than you are scared. What's the big deal anyway? Who will ever know?

Your visits with Mark continue over the next few weeks. You don't notice they are on the same two days of the week, days when his mother works and no one else is home. Mark teaches you how to make yourself feel good. He teaches you some other things that you're not comfortable with and although he tries to make you do them, you tell him, "No."

Then one day he gives you a dollar and tells you that putting his thing in your mouth is the same as putting your thumb in your mouth, no big deal. He says he'll give you his bag of soldiers if you just give it a try. He says, "Watch," then gets down on his knees and says, "It's no big deal. It just feels good."

He puts you in his mouth. His head goes back and forth a few times before he stops and says, "See? No big deal."

He gives you another dollar and you do what he says. He will give you more money the next few times you're alone with him in the apartment, but he forgets about the soldiers and you're still too shy to ask.

He reminds you each time before you go home not to say anything to anybody because you're not supposed to make yourself feel good until you're his age or older. He tells you that somebody at his school taught him, one of the teachers, and they made him swear an oath of secrecy, and that's what everybody has to do when they get older. He tells you to make sure when you make yourself feel good it's only in the bathroom with the door locked, and never do it in the bedroom, because you will stain your bed and your mother will know what you're doing.

"Tell them you're sick if they ask why you're in the bathroom so much," he says. "Tell them you don't feel good."

You do exactly as he says when your mother asks what you're doing in the bathroom all day and night. You tell her you don't feel good.

One day you hear your mother talking about Mark's parents. Someone told her they are moving. You forget yourself and mention Mark's parents have the cleanest apartment you've ever seen. Your mother asks how you know that and you tell her about going up to play with Mark's soldiers, and that he might even give them to you. You still believe he will give them to you, especially since your mother said she heard his family is moving.

Her eyebrows furrow and she wants to know why a sixteen-year-old is playing with a ten-year-old. You become nervous when she asks you more questions, but you don't tell her the secret. You ask if you can go outside and ride your bike and she frowns and says, "Okay, but I don't want you going up there anymore or I'll tell your father."

The thought of your father interrogating you about Mark terrifies you. Your adult brain has clearly discerned what you've been doing is wrong, and it is confirmed by Mark's continually swearing you to secrecy. If your father finds out, you will add to the disappointments you've already compiled in his life. It is bad enough Jesus already knows and is probably crying every time you visit that apartment or step into your bathroom. What if Jesus lets your father find out? What then?

The risk is too great. The next time you see Mark it's on the corner of 95th Street and Avenue M, just up the block from where you both live. You mention that you can't go upstairs anymore and Mark gets defensive and is angry.

"What are you talking about?" he says.

"Someone told my Mom they saw me going into your building."

He squints as he leans into you. "What did you say?"

"Nothing. I swear. She just said you're too old for me."

Mark looks up in the direction of your house and then back at you.

"I swear," you say again. "I didn't say anything. Ellen next door must've seen me going in the front door and told my mother. I told her you were showing me your soldiers and she said she didn't like that your mother wasn't home. Then she said you're too old for me and that I can't go up anymore."

Mark isn't looking at you when he says, "Okay." He crosses the street and leaves you on the corner without saying goodbye.

A few weeks later you see Mark in the street again and his right arm is in a cast. You ask him what happened to his arm and he tells you that he broke it playing softball. You ask him how it happened, but he says he can't talk now, he has something to do and he runs home.

The next day you're taken to stay with your cousins on Long Island while your parents go on vacation and try to save their marriage.

When you come back the first thing you see is Mr. Gallo, the man who owns the building Mark lives in, scrubbing something off the front steps. You look closer and can make out the following letters:

PERVERT LIVES UPSTAIRS.

Your adult brain sends you into your house to look the word PERVERT up in the dictionary. You're not sure what "alter something from its original course" means exactly, but you know it can't be good.

Later the same day you learn that Mark's family has moved. Your mother and father are talking about it over dinner. It doesn't sound as if your parents liked Mark's parents very much, something about them acting superior to everybody.

Within a few days you forget about Mark and his family. You forget about all the neat stuff in his room and the fact he never gave you the soldiers he'd promised. Most of all you forget all the other things he did to and with you.

Ten years will pass before you see Mark again. When you do it is on the L train, during the subway rush hour leaving Manhattan. You see him at the opposite end of the car. There's a thick crowd of passengers between the two of you. He is wearing a suit and tie. You are wearing your window-cleaning uniform. You haven't thought of him much, except when all the stories about pedophiles in the church were covered in the news. From that point on, every so often you thought about Mark and what had happened in his room.

You've since wondered if he was a pedophile in the making all those years ago. Is he one now? Has he changed? Is he married? Does he have kids? Does he abuse his kids? Does he abuse other kids? You can't be sure because none of that happened to you. You're not even sure if what he did to you qualifies as pedophilia. Your adult brain has developed beyond your adult years and there's nothing much you'll ever be sure about again.

You want to ask him a few questions, but you're afraid of hating yourself for it. You want to know why his parents moved so suddenly. You want to know why his arm was broken that time right before his family moved. You want to know if his father was a pedophile. You want to know about his mother as well. Did she know what was going on?

You've yet to tell anyone what happened when you were visiting Mark in his parents' apartment. It is something you've buried? You don't know if you've done that consciously or if something triggered your lack of recall. You wonder if it is embarrassment. The more time that has passed, the less you understand.

You are staring at him too long to remain in control. You're thinking back to the time when he told you how putting his penis in your mouth was like sucking a thumb, no big deal. You're thinking about how he used you, how he tricked you into going upstairs into his room and how he fondled you and then paid you a dollar to let him abuse you.

Your adult brain isn't functioning the way you know it should. Was it really bad? You aren't a pervert or a pedophile. Maybe it was just what happens to kids, or at least some kids. Maybe it's part of growing up.

Still, you have an urge to confront him.

Why? Were you really abused? Was it really pedophilia?

You don't know why, but your hands are clenched into fists. When you finally make eye contact, you can see his face blanch. He's nervous. He begins to fidget and turn away from you. Is it shame? Does he know what happened so long ago was wrong? Is he afraid of a confrontation?

Seeing Mark as a victim of fear is empowering. You continue staring, and he can only glance back, then quickly look away again. He looks down at the floor and then up at an advertisement. Is he making believe he's reading? Is he trying to fool you?

He's either embarrassed or a chicken-shit, but when he glances your way again and you make eye contact a second time, he turns his back to you. It makes you furious that he's turned his back. You lean forward and have to excuse yourself for bumping into another passenger. You're so angry you don't realize the train is slowing down as it pulls into another station. You begin to wade through the crowd of passengers, but there are too many people. Everyone sways as the squeal of metal against metal fills the car, and the train comes to an abrupt stop.

It's the fact he won't look at you that pisses you off.

You call his name as the doors open, but he doesn't respond. He hurries off the train instead. By the time you make it to where he was standing, the doors have closed, and the train is moving again. You try to find him on the platform, but he's gone. You missed your chance.

It doesn't take long, not long at all, before your adult brain returns to normal and you feel relief for missing your chance. Maybe you never wanted to know what any of it was about.

Sing, Sing, Sing ...

At age eleven, music reenters your Little Jesus life. Your mother doesn't like Buddy Rich because he's ugly. Your father doesn't like him because he's a braggart, and neither has a clue who Max Roach is, so when you follow a friend's lead and take drum lessons, you're given a new nickname—Gene Krupa.

Your drum teacher lives on Avenue N between 96th Street and

Rockaway Parkway, literally across the street from where you proved yourself a coward less than a year ago. The same spot is just half a block from the Bamboo Lounge made famous in the gangster flick, *Goodfellas*.

Your drum teacher has a set of aquamarine sparkle Premier drums he keeps in what must be a tiny second or third bedroom on the second floor of his one-family house. The room has its own fragrance, the same as in the music store around the corner on Rockaway Parkway, especially if you stand near the music books.

Your drum teacher's cymbals are big and worn from playing. So are the drumheads, which impresses you all the more, because you know this guy is a real drummer. It doesn't take him long to figure out you're a natural with a pair of sticks. You adapt to the bass and hi-hat almost instantly, and within a few lessons he's got you playing basic rock-n-roll beats with simple drum fills to "96 Tears" by Question Mark & the Mysterians, "Time Won't Let Me" by the Outsiders and "Apples, Peaches, Pumpkin Pie" by Jay and the Techniques. A month later, he's got you playing an off-beat tune like "Mickey's Monkey" by Smokey Robinson and the Miracles. The coup de grâce is when you can double-pump your eighth notes on bass to "Devil in a Blue Dress" by Mitch Ryder and the Detroit Wheels.

You enjoy practicing rudiments but really don't need to read music to play drums. Once you learn you can play along to records, you have little use for a drum book you will come to love later in life. After a few months of lessons, your teacher convinces your father to rent a drum kit from the music store on Rockaway Parkway. Little Jesus has found a new talent and this time even his father can see the progress. Your parents follow through and you're the proud renter of a blue sparkle, 4-piece Stewart drum kit with a mounted tom-tom and ride cymbal, a set your parents will purchase for one hundred dollars at the end of the yearlong lease. You can't play them enough. They have replaced your soldiers, toy trains, and bike. Your basement becomes Madison Square Garden. You rehearse walking down the stairs, drumsticks in hand, as if a camera is following your every step. You sit behind the kit on your drum throne, turn on the stereo, and set the needle on a record.

R&B captures your musical ear, but in the late 1960s, when some of the rock groups reinvent blues tunes you've never heard before, your music making energy refocuses. The three piece super group, Cream, is the band you will follow. Their ability to jam with improvisational skill is what you long to do some day. On nights in the near future, when you head down the basement to perform, you're on stage with Eric Clapton and Jack Bruce. As much as you admire Ginger Baker, you're his substitute for the evening and imagine that announcement to the fans at the start of the concert.

Your adult brain loves this shit. Nothing can touch you while you're in the world you imagine.

Your love of music blossoms even more the day you hear the Benny Goodman band's "Sing, Sing, Sing" on the radio. The opening drum beat catches your ear. When you learn that it's Gene Krupa on the skins, you take pride in the nickname and make a point of learning how to pound out the same beat. Things are going pretty good for little Gene Krupa/Little Jesus.

The Stella family has turned that first corner and there's money awaiting them. Your basement Madison Square Garden will soon be displaced. The American dream is about to flourish as the pursuit of happiness takes the form of mean green.

"Hey, Gene Krupa," your father yells to you one day. "Move those drums out of the way."

The Store ...

A man you were told to call Uncle Al brought the merchandise every Saturday morning. He was a curly-haired man with dark eyes. Your mother used to make him a fresh pot of coffee as soon as he arrived and served it to him as soon as he was finished unloading the booty. He often rubbed your head and asked if you were going to be the next Mickey Mantle, forgetting sometimes for weeks at a time he'd asked the same thing the week before. You told him you were a Mets fan and that you liked Joe Christopher. He said, "Who's Joe Christopher? Stick with the Yankees, kid. They're the ones with the *gelt*."

You notice how Uncle Al is always in a rush and that he occasionally puts in a bet with your mother, who you will later learn, was taking small action for a local bookmaker friend of her connected first cousin.

In the meantime your basement is converted into a store with swag hot off the Brooklyn docks. There are pillowcases, bed sheets, table linens, underwear, panties, bras, nightgowns, housedresses, shorts, t-shirts, polo shirts, pants, dungarees, socks, windbreakers, hats, slippers, cheap perfumes, radios, fans, razors, shaving cream, toilet paper, towels, cigarettes, lighters, and so on—the stuff that falls off the backs of trucks.

Last summer your father was selling fireworks, and you were told to never say anything about it to anyone because he could be arrested. Now that the stakes have been upped even higher, your father sits you down in the basement for one of life's lessons.

THE VOICES IN MY HEAD

THE VOICES IN MY HEAD

"This is serious business, Mister. You never tell anyone about this stuff. Not ever. Understand?"

You nod.

"Let me hear you say it? You understand, yes or no?"

"Yes."

"This is nothing to discuss with your friends or anybody else. Not ever. I can get arrested. And the people who we get this stuff from, they won't like that."

"Uncle Al?"

"I'm not talking about Uncle Al. He's a nobody. The people behind Uncle Al, who he gets this stuff from, they're dangerous."

You have no idea he's talking about your mother's first cousin, but you go from feeling nervous to absolute fear for your father's life.

"If anybody ever asks you something about the basement, what goes on down here, if they ask if there's a store down here or anything else, you tell them no. You don't know what they're talking about. It's where you practice your drums. That's all the basement is, where you practice your drums. *Capisce*."

"Okay."

"Remember, if anybody asks you about a store, you'll tell them you don't know what they're talking about."

He points to your drums. "And I want people to hear those when they pass this house. You practice them every day. Take them out to play, and then put them back out of the way."

It isn't hard for your adult brain to figure this shit out. Your Mom and Dad are doing something illegal.

Lots of customers come to the basement from word of mouth, and there are lots of big mouths in the neighborhood. Soon the basement is flooded with shoppers looking to save coin. You even recognize a few of the parents of your schoolmates. Some make believe they don't know you, others nod hello.

It'll be a while before the stores on Avenue L learn about their illegal competition, but by then some of the local police are more than happy to look the other way for a free shopping spree of their own. The basement on 95th Street has become a discount paradise.

When you're asked about the store in the basement, you respond like a soldier, "What store? I play my drums down there."

It isn't hard to notice how your parents are suddenly flush with extra cash. Even you notice the extra money from the all-night card games you mother plays on weekends, because mornings after you crawl around on all fours under the table and find the dropped coinage, what were once nickels and dimes have become quarters and half-dollars.

Uncle Al's Saturday morning visits also equate to brand name sodas replacing the C&C swill they sell at the A&P. Fresh containers of Tropicana orange juice replace the frozen brand, and suddenly there are small Wise Potato Chips bags in your school lunch bag along with Yoo-Hoos. There's even Breyers ice cream in the freezer, sugar cones, U-Bet chocolate syrup, and rainbow sprinkles in one of the kitchen cabinets to decorate your mother's creative desserts. Some Friday nights, instead of the usual pizza or fried fish, because the Church is still holding to a no meat on Friday policy, your father orders Chinks, and it will be years before you realize that word is derogatory slang for Chinese people and/or their food. Nobody mentions or realizes, or maybe they just ignore the fact there is meat in pork fried rice. You're supposed to confess to eating meat on Fridays, but that isn't going to happen. Instead of making up the usual lies to have something to confess, you opt for a sin of omission and never mention the pork fried rice.

Come the weekends, your mother hands you and your sister extra money on top of your one dollar allowances. The movie money is enough for a ticket, popcorn, soda, and a frankfurter.

Even the kitchen starts to smell different. Your mother is using a spray that temporarily dilutes cigarette smoke. You overhear plans for maybe buying a second house.

Although you never see your parents smiling together, they do seem happier in their own way. Your mother plays cards while your father is out doing whatever keeps him from coming home.

Money must be the answer you're starting to think, because even you are walking a little taller, Little Jesus. The road to happiness must be all about money. Your adult brain is being sold out just like those cops and their free shopping sprees for the sake of looking the other way.

Making Your Bones 101 ...

What you didn't count on with the new economic status your family has achieved, what you never would've expected, is the extra shit you're starting to catch from your sibling. Your sister has figured out a new way to screw with your head and it's becoming frustrating.

"Charlie cursed," she tells your father one night.

"I did not!" you yell.

"What did you say, Mister?" your father asks.

"Nothing, I swear."

"He did, too," she says. "He said the F word."

And just like that, your face feels the sting of a quick left-right open hand combination. Your father's hands are rough and callused and smell of cigarette smoke as they slap your cheeks. He's left his mark, fingerprints that turn white and then red. In the bathroom you stare at yourself in the mirror, fighting back tears of frustration while clenching your teeth.

Your adult brain doesn't quite understand this shit.

A few days later, your sister threatens to tell your father you cursed again.

"But I didn't," you say.

"And who is he going to believe, you or me?"

Another few smacks from your father with a bit more energy behind them are the result, and it is a much more complex situation than your Little Jesus brain can process. You love your sister, in spite of her being so goddamn mean to you lately, but she seems to go out of her way to get you into the shit. This lying for the sake of showing her power is particularly annoying, but mostly because when you tell the truth nobody believes you.

A few more Charlie cursed again lies does the trick.

"Then fuck you," you say. "How's that?"

She smiles. It is a smile you will see again and again, one you won't ever forget, one that will appear the day her girlfriend/lover calls the police on you and nearly gets you arrested, something you can't afford because you've already begun a life of crime. A smile that says, "Now I got you. I got you good."

But on that day way back when she accuses you of cursing one time too many, you realize you can't win, and that if you're going to get smacked, you might as well make it worth your while.

"You're a shit, bitch, fuck!" you say.

"Now I'm really telling Dad," she says.

You flip her the bird.

That night you're prepared for the slaps and take them with pride. You don't sniffle. You don't even flinch. The fact is, you're starting to like getting slapped. Standing up to them has become an issue of pride.

That night when you stare at yourself in the mirror, you're smiling.

Your adult brain has figured it out. He won't kill you. He can't kill you. The worst he can do is slap you, but you'll still be there after the sting is gone. So, why cry?

Take that, *Sorella*.

Mr. Stella, meet Thomas Rocco ...

As the basement business continues to boom, your father continues to ignore the weekend card games your mother seems to live for. He's gone most nights after dinner and almost all-day Saturday and Sunday. At some point your mother also notices he's not around. She starts acting strange again, once more going up on her toes to watch the phone numbers he dials from across the kitchen. There are incoming calls with hang-ups, and eventually you overhear your mother tell your father, "Go if you want out, but don't you dare think these kids are going to suffer."

This marital discord is intensifying, but it's still something your brain isn't understanding, not yet anyway. You're not sure why, but seeing your mother spy on your father is upsetting.

You wonder why all this shit is happening.

One day your father builds shelves for some of the extra swag displays in the basement, and he breaks your balls for not paying attention. He sees you leaning against a wall while he hammers home a nail, and he says, "What's the matter, afraid you might learn something?"

You, Little Jesus, will be anything but a carpenter. As has already been established, you're a hopeless daydreamer, soon to be a hopeless romantic, and none of it gets past your father. Your inability to pay attention or care about the more pragmatic things in life is a constant annoyance to his being. When he attempts to teach you things by allowing you to tag along on some of his weekend swag runs, dropping off boxes of stolen goods at different stores on Delancey Street in Manhattan, you can't even feign interest until he tells you a few stories about his life as a kid: how he used to work in the Sugar Bowl, his father's candy store on Second Avenue, how he used to have to wake up extra early in the morning to pick up newspapers from a corner drop-off and bring them back to the store, then clean the place before his father opened for business, how he wasn't allowed to take any of the candy his father sold because it was business and nothing in life was supposed to be free.

You like hearing those stories about your father. He doesn't share anything else with you, so the stories are special. Your brain can process these stories into images. You can see your father as a young boy performing the errands necessary to becoming a man someday.

He even tells you how he never finished high school and went straight to work as an apprentice lithographer on Hudson Street, and how the old German who taught him how to run a press was a master at his craft. There aren't any pictures of your father as a young man, but you manage to paint them in your noggin anyway. This short, stocky, man with the curly hair and angry eyebrows is your God. You wonder what his life was like when he was your age. Was his father strict? Was his father happy? Was his father disappointed in him the way your father seems to be with you?

Eventually he can't take watching you not pay attention to his handiwork on the new display shelves and he tells you, "Go 'head, get lost."

Getting away from him at times like this is something you do gladly. Getting away from the confusion of your world is something you've begun to do without reservation. On the flip side, it brings you some extra grief at school when your daydreaming gets worse.

Between the television series *Combat* and the John Wayne movie, *The Longest Day*, which you and your equally propaganda loving friends see at least half a dozen times at the local theatre, you dream of being a war hero in Europe. You almost can't wait to get there. You have no clue that the war has been fought and won, or maybe you think the next war will be the same.

In fact, until baseball becomes the primary interest in your life, and you daydream about playing for the New York Mets someday, you become a Sergeant Saunders wannabe while teachers try their best to get you to pay attention. When you aren't staring at the clock on the wall above the blackboard, urging it toward three o'clock, you're either daydreaming about being Sergeant Saunders or being a class clown by recreating the sounds of war you've learned to mimic watching television.

It isn't long before your name changes from Charlie to Mr. Stella—not a good thing.

"Everyone turn to chapter five," Mrs. Craig says. "Who wants to read first?"

"Da-dush, da-dush, da-dush."

"Who did that?"

"Ba-kwah, ba-kwah, ba-kwah!"

"Who made that noise?"

Imbecile you've become, you can't stop laughing, and give yourself up in the process.

"Oh, I see. Mr. Stella. Fine. You can go down to the principal's office and wait for me there."

"Da-dush, Ba-kwah!"

"Then we'll call your parents and discuss it with them."

Those phone calls are hits and misses. Sometimes your mother answers and she doesn't tell your father, or sometimes what you've done, like farting during an assembly, offends that angel of mercy's sensibilities, and she passes the message along. The smacks are harder, but they no longer sting as much, and you prefer them to the punishments that keep you from watching *Combat* or WOR channel 9 wrestling or the *Million Dollar Movie*.

Adding to your confusion are the twins in your class, Sarah and Sonia Levine, Jewish girls who are dressed identically every day. Sarah clearly can't stop looking at you. Nor can you stop looking at her. She marks your first official flirting, and now that you know she's watching, the daydreaming and class clowning become a trademark. Your adult brain is still a bit behind on the sex front. At least it hasn't sparked any horniness or enough pubic hairs for you to notice. Having been the possible victim of a possible pedophile in your recent past doesn't urge you to urge, so to speak, but you sure are finding Sarah's attention divine.

Eventually, from all the horsing around you've done in class, your notebook needs to be signed by your parents every weekend. Mrs. Craig will write: Charles was good this week or Charles was bad this week, and because you're bad for a record four weeks in a row and never get your book signed, Mrs. Craig warns you if it isn't signed the following Monday your ass will be grass.

"I'll be calling your father, Mister Stella," she tells you one Friday.

When Monday rolls around and you remember your ass will be grass, you come up with a creative bullshit story.

"I swear, Mrs. Craig, my father signed the book, but I was late coming to school this morning, see? I was running, and I slipped near the corner, and the book went down the sewer. Really." You make the sign of the cross. "I swear on my mother, Mrs. Craig. I'll get it signed tonight, I promise."

The thing is, you actually see this bullshit story as you're telling it. You can see yourself running and slipping, and the rubber book binder breaking, and the one book you need, the one with all the signatures that aren't there, heads straight for the corner sewer on 94th and Avenue M, a block from where you live.

After listening to your fantasy born of necessity, Mrs. Craig doesn't respond. Maybe she bought it. Ever the desperate optimist, you find hope in her silence. You think: *Little Jesus may not turn water to wine yet, but he sure can spin some bullshit, yeah?*

And that day after school you're in your backyard with a friend tossing a baseball. At four-thirty-five in the afternoon, exactly five minutes after your father gets home from work, you and most of the neighborhood hear his voice:

"Charlie!"

You look at your friend and swallow hard. He looks at you, his eyes suddenly big with fear for you. He knows the story about the book and Mrs. Craig, but he's forgotten all about it the same way you did because it's your nature, as most Italian-American boys brought up in Canarsie, to not give a flying fuck about anything involving school.

You swallow hard a second time and hope it's something else until there it is again, louder this time.

"Charlie!"

"I'm dead," you say.

"I know," your friend says. "Good luck."

Your father is no athlete, but he does have the quickest hands in the world. All he needs is to get you within reach, and it's a done deal, Little Jesus will get clocked.

"How you doing in school?" he asks once you're standing in the kitchen.

You shrug and say, "Okay."

He's sitting at the end of the table, a good two feet from where your sneakers seem stapled to the green linoleum floor. Cigarette smoke swirls from an ashtray strategically placed on the table, just far enough from the edge for you to assume he's comfortable where he's sitting.

"Yeah?" he says. "You doing your homework?"

Another shrug. "Sometimes."

"Sometimes?"

"Yeah, you know."

You see his face tighten. "Come closer," he says, "I can't hear you."

Your adult brain may spin some epic fantasies, but it's not exactly dead to reality. You know what's coming and try to stall. You move about two inches.

"Closer," he says.

You shuffle another inch, maybe two.

"I said closer."

You're mid inch-step when he leans forward and connects with a flush one.

Smack!

This smack has force and your face stings. *Ouch, motherfucker*, is what you want to say, but you don't. You clench your teeth and take another few left-right open-hand combinations before this life's lesson is over, and although he manages not to draw blood, your head is swimming pretty good when you finally get banished to your room to study.

Study? The fuck is that? You can't even think. All you can do is dream of something dramatic that will make him hate himself for hitting you. That slapping shit was embarrassing. You're wishing, literally, except not really, that you can die and watch everybody get sick with grief, even your sister, who seems to hate you anyway, but mostly him, your father, you want him to really suffer for the loss of his only boy.

Your adult brain daydreams on overdrive as you envision this great vista of grief from the ceiling of a funeral parlor, as if the ceiling is a dome, and you are pinned to the epicenter like a butterfly pinned to a mounting board. You can almost smell the flowers. Your mother is a wreck, and you feel totally rotten and guilty about that, but so is your father a wreck and you can hear him saying: *"My son. My son. What did I do?"*

The next morning reality creeps into your life of delusion. Once again you overhear your mother say to your father, "You think I don't know you have a girlfriend? You think I don't know who it is?"

You overhear him speaking into the phone. "I'll call you later," he says. Your mother is yelling something as he turns away from her. His eyes and frown meet your eyes and your frown.

He says, "What do you want, Mister?"

"Nothing," you say.

"Then get lost."

You begin to wish you could. You're thinking about that funeral scene again, your funeral, except would he even give a shit?

"Fine," your adult brain thinks, *"if I'm mister, then you're Thomas Rocco, motherfucker."*

Strat-O-Matic ...

Before there's an official leap into the world of Little League baseball, while you're still throwing sponge balls against the side of the garage, you're introduced to a baseball card game called Strat-O-Matic, and yet another obsessive disorder is born.

You form a league with a friend, and before long the two of you are playing the game five hours a day when it's beautiful outside, ten hours when it rains. Because there are so many teams, 20 at the time, you both take a league each and play the solo version of a season. Your friend is a Yankee fan, but has the National League. You, a Mets fan, have the American League, the idea being neither of you have any reason to cheat.

You use composition notebooks to make box scores. You perform the tedious work of lining each page with a ruler and pencil. You keep statistics daily, including everything but errors by position. You create schedules for each team, writing them out neatly on loose leaf paper and keeping track of home and away games for each team. Nobody notices the details and organization you employ, not to mention how your basic math skills are greatly enhanced, something that will come in handy down the criminal road you'll take for a dozen or so years before a genuine come to Jesus moment sets you straight again.

In the meantime you can look at a column of numbers and do the math in your head. You enjoy double-checking the old-fashioned way, adding the numbers one-at-a-time, and then you take pride in finding you're right. You take pride in creating statistic sheets for each team. You take pride in managing each team and making sure the substitute players get more than pinch-hitting playing time.

Why couldn't school be this interesting?

Because you have no confidence in yourself.

Before long your daydreaming takes on new dimensions, and you begin broadcasting the games to yourself, whispering the play-by-play while seeing the action in your head.

"That's a deep drive to left-center field. It's going, going, gone, a home run! Joe Christopher hits his tenth home run of the season, and the Mets take a 3-2 lead."

Many years later you will read how Ronald Reagan did this for a living for a time. Might you become an actor some day? President?

The delusional broadcasting isn't all bad because eventually you put two and two together and begin writing sports articles like the ones you read in the *New York Daily News* every morning.

Last night at Shea Stadium, before a crowd of 22,000, Joe Christopher led-off the bottom of the eighth inning with a tremendous drive over the left-center field fence, giving the Mets a 3-2 lead. Lefthander Al Jackson held on to win his third game of the season, striking out two in the ninth.

Little Jesus is pretty sure he's found his calling, broadcasting and writing about Strat-O-Matic baseball games, but it isn't something Thomas Rocco enjoys seeing. It is, in fact, something Thomas Rocco cannot stand to see, his first and only son playing a game all day and night.

Thirty years later Spike Lee will direct and co-write a movie called *Crooklyn* about an African-American family in Brooklyn struggling through the same life situations as every other working class family. One of the kids, the one Spike Lee plays in the movie, also plays Strat-O-Matic, and his father often repeats a familiar phrase a few times during the movie: "That goddamn Strat-O-Matic."

Thomas Rocco will add a few of his own phrases to those used in the movie. Upon returning from work and seeing you playing the game, he will say:

You think they're gonna pay you for playing that?

Enjoying yourself, huh?

It's a good country, America.

Not only does Thomas Rocco not like you playing Strat-O-Matic all day and night, he especially doesn't like the fact your favorite Met is Joe Christopher, a black man. It isn't that Thomas Rocco is prejudiced. At least you don't think he is, but he cannot understand why or how you can like a black player more than the white ones.

You explain that you not only like his name, which has *Christ* in it, you also like his accent, and that he wears a cross around his neck and is always smiling.

"He looks like a real nice guy," you say.

Thomas Rocco frowns. The racism that is at the core of the town you live in has begun to seep into your life via Thomas Rocco. You don't understand the economics of it yet, nor do you have a clue about real estate values, the American dream, and why capitalism is the most surefire way to enhance hatred and prejudice, but you aren't comfortable with this new experience. Maybe there is a bit of racism in Thomas Rocco after all.

You eventually put Strat-O-Matic away, at least out of Thomas Rocco's view, but you will come back to it several times throughout your life. The statistics and fantasy of this baseball card game will provide the occasional opportunity to escape the real world. It is too great to ignore, even as an adult.

When Major League Baseball changes the rules and challenges your purist nature, Little Jesus can return to his own world, and it doesn't take six days and six nights to recreate. Best of all, if it's your world, you can play by your rules.

One thing is for certain, you will never make any of the players prove their love for you by telling them to kill one of their kids.

When the Strat-O-Matic game company enters the computer age thirty plus years down the road, you will teach one of your sons the game with dice because you're still old school when it comes to dumb shit, and the idea of a machine doing the work for you is repugnant. You will remember a Marxist quote from a course on communism you took at Brooklyn College in your mid-twenties that will make more and more sense in the future: *"The production of too many useful things results in too many useless people."*

Will Little Jesus really go from a bought and sold capitalist to a Marxist someday?

Batter Up ...

Your daydreaming eventually turns to full blown delusions of grandeur. Perhaps you carry some of Thomas Rocco's cousin's fucked-up genes? Your nervous energy runs full-throttle as you pace the floor back and forth, over and over. You especially like the hallway from the kitchen door to your parents' bedroom. You talk to yourself while pacing, engaging in full back-and-forth conversations with imaginary interviewers after you've won some famous award: the MVP, the Triple Crown, Best Actor in a Leading Role, Longest Drum solo, the Medal of Honor, Best Baseball Game Announcer, and so on.

These dialogues become a new escape. You need to feel good about yourself, Little Jesus, and nobody is looking to help you out. Your Mom would throw herself over hot coals to help you feel better about yourself, but she's having her own self-doubts. Thomas Rocco has stepped up his stepping out, and this time it appears to be serious. Your mother doesn't notice how you've become one isolated motherfucker, talking to yourself when nobody else is around, but it's best you keep that shit to yourself.

The other thing racking your Little Jesus mind is guilt. You're confused and feeling guilty. If you're not a good student and you're not a good son, then you must not be good, and it's all your fault. That Abraham-Isaac story really fucked with your head, not to mention the forsaking of a son by his father.

Maybe Isaac was a fuckup, too. Maybe he deserved to die.

You're not on the cross yet, but you're starting to imagine your skin being pierced by the nails to be hammered through your hands and feet someday; the nails being guilt you will never shake. Reality is busting your bubble, Little Jesus. Your romanticized worldview is being tested slowly but surely. Nothing makes sense except to daydream whenever possible and avoid reality at all costs.

Sometimes you'll converse with yourself while pacing from the front of the house to the back, over and over. Sometimes you'll do it while walking to or from the store. Sometimes your dialogues will occur in bed before falling asleep and/or again when you wake up, and in the mornings you'll lie there an extra hour or two instead of getting up and facing your day. You'll do this lying-in-bed routine until even you feel silly for all the effort it takes.

Fortunately, you've come of age and can step out of the daydreams at least long enough to get out of the house and play some Little League baseball. The dialogues you have with yourself won't end just yet. Safe havens aren't easily discarded, but you will get some exercise and oxygen, as well as learn to play and socialize with others.

After years of throwing a sponge ball against the side of your garage, you're about to get your first taste of genuine competition. Although it will not come close to obliterating your romanticism, what Thomas Rocco perhaps hopes for, it will certainly unleash some natural athletic talent you wouldn't dare to believe you ever had.

It will leave you no less confused about this strange world you're supposed to save some day, but you'll have moved from the theoretical to the empirical, and as you'll learn over time, there's no substitute for getting your hands dirty.

The time to put up or shut up has come. You and a hundred or so other kids around your age bring your baseball gloves to the local high school where officials of the Canarsie Little League will usher you to the gymnasium and perform a general evaluation. It is a Little League combine where dorks are screened from athletes, and the last place finishers from the previous season get to pick first.

The gymnasium is huge and mostly barren. There's a distinctive smell you can't yet recognize, but the hardwood floor is somehow comforting, and you perform with confidence. You're good at throwing and catching, and you do even better in the batting cages. You're picked early on in the process by a last place finisher the year before, the C-Vue Cleaners. The manager lives up the block from you on 95th Street and Avenue N, and he's known to have a good baseball mind. He's had champion teams in the past, but last year suffered the loss of a ton of talent when his best players aged enough to join the Pony Leagues, ages 14-16. When the draft is finished, with the exception of a few kids who aren't very good athletes, the C-Vue Cleaners are pretty much an all-star team.

Mid-season, with the team 6-0, the good baseball-minded manager suffers a heart attack and Thomas Rocco, of all people, steps in to take over. This is good and bad. Except for boxing, Thomas Rocco was never a big sports fan. He was loyal to his New York Giants when they played in the Polo Grounds, and he continues to like them even after their move to San Francisco, but he knows as much about the intricacies of baseball as he does about botany.

On the other hand, Thomas Rocco is also extremely fair about playing the kids who had only played the minimum amount of innings required by Little League rules. He doesn't have a baseball ego like too many of the other managers, and he isn't worried about being considered a good manager. He'd rather be a fair one. Most of the kids who aren't very good haven't played much, but now, because the C-Vue Cleaners are unbeatable in spite of Thomas Rocco, he plays those other kids, sometimes starting them and making you ride the pine along with some of the other all-stars on the team.

He will let the single black kid on the team, another bench rider, play even more than the other bench riders because he says, "Those people have it tough enough," which confuses you even more about just who the fuck Thomas Rocco is.

Midway through the last half of the season, the catcher breaks a finger on a foul tip. Nobody else wants to catch. Thomas Rocco pulls you off second base and says, "Put on the equipment."

You ask him if he's crazy and he smacks your face faster and harder than ever before. Years later the Yogi Berra quote regarding catching equipment will make a lot more sense: *they are the tools of ignorance.* And there you were, a catcher.

The sting from his slap leaves a red welt on your face for the remainder of the game, even under the catcher's mask you wear. By season's end, you're the second-string all-star catcher, and you forgive Thomas Rocco the smack because you know why he did it. There was no way he was going to be accused of favoritism by forcing some other kid to wear a catcher's mask. When all is said and done, neither the original catcher's broken finger nor you becoming the catcher can stop the C-Vue Cleaners from winning. Nothing does until it rains four innings into the last game of the season with C-Vue winning 8-0, except the other team's manager wants to keep playing. Thomas Rocco says, "No, the kids will get sick," and he pulls his team off the field and forfeits. Later he claims it was to teach your team a lesson in humility, that no team is perfect.

You know it was the right thing to do. The C-Vue Cleaners had already proved they were the best team in the league. What was the big deal of going undefeated?

The rest of the team hates him for what he did, and you think: *forgive them, they know not what they do.*

You admire Thomas Rocco for his decision, adding yet more puzzlement to your already bewildered little Jesus brain.

Although Thomas Rocco will mostly disappear from your Little League life over the next few years, you will learn to switch hit on your own and play in two more baseball leagues over the next few years. You will make the all-star teams in all three leagues and hit eight home runs in a fourteen-game season for St. Jude's CYO team. You'll get a trophy at the end of the year, signed and handed to you by Tommy Holmes, a back-up Yankee outfielder from back in the day. In civilian clothes, Holmes looked no different than any other man, and you started to believe baseball might just be your calling after all.

Unfortunately, your Little League accomplishments aren't enough. There's no praise when you hit a grand slam in one game or when you hit two home runs in another game. After a game when you go hitless, you feel the need to lie to Thomas Rocco about getting two hits, a single and a double, and going so far as describing the line-drive you didn't hit down the third base line. Later the same night he sees your coach somewhere and brags about your hits, something you never thought for a second might happen. The next day he cracks you one across the chops.

"Don't ever make me look like a fool again," he says.

You don't know why you lied, except to make him feel proud. You're a good ballplayer and shouldn't have to lie, yet you did. The shameful lesson you learn from getting caught in the lie is secondary to a feeling that you'll never make this man proud of you. It's a feeling you'll have over and again, that he's sitting in ambush waiting for you to fail.

A few years earlier, in August of 1965, before he was Thomas Rocco, your father took you to your first major league baseball game at Shea Stadium, the only game you would ever attend alone together. His Giants played your Mets, and you sat in third base box seats that cost $3.50 each. You were six or seven rows behind the Giants' dugout and were completely mesmerized by the scale of it all. The Giants players returning to the dugout looked like actual giants, and the field itself was beautiful, the lawn cut perfectly around the infield, and the base and foul lines regally white-lined. The home run fence and the scoreboard made you dizzy, fueling future daydreams about playing professional baseball for the New York Mets someday.

You were in heaven, Little Jesus, until the game started, and you noticed your father was watching the women in the stands rather than the game.

That day both Willie Mays and Joe Christopher hit home runs. Number 41 for Mays and number 5 for Christopher. Both also had two hits in the same game, a Giants 8-3 victory. Later, on the way home, when you tried to engage your father in conversation, you talked about how fast Willie Mays was, and you asked him if he thought Mays might make it to 50 home runs before the end of the season.

"Willie Mays is nigger rich," he said, stunning you.

You didn't know what he was talking about, but you knew the word nigger was bad, something you never should say. Your father had told you so himself.

"You know what that means?" he asked. "He spends his money faster than he gets it. Color TVs and Cadillacs, that's what Willie Mays does, pisses his money away."

You couldn't imagine anyone not liking Willie Mays. You swallowed hard and said, "I like Willie Mays, Dad."

"What?" he snapped.

Too frightened to engage him any further, you froze in anticipation of the frown you knew was already on its way.

The conversation was over for the rest of the trip home. You had to wait until you were in the house again before you could thank him for taking you to the game, but his response, even to your thanking him, was one more frown to add to the collection.

You did your best to ignore that frown because otherwise the day was a total loss. It had happened in the past, going back to the train board Christmas. Your father does something fatherly, something you can love him for, and then a look, an insult, or a lecture turns your enthusiasm upside down and you feel like shit.

That night your dream is a nightmare and you get to eavesdrop on what he's thinking about and it isn't pretty.

"Bad enough I had to sit there all day in that stupid stadium, wasting money on programs and soda and franks. We're coming home and I try to teach him something, and the kid tells me how much he likes the shines, Willie Mays and that guy on the Mets. I can't believe he's my son."

You push the dream out of your mind and remember that he took you to a Mets game. It's one way to survive, pushing the bad out of your head. You were secretly rooting for his team in the hope it would keep him happy that he took you to the game. He probably felt that he'd wasted one of his valuable Sundays off, but if you ignore that aspect of the day, the fact remains your father took his son to a Major League baseball game.

The fact he never takes you to another game is something else you'll have to ignore.

Once more your adult brain learns a survival trick.

The Sweet Science ...

Billy Castro is two years older than you and a bully. One week after he gives you a shiner, Thomas Rocco brings you to a sporting goods store on Pitkin Avenue in Brownsville. It is an area where Hasidic Jews own most of the stores and are keen on bargaining. You've been there before for school clothes, before there was a store in the basement, usually socks, underwear and shoes, the essentials that could be purchased in bulk because Thomas Rocco claimed he could "Jew down" a salesman to save money.

Pitkin Avenue is mobbed with people traffic, and he tells you to wait outside the store while he negotiates the price of boxing gloves. The smell of dirty water frankfurters from a nearby street vendor works on your hunger. You do your best to ignore the smell, because you've started to gain weight, and Thomas Rocco has already commented on it. You focus on the sports equipment in the display windows instead of your hunger, but shy away from the football, boxing, hockey, and basketball equipment. You're focused on the Mets baseball uniform, the blue leggings, the white pants and shirt with blue pinstripes. You smile at the orange lettering framed in blue that spells *Mets* across the front of the shirt. The Mets emblem on the left shoulder sets off another daydream—you wearing that Mets uniform while playing in Shea Stadium. You're running off the field after making a great catch, the Mets patch visible to the television camera before panning to the back of your uniform and name above your number, which you want to be Joe Christopher's number, 23.

The look of wonderment on your face draws the attention of a hustler standing nearby, a man with larceny in his heart.

"You a baseball player, huh?" he says.

You never noticed him watching and are surprised. "Excuse me," you say. "Oh, yeah. I love baseball."

"You look big enough. What position you play?"

"Catcher now. I used to play second base."

"You a long ball hitter, I bet."

You don't handle compliments well and blush, but you do feel good about what he's said. "Sometimes."

He points to the Mets uniform. "You get me a ticket when you play for them?"

You're immediately on a high because an adult is not only talking to you, he's complimenting you. "If I make it, sure," you say.

"In the meantime, I'm a little hungry," he says. "Haven't had breakfast yet. Maybe you can—"

"Inside, Mister," Thomas Rocco's voice booms from behind you. He looks at the man and says, "Take a walk."

The man quickly turns away and heads off, leaving you baffled at what just happened. The man was being nice. Why did Thomas Rocco tell him to take a walk? On the way inside the store, he says, "You need to learn when you're being hustled, Mister."

You're not sure what you did wrong. You were being polite to the man, but there's no doubt it upset your father. You aren't street smart enough yet to recognize the hustle, and it becomes one more check mark on a growing list of things you're sure you're failing at.

Inside the store, a salesman wearing a yarmulke helps you try on the boxing gloves. Thomas Rocco pulls down on them to make sure it's a tight fit. They are cranberry colored and leather and smell funny, like a horse.

"You be a champ mit those," the salesman says in a Yiddish accent.

"Yeah, right," Thomas Rocco says dismissively.

Was he telling the store own to forget blowing smoke up his ass for the sake of a sale, or was Thomas Rocco using sarcasm to suggest the kid he's buying the gloves for doesn't stand a chance?

On the way home he reminds you, "The gloves *aren't toys*, don't *ever* lend them out, and make *damn sure* you take care of them because *they were expensive*, Mister."

Your adult brain is used to this shit by now, so although it's upsetting to hear yet again, you know how to handle it.

The lessons start as soon as you're home. It's a side of Thomas Rocco you never knew until now. The only organized sport he ever engaged in was boxing when he was a kid. He learned in the old Greenwich House, a gym in the West Village. He doesn't tell you much about how good or bad he was, but he does know the basics. He teaches you to throw a straight jab and right cross without the gloves, and they are heavy when he makes you put them on. He has you hold your arms out, not throwing punches at all, to measure your arm strength. It isn't long before your arms are tired and start to drop.

"You have sissy arms," he says. "You need to build them up and lose some weight. You're getting fat, Mister."

Hey, it's not like he's teaching you ballet, right? Your adult brain can deal with this. You try again, but your arms start to sag, dropping at your elbows.

"Keep them up, I said."

You start to hate this shit and feel about to cry, but there's no way you can do that without making it ten times worse. You hold the gloves up until a tear finally does slip from one of your eyes and your nose begins to run.

"Okay," he says. "Rest a minute."

When the minute is up, he tells you to hold them up again, straight out, no flinching. He's watching the second-hand on his watch and lets you rest after 30 seconds have passed. You do this routine for nearly ten minutes before you can't keep your arms up for more than 15 seconds. It becomes ten minutes of total failure, the most time you can remember him teaching you anything sports related one-on-one since you were born, and you couldn't hate it more.

"You're gonna do that every day until you can throw a punch with those gloves on," he says. "It's time to grow up."

And he follows through, each day for the next several days, adding sit-ups and push-ups to your routine. The boxing lessons preclude your drum time and instead of setting them up every night to practice, you're forced into the torture of building arm strength. It is something he knows you'll never do on your own, so he makes a point of taking you to the basement and making you go through the exercises every night while he smokes a cigarette and times you with his watch. The basement store is closed for the day before he returns from work, so there's no chance of these boxing sessions catching a merciful break. The free time you had after dinner is gone. It has become a relentless gym session in the same basement you once daydreamed was Madison Square Garden, when you were playing drums with Eric Clapton and Jack Bruce.

The last few days he teaches you how to throw a left hook by quick-slapping your face over and over as you try to defend yourself. They aren't hard slaps he's landing, but they are humiliating.

The other thing those slaps teach you is how to throw that quick left hook. Somewhere in your Little Jesus brain, you know that if you want, you can tag his jaw with the same left hook he's play-slapping you with.

Low and behold, a month or so later, your boxing gloves are the talk of the block. Not that you're a good boxer, or have fought anyone with them yet, but because you were dumb enough to mention to one of your friends how much you hate what your father is doing with you every night after dinner. Word spreads: Charlie has regulation gloves, and before you know it, everybody wants to try them out. When Billy Castro makes a challenge to "you and your fancy new gloves," the tiny yard in front of your house becomes a ring. Several kids are watching as you land a few solid punches, including a left hook that surprises the bigger Castro and he lands on his ass. You're declared the winner when your older foe's mother yells from their apartment window for her son to come home. It's a confidence boost you never expected could come from fighting.

A few days later, the same Castro catches you in the schoolyard without the boxing gloves and kicks your ass pretty good. You don't cry though, but you do swear you'll get him back someday.

Between the slaps to the face Thomas Rocco had delivered over the years, the scraps you had in the street, winning some and losing more, Little Jesus is learning how to fight. It is a requirement to overcome the coward you were when that bike was almost stolen a few years earlier.

You will learn how fleeting fame is when you are humbled in a dozen or so fights your freshman year in high school, but you will retain that quick left hook Thomas Rocco taught you. It is a punch you will land successfully, even when you get your ass kicked, because nobody expects a well-executed left hook in a street fight. It is a punch that will catch the eyes of a friend's father the day you break the jaw of a nineteen-year-old dropout robbing kids in the high school schoolyard. Ultimately, ironically, it is a punch that will enhance some much needed confidence and eventually change your life.

Your adult brain, for better or worse, likes the way it feels when you connect with that left hook.

Death of a Salesman ...

Upon hearing you win a few fights, the boxing lessons come to an abrupt and merciful end, but tensions continue to sour at 1505 East 95th Street. Thomas Rocco never comes home on time anymore. Sometimes he comes home so late, you don't see him for days. Your mother is losing weight and looking exhausted. Your sister has turned her room into a safe house and doesn't come out unless it's time to eat or leave for school. When she does cross your path, she heaps new, more sophisticated insults on you to replace the ones you're missing from Thomas Rocco.

"You know who you are? You're Happy."

"Who's Happy?"

"Read, idiot. In *Death of a Salesman* there are two brothers. You're the big dope, Happy."

You won't know who Happy is until you become an avid reader later in life, and when you do, you'll realize one of two things about your much smarter sibling: either she's an incredibly poor judge of character, or she's a lot meaner than she is smart. It'll be Biff you relate to, and it'll be the ghost of a father exposed as a fraud you will fight most of your life.

And when Thomas Rocco dies, it won't be the death of a salesman, it'll be the death of a hustler and an emotion bully. Similar to Willy Loman, there won't be any crowds at his funeral. You'll go to the funeral parlor two hours before the viewing. You'll leave before anyone sees you. Your sister won't go. Your mother won't go. It'll be his wife, the woman your mother had named Gang Bang after he leaves his family for her. It'll be Gang Bang and her brothers and your paternal cousins, the same ones he seemed to adopt when he turned his back on his own kids, those are the people who will attend his funeral. The same people you wouldn't piss on if you saw them on fire.

And when Gang Bang sends you what Thomas Rocco left you, a watch, a ring and the death certificate, she'll also leave a note about where the ashes are going to be spread, the time and date, but there will be no attention paid to this salesman, not by either of his children.

You'll be Biff all right; Biff minus the pipe dream support and encouragement, Biff nearly ruining his life trying to impress his father, Biff finally coming to terms with reality and accepting his lack of greatness and a determination that leads to as much bad as it does good.

Biff, through and through.

Sex Education 102 ...

"I know this kid who doesn't have hair down there yet," you say to a few trusted friends one day. "Believe it, at our age?"

It has to do with the peach fuzz you have between your legs, especially after playing a strip poker game with Nick and Lisa Schmidt in their basement and seeing that the brother and sister have thick pubic hair. The fact they're a couple of years older than you doesn't dilute your shame, but you do feel a need to know you're not alone.

"I know a kid who's fucking already," one of your trusted friends says, taking the conversation completely off course. "He better be careful or he'll get his girlfriend pregnant. Imagine becoming a father now?"

Naive Little Jesus that you are, you're not quite sure what he's talking about. Fucking doesn't lead to pregnancy. God, your father, he does that stuff, gets women pregnant.

Doesn't he?

"The fuck are you talking about?" you say, and one embarrassment soon pales by comparison to a new one.

"What do you mean?" your friend says.

"You know some kid fucks, so what? What does that have to do with getting pregnant?"

You can't imagine Thomas Rocco did that to your mother, and it isn't until they're all laughing at you for being such a dimwit when you come to realize there might be something to that fucking-leads-to-pregnancy theory.

Still, the damage has been done. Not only are you barely sprouting where it counts, you were clueless about how babies are conceived. Learning that it has nothing to do with God, and that your earthly father had to fuck your mother to have your sister and you, makes it even more revolting. Maybe it is best you avoid what everyone else seems to think is so cool.

Maybe getting laid can wait.

While your sister continues to hide in her room singing to records, your safe house has become the bathroom, where you continue to sneak off with parts of the *Daily News*, and not the sports section. You'll check the standings of the clubs and box scores to see if the Mets won, but not in the bathroom. Baseball is kitchen table reading. *The Daily News* pages reserved for the bathroom are the ones with advertisements for Playtex Bras, the new fodder for your overly enthusiastic journey through puberty.

Your adult brain may have blocked how you first learned about masturbation, but it's a lot safer taking care of business in the bathroom than it is making a fool of yourself talking about sex in public. In the bathroom, after watching a Marilyn Monroe movie, you can daydream you're making babies together. When it's not Marilyn, it's Dorothy Provine after you watch a rerun of *The Roaring 20's*.

So, who has it better than you, banging Marilyn Monroe and Dorothy Provine pretty much whenever you want?

Steve and Eydie (without Steve) ...

One day you hear your mother crying while she's talking to her younger sister on the telephone.

"I think he's going to leave me, Franny," she says, and your heart breaks for her.

Not only does your mother continue watching Thomas Rocco dial the telephone, she's singing songs of marital woe whenever he's about to go out for the night and/or when he comes home. An *Ed Sullivan Show* with Eydie Gormé belting out "What Did I Have That I Don't Have" is the catalyst behind the drama. You're clueless about all the singing going on, but your mother is dropping hints the way B-52s will carpet bomb Cambodia in a few more years.

Mom isn't skinny, but she isn't fat either. She's a big boned woman just like her sisters, and although she's almost forty now, she's still attractive enough to catch looks from men on the street. Her problem, of course, is she's still in love and way too loyal to imagine having an affair. But in the late 1960s, she's turned to her drama gene to try and keep her husband from leaving. She performs live theatre whenever she catches Thomas Rocco coming or going, and too often breaks out in song.

"What did I have that I don't have now?" she sings, over and over.

It is sad and pathetic to witness, but you're too compassionate to tell her to please shut the fuck up already. Even you can see it isn't working; Thomas Rocco can't get away from her fast enough.

She's always sad and you wish you could do something to make her happy enough to lay off the Eydie Gormé woe-is-me tour. The Victrola is moved to the living room and albums are spread all over the place. She plays them until they are worn out, one victim of love dirge after another, a relentless barrage of women dumped by their one true love.

What did I have ...

You wish she would can it before your father never comes home again. You're still too attached to your need for fatherly acceptance to place the blame, if there is any, where it belongs. Your first thoughts are to shut your mother up, but for all the wrong reasons.

The drama develops its own smell, cigarettes and Dewar's White Label. Your mother isn't a drunk, but she's feeling desperate and is putting on shows you can smell from the moment you wake up Sunday morning until the moment you're forced to go to sleep after Ed Sullivan, whom you've come to hate now for his allowing Eydie Gormé to ruin your family. Both your parents smoke Marlboros, but Mom isn't a Marlboro Woman. She doesn't crush them out the way Thomas Rocco does. Nor does she smoke them all the way down to the filter the way he does, but she sure can blow smoke the way some of the movie queens on television do, and it's always melodramatic.

She inhales deep, holds it a long moment while squinting at him, then exhales slowly before delivering her lines as she dangles one hand out to her side holding the cigarette.

"Oh, you're tired now? You came home? You going out again? Should I bother to leave a light on?"

Your sister isn't observing any of this because of her own singing in front of the mirror in her bedroom. You're the audience, Little Jesus, like it or not.

What did I have ...

And when she threatens to divorce him, there's a last-ditch attempt at reconciliation. Poppa car Carmelo sits with your mother and tries to talk some sense into her.

"What are you doing? You've got two kids together. You can't break up your family."

"He's got a girlfriend, Dad," she says. "I know he does."

"I don't believe it. And even if he does, that's nothing to worry about. You think he doesn't love you or the kids? He's not going anywhere, trust me. I'll talk to him and set everything straight again. Don't be foolish. You have a nice family here. My son knows that."

What he tells his son is anybody's guess, but shortly thereafter your mother and Thomas Rocco head off to Whaley Lake in upstate New York. A second honeymoon perhaps? Their first was in Washington D.C., and your mother fondly remembers the cherry trees were in full bloom. You try to picture your mother and father happy on their honeymoon, but it's an image that doesn't hold.

Whaley Lake, where they're headed to save their marriage again, isn't too far from Monticello Race Track. Maybe they'll win a million dollars and come back happy after all.

Maybe.

You can't tell if they're happy once they return from Whaley Lake, but your mother isn't crying the next time she speaks to her younger sister on the phone.

"I followed him at the track when he was supposed to be making bets at the window. He went straight to a telephone instead. He must've used four quarters, a long-distance call for sure."

You're in the bathroom listening through the door. This is the toughest you've ever heard your mother sound, and there's the F word, so you know it's serious.

"I catch him again, I'm throwing him the fuck out. I had it. Let him send his father to talk again. He does that and I'll call Gazut and ask him to do my talking."

You have no idea what or who she's talking about, but when you finally learn many years later, you can only wish she had followed through on her threat. Her first cousin, Gasper, nicknamed Gazut, was with the Genovese team, and one of the toughest street fighters in New York City. He would eventually be a mob murder victim some years later, but in 1969 he would've kept Thomas Rocco from robbing his favorite first cousin, Speranza.

"I know," you hear your mother say into the phone, no longer angry. "I'd never. It's just Tommy makes me so mad sometimes. I guess he can't help himself, my husband."

You stay in the bathroom until you hear your mother step outside onto the back porch. You don't want her to know you've overheard her conversation. You know you shouldn't have listened, that it was something she feels bad about, and you don't want her feeling guilty for you're having heard it. You wonder who Gazut is and what it is your father can't help himself about.

You wait a few minutes before you approach the back door. You see your mother is crying and your heart breaks for her all over again.

Meantime, your sister continues to disappear in her room, singing to Jonnie Mitchell now, occasionally bringing home a friend or two she's made at school, girls you assume are as sophisticated as she is. Although they're mostly polite, your sister makes sure they don't get too friendly with you. She's got turf to protect and a reputation to maintain, and you're still the enemy, Little Jesus. Even your mother isn't spared your sister's mysterious wrath. Somewhere along the line, your sister has chosen sides. She's her father's daughter, and you're your mother's son. It's a Eugene O'Neill tragedy unfolding one day at a time.

Some twenty years down the road she'll suffer the same rejection her mother does and for the same woman Thomas Rocco chose, Gang Bang. It is a rejection you'll be drawn into because you're a fool for love. Your sister and Thomas Rocco won't speak for ten or so years before he dies, yet you'll learn from your kids how she kept a picture of him hanging in her living room, how she was haunted the same way Lavinia Mannon was haunted by her father, how mourning eventually became your sister. You're no Eugene O'Neill, but you'll try to write theatre pieces about the Stella curse within days of learning about the picture of your father your sister seemed to treasure. You will call the play *Marlboro Man* and begin it with Thomas Rocco's dead brother sitting at a table with your sister, but it is a table full of ghosts. Your sister and his brother will be ghosts for Thomas Rocco, your sister and Thomas Rocco are ghosts for you.

What did they have?

And the winner is ...

Your tendency to drift away from reality continues to impede your education in and outside of school. You hate school. You hate homework. You can't focus. You remain, in fact, a daydreamer. Taxpayer dollars are being flushed down the toilet while you stare at the clock and wish the final bell would ring already.

The teacher talks and you're out to lunch: "Today we're going to discuss the thirteenth amendment," the teacher says. "When Lincoln ..."

You're thinking: *How cool would it be if I could stop the world, get up and walk out of here, grab some free pizza and a Coke, and get some of the guys to come play stickball?*

Months after your parents' return from the second honeymoon there's not much of a change at home. Thomas Rocco continues to disappear nights and weekends, and your mother remains terrified he's about to leave her. You're in your last year of Catholic school, the 8th grade, and it can't end soon enough, although the next year will prove the most tumultuous of your life. You're sick of the uniforms, the nuns, the

Mother Superior, the priests—except for Father Scavo—the detentions, the phone calls home, the smacks off the head, the pulled earlobes, the religious instructions, and just about everything else that has to do with being in the first graduating class of St Jude. Most of all you're sick of being a fucking altar boy.

Serving six o'clock morning Mass blows worse than homework. It isn't so bad when it's Father Scavo, but working with Father Coyne or the Giant, Father Nolan, is torture. They are mean and angry in the morning, sometimes all friggin' day, and the only ones they can take it out on, the only ones they don't have to wear their frozen smiles for, like the parishioners dropping coin in the collection baskets, are you and the poor bastard serving with you, usually Marco Panello, your ordained partner in goofing off in church.

You have just a few more months of this church bullshit you've come to hate, but until then you're expected to be on your best behavior. You almost try, you almost really do, but the roar of laughter, both inside and outside of church, is like crack, or Yankee Doodles, and you can't resist fucking off.

"Ouch!" a kid in your class yells when you nail him in the back of the neck with a paperclip slung from a rubber band.

"Who did that?" your teacher yells after the class has laughed hysterically. He's stood up from his chair to write on the board and the seat of his pants is white from the chalk you crumbled into a fine dust on his chair.

Smack! Smack! Smack! It's a ruler off your knuckles the day you cut a fart so loud in class, even one of the nuns started to smile.

The other thing is how you've come to enjoy getting slapped. It no longer hurts and so long as you're expecting it, you take pride in not flinching.

And when the school holds a writing contest, the winner of which will get a big-ass electric race car set, you go home excited about it. Everyone has to write an essay on something to do with religion and/or what it means to be Catholic. You're not thinking selfishly about winning. You want to win because it would validate your ability to do something, anything, well. You write the essay instead of watching *Dark Shadows*, a show your Little Jesus mind enjoys because of all the lingerie the lady vampires wear. The essay was mostly bullshit, you writing what you're sure they want to read, but when you made it to the last paragraph, what you had to say flowed on its own:

> *In the end, Christ sacrificed his life for all of us, and while some*
> *of us may question our faith, the truth is that Christ set the*

example of sacrifice. Sacrifice is something each of us must be willing to do for each other, doubters and the faithful alike, no matter our color or creed. Sacrifice is what it means to be most Catholic, most Christ-like.

It was some corny shit, but you felt good when you handed it in. You forgot about it within a day or two, and then a month or so later you learned you were one of three finalists.

Great news, except nobody believes you wrote your essay. Partly because your competition happens to be two of the three smartest kids in the school, and partly because, let's face it, you're a dumbski by comparison. There has to be an explanation other than you wrote that essay.

You don't win the race car set. Jerry Galante does, which is cool with you and the other finalist, not only because neither of you gives a shit about race car sets, but because two weeks before the winner was announced, Jerry Galante's father died of a sudden heart attack. You and the other kid get rosary beads. This should be good news all around, except it isn't because you hear the commentary from a few of the parents, and you're sure they wanted you to hear it.

"He didn't write that. Charlie? Come on. People shouldn't cheat to win rosary beads."

It is bad enough they refuse to believe you could do something well without cheating, but cheating to win rosary beads? You want to tell them what they can do with their fucking rosary beads.

And it only gets worse at home. Even Thomas Rocco doesn't believe you wrote the essay. You lose for winning, then lose for losing.

A week after the contest you bring a magic marker into the confessional and are prepared to write *Bullshit Box* on the wall separating you from the priest. Once you're inside you hear Father Scavo's voice and you don't do it. Father Scavo is a young priest, in his early 30s, and he smiles whenever he sees you. He seems to understand your desire for attention. At least he takes interest enough to ask you how things are going at home from time to time. You like Father Scavo. Everybody does. You especially like him a few months later when you learn he took off with one of the nuns and left the church, but at that moment you do what is expected of you and make up a bunch of lies to have something to confess.

"Bless me father for I have sinned, my last confession was two weeks ago."

"Begin."

"I cursed fifteen times. I cheated on a science test once, and I stole three quarters from my father's change can."

"Is that it?"

"Yeah. I mean, yes, Father."

"You sure?"

You don't answer fast enough.

"Charlie?"

"Shit," you mouth without saying it. "No, father, there's more."

You tell Father Scavo how you cursed everyone who didn't believe you wrote the stupid essay, and he says, "It's really not important what other people think, Charlie."

You appreciate the personal touch, but are concerned about being so exposed.

"Did you hear me?" he says.

"Yes, Father."

"Good," he says. "Say ten Hail Marys ..."

You wonder if it applies to Thomas Rocco, Father Scavo's advice about it not being important what other people think. You can't help but worry about what Thomas Rocco thinks. It is a life lesson that won't really sink in for another thirty years, not until a court officer tells your third wife that instead of crying while waiting for your arraignment, she should keep better company. For whatever reason, when she told you what he said, you felt one thousand times better about yourself. At least you didn't have to insult somebody to make yourself feel better, at least not then.

Gaining confidence that day will be a watershed moment. Like everyone else, criminals work best when they're confident.

As soon as you're outside the confessional and on your way home, you realize you didn't confess that you were about to write *Bullshit Box* on the wall inside the confessional, and you feel guilty, but only because it was Father Scavo.

That night you approach Thomas Rocco while he's smoking a Marlboro on the porch. You can already tell he's in a bad mood because you can see the crushed cigarette butts in the ashtray. You approach him anyway and say, "I really wrote that essay."

He frowns, then nods. It's as much an acceptance as you'll ever get from him, and you can't be sure if the nod was worth more than the frown. Once again you go to bed frustrated for wanting to be liked, never mind loved, by Thomas Rocco.

And to confuse your adult brain a little more, a month after Jerry Galante's father died, Thomas Rocco let his mother move upstairs in the house on 95th Street because she could no longer afford the rent she was paying on 94th Street. How can a man be so indifferent to his son, yet find compassion for others?

It isn't rocket science. He must be a good man.

And if he's good, it must be that you're the bad one.

Maximum Torque ...

A few weeks pass and it's the weekend before you're to serve your last set of six o'clock masses. You're feeling your oats and looking for something more outrageous than normal to do. You and the other three trouble-makers, what the Mother Superior calls you and your friends, are supposed to be practicing for your last CYO basketball game against St. Thomas Aquinas. You're all goofing off because you already played St. Thomas, and they won by 30 points, 42-12. Your team sucks. There are only two good players on it, and you're not one of them. You're a doofus on the court, an absolute liability.

You scored two points in one game, which will remain your total for the season—ten games, two points. No wonder you don't give a shit about practicing for St. Thomas.

Instead of practicing, you and your teammates are goofing off playing dodge ball in the school basement. The basement is enormous and when one of you dodge a throw, the ball bounces and rolls a long way to the wall. It gets old fast until you realize the basket and backboard are attached to a portable rig.

"Hey, let's ride it," you say.

Your altar boy partner, Marco Panello, kicks off the brakes on the rig, and all of you begin pushing it from one end of the school basement to the other, gaining speed and momentum as all four go from pushing to running to jumping onto the rig's railing 20 yards from the wall. Not one of you has thought about how to stop the thing. Little geniuses, all four of you.

All of a sudden there it is, the wall. The front of the basket hits and chips the cinder block, bends the hoop and the entire rig rebounds so fast and hard the two morons on the back, you and Panello, are thrown back onto your asses. You look at each other dumbfounded and unsure of what has happened, until one of the others laughs and then everybody laughs. It's a laugh fest, all of you hysterical over this new form of being clowns, and it all comes to an end when a booming voice yells from the stairs on the opposite end of the basement. You all turn and gasp. It's the Giant, Father Nolan, all six-foot-six, two-hundred seventy-five pounds of him, and he's pissed off. You can still envision the smoke coming from his ears as he stomps his way across the basement and the four of you scramble to look repentant.

"Get over here!" he yells. "All of you. Right now!"

The four of you shuffle into position. Left to right: Ryan, Panello, you, and Pinto. The Giant is glaring at each of you, one at a time, not saying a word; extending the suspense just long enough for one of you to say something really stupid like, "We couldn't stop it, Father."

Wham!

Panello is spun into an about face. His left hand goes to his left cheek where his skin has gone from its usual pasty white to a bright red. He is stunned. He turns around, still holding his cheek and defensively leans away from the Giant.

All of you lean forward to take a closer look.

The giant turns and points to the bent basket. "You see what you did? All of you. You see what you did?"

"Holy shit," Panello whispers, but loud enough for the Giant to hear.

Wham!

Another one. Down goes Panello, this time from a short left that came from the Giant's waist. The slap has watered Panello's eyes, but he's tough and isn't about to cry, not in a million years. He covers up and seems to be waiting for a kick, what it looks like, but the Giant yells for him to "Get up!"

The four of you are back in line, and this time the Giant steps toward the other end of this St. Jude squad of misfits. He glances into your eyes but only for a second, then looks at Pinto and yells, "Idiots!"

Pinto does what you're too scared to do. He loses eye contact with the Giant, giving Nolan just enough time to reach back, and then it comes, the Giant's sweeping right.

Wham!

It's maximum torque this time, the smack so loud and hard even Nolan takes a step back as Pinto spins like a top, does a complete 360, and corkscrews down to one knee. His face is welted red where the Giant's paw has struck. He is clearly dazed and tearing, but he won't cry either, no way. You've all got street creds to earn. Crying isn't something you can do, at least not in public.

You figure you're next, but the truth is the Giant seems fearful of what he's just done. Instead, he orders the four of you to the rectory for punishment the following day, a Saturday, where you will all have some chores to keep you busy, he says.

Considering you were probably next, and you were the genius who came up with the idea of riding the portable rig, you're the lucky one. Pinto is clearly not lucky. He still looks stunned. He may be concussed. He will die thirty years later from a brain tumor, and the Giant's slap is the first thing you will think about when you visit him in the hospital after his first brain surgery.

Back outside of St. Jude School, all of you are watching Pinto without letting him see you watching, because you all know he wishes he could just scream out and have a good cry. It's what you all want to do, let out a primal growl to vent your frustrations and serve warning to those who'd fuck with you again, but Pinto is still in shock from the force of the Giant's blow. You're starting to worry it may be something more serious than embarrassment. There's something weird going on with his eyes, something that doesn't seem right, that straight ahead stare of his can't be normal. His eyes are glassy. Something isn't right.

And he's not saying a word.

Ryan breaks off before 96th Street and Avenue N. Panello heads for the bus on Rockaway Parkway. It's you and Pinto for the stretch of 96th Street between Avenues N and M and you don't know what to say. You're feeling extra guilty for escaping the Giant's wrath. Why Pinto and not you? You're bigger. You caused the mess, and you're usually in trouble anyway, especially in school. What kept the Giant from taking another swing? If he was afraid of his own strength, he could've nailed you with a quick smack the way he caught Panello the second time he hit him.

It will be a question that stays with you through adulthood: Why was it the Giant didn't hit you?

The closer you get to Pinto's house, the more you feel the need to say something.

"You gonna be alright, man?"

"I hate this fuckin' school," he says through some obvious sniffling. You're relieved he can speak, and you understand his sniffling. You'd be sniffling too if it was you. You'd be just as angry too.

"I hate it all," he says.

You know he's embarrassed, so you keep your trap shut as you both approach his house. He turns into his driveway without saying goodbye. You stand at the fence outside and watch him walk the length of the driveway, a soldier returning home in defeat.

By the time you make it to the corner of Avenue M, you're a nervous wreck. You're seeing and hearing the Giant's smack, Pinto corkscrewing to a knee, his left hand barely touching his red cheek as he comes to a stop.

And that glazed look in his eyes. You can't get it out of your head.

A car horn interrupts your thoughts. You look at your watch and see it's close to four o'clock. Thomas Rocco will be home in half an hour. You're going to play your hunch and not say a word about what happened back at school. The Giant may or may not say something. If he does, you'll catch a beating. If he doesn't, you'll be home free.

A week passes without incident, lecture or punishment. You are, in fact, home free, except now you'll carry an extra dose of guilt around because you were the one who deserved the slap Pinto caught.

Your adult brain can process a few things pretty well by now, guilt being at the top of the list. Later in life a psychologist will tell you how guilt is nothing but resentment and there's some magic formula to release it you can never quite grasp. Your way to deal with guilt and so much more in your life is rage, and there isn't much of a thought process behind it. The first Jesus must take notice of this issue, so he sends you the first of two visitors to keep your crazy ass in check.

St. Patrick ...

"You can be a quasi-renaissance man or a complete jerk-off," a voice says to you.

You're dreaming, but you don't know it.

It's you and some pale kid who looks to be about your age, give or take a year. You sit across from one another at the kitchen table on 95th Street, a bowl of peanuts on one side of the table and several cold bottles of 7-Up on the other side. You're sitting on the peanuts side and feed yourself one at a time. The pale kid is sitting across from you, a bottle of 7-Up in his hand. He takes a long drink, belches loud and long, then sets the bottle down and winks at you.

"Think you can match it?" he says with a hint of an Irish accent.

Your brow furrows.

"What, I say something confusing? Here, I'll do it again."

He takes another long drink from the 7-Up bottle, except this time he sets it down before he belches long and loud.

"You want a parade?" you say.

He smiles. "Clever," he says, "for a wop."

"Who are you?"

"St. Patrick."

"Yeah, right."

He downs another hit of 7-Up and belches again, but this time it's short and not as loud. "Don't believe me?"

"What's your name, asshole?"

"Losing it already, are you?"

You suck your lower lip under your upper teeth, then run your lip back out. "Jerk-off, your name. What is it?"

"I already told you. How many times you need to hear it?"

"Asshole," you say, then yell. "Who!"

"First base."

You let out a breath of frustration.

"What, you don't like Abbott and Costello?" he says.

It has become more than confusing to your adult brain, mostly because this pale kid isn't familiar to you. Why would you have a dream with him in it?

"I'll make it easy for you, Guido," he says. "We'll meet again, like it or not. In the flesh, though. At least for a little while."

You stare at him a long moment, then shake your head.

"What?" he says.

"Let me sleep."

"That's all you been doing, dumbass. Time to wake up. It's a big world out there and you're making it a lot smaller being an Eejit."

You've had enough. "Fuck off."

He frowns. "Look," he says, "I'm here to explain something. It's some of what you'll remember about this dream, except it'll be subconsciously remembered. You'll think it was an anxiety dream about you, your father, and the sharks in Florida."

"What the hell do you know about that, the sharks?"

"Not important," he says. "Point is, Guido, if you don't start broadening your world, you'll be a one trick pony."

"The fuck are you talking about?"

He swings his backpack around, sets it on the table, and pulls a few books from it. "These," he says. "Books, they're meant to be read, not avoided. You need to broaden your reading beyond the Daily fuckin' News and baseball scores. It's good you were writing your own articles there for a while, but now it's time to look beyond a fucking baseball game. There's a world of culture out there, Dago. You tasted some of the music, but there's more. There's also literature, languages, art. You name it, you're ignorant of it."

You ignore the insult. "What are those books?"

He holds them up, one at a time. "*Windows for Dummies*, but it won't be available for a couple of decades. This is a comic book, *Superman*. That's been around, but you think you're too macho to read it. At least you know who Superman is. This one is a Russian novel, *The Brothers Karamazov*. You're gonna like this one a lot. Then there are these, *Revolutionary Road*, *The Winter of Our Discontent*, and *A Christmas Carol*. You already like that one and might've read a page or two."

"More than that," you say.

"Want a parade?" he says, then pulls out one more book from his backpack, a thick one. "And this one," he said, "but you've already read the cover, right?"

"*The Bible*," you say.

"It's a tongue twister, but it might do you some good."

"Fine. Whatever."

"Look, I know you don't have it yet, a fully activated adult brain, so you're excused for sometimes being a moron and an Eejit. Next time you're in class, try not to stare at the clock and dream about playing for the Mets. Pay some attention to your teachers. Eventually even you will find this stuff interesting, Guido."

"My name isn't Guido."

"No, I know, and you don't even get the insult because you don't read or socialize enough yet. It's an insult, leave it at that."

"Florida, the sharks. How do you know about that?"

"That's important?"

"Fuck me. When does this dream end?"

"When I say so."

"I'm really tired."

"Look, you like Scrooge, right, the way he turns out? Don't act so dumb. I'm talking about Dickens' *A Christmas Carol*. You can jump a few brain grades just reading that one by Dickens. Forget the Alastair Sims movie and read the fucking thing. The others are also good, but they're big and bulky and you're too impatient yet. Aside from a few asinine detours, you're heading in Dickens' worldview anyway."

You're grinding your teeth, totally frustrated with this dream.

"You think Marley was hauling iron? You'll be hauling steel, you ignorant wop. You're lucky I'll be around."

"Can I sleep in peace now?"

"No, not until you're dead."

You yawn.

"Yeah, it's real excitement for me too, moron," he says. "Shame you won't remember most of this, but the bug's been planted and I've done my job, so fuck you too."

A deep uninterrupted sleep returns. It lasts for eight hours, two more than usual, so you're in a fog come morning. All you know is that you have to deliver newspapers and get back in time to change for school, then attend school and be bored to the point of staring at the clock in desperate anticipation of the three o'clock bell.

It's all your adult brain can process, except for a lingering thought about Ebenezer Scrooge and his partner Jacob Marley, and something about hauling metal.

Something about a ponderous chain?

That Second Corner ...

The day your family closes on the new house on Canarsie Road, an attached, brick, split-level, two-family, with a two-car garage that cost $50k, Thomas Rocco is pinched moving a truckload of Chivas Regal scotch. It is a beautiful sunny day and you are pushing a grocery wagon filled with *Long Island Press* newspapers. You are completely oblivious to the world around you, except for what is left on your paper route: a right on Schenk Street at the end of Canarsie Road. It is a paper route never completed that day because you are stopped on the first leg of the Canarsie Road deliveries by Poppa car Carmelo. He pulls up at the curb half a block from where a bunch of police cruisers are parked in front of the house you are moving into that upcoming weekend.

"Get in," Poppa car Carmelo says.

"Huh?" you say.

"Get in the car."

"But my papers."

"Leave them."

"But—"

"Get in the car!"

You aren't about to test Poppa car Carmelo, father of Thomas Rocco. You get in, shift on the front seat so you can look back at your shopping cart filled with *Long Island Press* newspapers as it grows smaller and smaller and finally disappears behind a parked car. As Poppa car Carmelo drives to the corner and turns left, you can see your new house with all the police cruisers out front. There is also a truck parked in the driveway you assume was a delivery for the new house.

You ask why all the police cars, but Poppa car Carmelo ignores you. This is big people shit and you're still too little a shit for them to have to explain anything to. Besides, Poppa car Carmelo already knows some of Thomas Rocco's game plan, and he isn't about to share that information with you. Thomas Rocco, after all, is his son and has become the official family earner, because Poppa car Carmelo went bust holding onto his properties in the South Bronx too long, some of which he had to donate to a church through the Mob to avoid the taxes that would bankrupt him.

You won't know what was going on with all those police cars outside the house on Canarsie Road for years, except when you finally do learn, it will have served, to your mind, as the metaphorical end of your family, the day when Thomas Rocco crossed the line and sold his soul for a better life that had nothing to do with you, your sister and/or your mother, the day when your family turned that second corner.

The day Thomas Rocco is arrested he'd been followed by undercover cops from the Brooklyn docks to the new house, where the Chivas Regal, several truckloads already, are stored in the basement. Your mother agrees to sell the house on 95th Street to pay his legal expenses. You will later learn, even later than learning about the Chivas bust, that most of the money from the house sale went south, some in Thomas Rocco's pockets and some in the pockets of the police to keep them from searching the house on 95th Street, where the basement remained loaded with swag from your mother's first cousin.

Your mother's troubles don't end with Thomas Rocco's using the money from the sale of the first house to save his ass or line his pockets. Thomas Rocco is a multi-tasking genius when it comes to fucking over his wife and kids. He's been skimming most of the cash from the store in the basement of the house on 95th Street for years.

After all was said and done, not only was your mother devastated by all that was going on around her, she'll eventually have to live with the knowledge that she had saved her husband from going to jail for the other woman, his first cousin's wife, the by then infamous Gang Bang. She's ten years younger than your mother, has a reputation for screwing around and getting what she wants, and you hear she's already put her kids into foster homes when she split from her husband during previous breakups.

The family scandal that will ensue is epic, but still a few months down the road. Thomas Rocco is released from jail, his lawyers are paid over time, and he's back living in the Spartan new home at 2186 Canarsie Road, where three of the seven rooms, the living room, dining room and den, have no furniture. Thomas Rocco won't be there long, but while he's home his extracurricular activities with his cousin's first wife continue with gusto.

You graduate from St. Jude's, but he isn't there. He's with his *comare*, pronounced gumarra, meaning mistress, who was supposed to be at her sister-in-law's son's graduation from the same school, your second cousin. Instead of either graduation, Thomas Rocco and Gang Bang are at the track betting on horses. It isn't a stretch to assume what they did after the track, because he doesn't come home until very late the same night to find your mother a nervous wreck over her fear that he'd already taken off for good.

The times Thomas Rocco is at home at the new house, he's more miserable than usual. You are in the way, Little Jesus, now more than ever. He has someone he wants to be with and it isn't you, your sister, or your mother.

The beginning of the end has gained momentum. The shit storm will come to a head and emotions will run wild as conflicting interests will first devastate, and later isolate your immediate family. Sides will be taken and accusations made. There will be winners and losers and emotional and mental breakdowns that will leave the future fertile for lifelong hatred.

Was it really the money, Little Jesus? Was it a sudden awakening by Thomas Rocco that he was in a place he no longer wanted to be? Was it your fault? Your sister's? Your mother's? The other woman? Could it really have been Eydie Gormé?

Why has he forsaken his family?

How could he forsake his family?

What did all of you have you no longer have?

You hear him tell your mother why he's leaving. He does it in a fit of anger the day she asks him through the most gut-wrenching crying you've ever heard.

"Because you're no damn good, Hope," he yells before he leaves for a few days.

You have no idea what he means, but you know what he said was cruel, and the way she's left broken and alone in her room that day, you promise to be her protector for the rest of her life.

Motherfuckers will pay.

Thomas Rocco will pay.

You're fast approaching adulthood, Little Jesus, like it or not.

Something To Prove ...

The confusing thing is Thomas Rocco doesn't leave, at least not yet, and you can't get into trouble fast enough. It's a fight a day you get yourself into, purposely hanging out where you know there'll be trouble, at the school yard at Bildersee Junior High, the Foster Market, or the projects on Ralph Avenue. You're not a bully and don't pick on younger or smaller kids. Instead, you wait for older kids to pick on you, which won't take long in a neighborhood front-loaded with teenage boys anxious to be tough guys.

Finding a kid they don't know is like manna from heaven.

"Hey, you got any money?" one kid will ask.

"Fuck you," you'll say.

"Oh, yeah?"

And the fight starts when he takes the first swing. Sometimes you do okay for yourself, but most times you lose because you're clearly out of your league. You go home with battle scars and bruises, and it isn't unnoticed, except for the guy you're trying to impress. Your frustration turns to raw anger the day an older kid smacks you off the head outside the movie theatre on Avenue L. Embarrassed and enraged, you charge him like a fullback attacking a linebacker, growling like a lion, and surprising him enough that he takes the charge in his chest and lands on his ass in the open doorway of the soda shop next door to the movies. You can hear people inside saying, "That kid must be crazy."

And they're talking about you.

When you go home that night, your mother sits you down and wants to know what's going on?

"Why all the fighting?" she asks. "Didn't your father talk to you? I spoke to him two weeks ago about this. Tell me what's wrong."

How do you answer without upsetting her even more than she already is? How do you tell her you've come to enjoy getting hit, the feel of a fist against your face, the feel of your fist against another's face? How do you explain you enjoy taking the first punch, or that you need to take the first punch? You have knots on your forehead from insisting on taking the first punch, because it makes you angry, and anger is what you need to hit back.

Anger is what drives you.

Anger turns to rage, and there's nothing like taking a cheap shot to set your blood afire. Somehow, in your Little Jesus brain, it's all about justice. You can't hurt someone until they've done you wrong. On the street it goes by the derogatory label known as "getting Japped," and for you it's the necessary ingredient to the chemistry of your rage. Unless there are extenuating circumstances, and from time to time there will be, taking the first punch permits you to release the poison inside your being.

It is embedded in your being: *Anger is what drives you. Rage is what sustains you.*

One diagnosis presented to you later in life claims that anger can be a substitute emotion for pain. Aside from hiding vulnerability, anger can generate a self-righteous power that makes one feel better about oneself.

And Lord knows, Little Jesus, the way you're getting your ass kicked in street fights, your self-esteem tank, at best, is running on fumes.

And if you think Thomas Rocco was frowning at you before, the day you come home to 2186 Canarsie Road with a pair of shiners and a shirt full of blood from a fractured nose, you get the extra special frown, the one with the furrowed eyebrows. Once again he's out on the porch crushing one of his Marlboros into an ashtray because he doesn't want to be in the house with your mother.

"The hell is wrong with you?" he asks.

Giving him your best attempt at indifference, you shrug.

"You ever win?"

Another shrug. "Sometimes."

"You want to be a fighter?"

"I don't know."

"Well, you're not any good at it, so you better get smart fast or join the Army, because I don't know what the hell else you're gonna do. There's no percentage in being a dumbski all your life."

Somewhere in your Little Jesus brain, there's a ping, and it is the mother of all pings. It will ring again in another fifteen years. Dumbskis, you've been told, do one of two things: join the Army or become criminals. You've already established an incredible inability to focus while in school, and you hate it. Judging from your win-loss record in street fights, becoming a carpenter is probably a better bet than continuing down the road of hard knocks, except you have zero skills when it comes to anything outside of playing your drums or baseball or daydreaming. You're still too young to join the Army, but you already know of kids in the neighborhood who are well on the road to becoming criminals.

Hell, this is Canarsie we're talking about, what will prove to be a Mob breeding ground.

Somebody say *Goodfellas*?

Ehhhhhhhhhhhhhhhh, no way. Even you know that can't be right. Even you know, after watching *Pay or Die* on Channel 9's Million Dollar Movie over and over again, that Mobsters are the bad guys.

In that movie, *Pay or Die*, the Mob was anything but romanticized. Ernest Borgnine played an Italian-American police Lieutenant named Petrosino who fought the Mob and was killed when his investigation took him to Italy. It is a story you always assumed was fiction until some thirty years later when you're standing outside of a tiny park on Kenmare Street in Little Italy waiting for one of your loan sharking customers to drop off his weekly vig. That day you notice a plaque on the wall outside the triangular fenced-in park where several homeless people are gathered. The plaque reads: Lieutenant Petrosino Square. It is at that instant you realize the movie you loved so much as a kid was based on a true story. You remember how the Mob was made up of bad guys. Standing there like some dumski who just learned the sun rises each and every morning, you realize you've become one of the bad guys, and you're finally shamed.

Way to go, Little Jesus.

But in 1970, after your father calls you a dumbski, you're still searching for your place in this world you're supposed to save. In 1970, you're still just a little shit and nobody is going to pay you any attention, not the Mob or anybody else, especially after all the beatings you've been taking.

Maybe the way to go is to lay low while you build yourself up, work with weights and do X amount of sit-ups every day. Train like you're going into the Army. Train like you're going to the Olympics. Train like you have something to prove.

You already know from the slaps and the street beatings that you can take a slap and/or a punch. Nobody has killed you, not yet.

It is the thought you take to bed that night, to build muscle, to recreate yourself for the sake of your salvation.

Many years later you'll research the life of the first Jesus and notice that historical gap, a few years while he was growing up that no one seems to know anything about, those lost years. Biblical references suggest he was growing physically, mentally, and spiritually, and that he was tempted like everybody else, but somehow remained without sin.

What were some of his temptations, you wonder? Were his parents going through the same shitty breakup as yours? Was Joseph finally questioning that bullshit about the virgin birth? Was Mary sick and tired of having to explain herself? Was Joseph stepping out on Mary?

Was the first Jesus blaming himself for his family's troubles? Was he going through a period of self-loathing? Was he getting into fights because of it? Was he losing those fights? Was he taking the first punch to fuel his rage? Did he have something to prove?

How are you supposed to save a world you still don't understand?

You need a sign, Little Jesus.

Voi sogno di Alan Rickman...

The same night you come home with those two shiners and a fractured nose, and are reminded you should probably join the Army, the sign comes to you in a dream about a movie script. It starts with an ...

ESTABLISHING SHOT: From above. You can see this happening as if you're pinned to the ceiling of your bedroom. You're that butterfly again, your wings pinned to a mounting board, and you can see yourself stirring in bed as a voice repeats itself a few times before you pull down the covers, sit up, and rub your eyes.

THE VOICE

Oh, Little Jesus.

A cloud forms at the end the bed. Its center is bright gold. You are forced to squint until your eyes adjust. Telepathically, without saying the words, the cloud asks if you're still sleeping.

YOU

I don't think so.

THE VOICE

Yes, you're still dreaming, but it's best you think you're awake.

YOU

Who are you?

The cloud takes the form of a man, someone recognizable.

THE VOICE

The Metatron.

YOU

Huh?

THE VOICE

A voice of God.

YOU

Alan Rickman? You the actor from the movie *Dogma*?

THE VOICE

You're too young for Mr. Rickman or *Dogma*. Think of someone else.

YOU

But you look like—

THE VOICE/ALAN RICKMAN

The actor in the movie, yes, I know. Okay, *Dogma*. Very astute of you. Fine, but you'll be writing this well into your sixties and have yet to see or know who Mr. Rickman is. Your mind is playing tricks on you.

YOU

I don't understand.

ALAN RICKMAN

You're not supposed to. I'm here—

YOU

Hey, is that Loki Character around, that angel of death creep and his fucked-up friend, Bartleby?

ALAN RICKMAN

Excuse me?

YOU

(Confused)
Am I dead?

ALAN RICKMAN

Hardly. You're dreaming, but it's a prearranged dream. I'm here to provide you with a heavenly valuation.

YOU

A what?

ALAN RICKMAN

A report card.

YOU

I hate school.

ALAN RICKMAN

Yes, GOD knows.

YOU

GOD?

ALAN RICKMAN

The father.

YOU

Thomas Rocco?

ALAN RICKMAN

Maybe we should start over.

You're trying to shake the cobwebs free.

YOU

I don't get it.

ALAN RICKMAN

(Sighs)
For now, let's just say I'm a voice of God. The Metatron. I'm
called the Metatron.
You are still confused and show it by huffing.

ALAN RICKMAN

The character Mr. Rickman played in the Dogma movie?

YOU

The Holy Ghost?

ALAN RICKMAN

Close enough.

YOU

But God was Alanis Morissette in that movie.

ALAN RICKMAN

(Sighs again)
GOD herself. Now, I'm here to—

YOU

Wait a minute. You're telling me—

ALAN RICKMAN

Wait a minute?

YOU

Alanis Morissette isn't a He.

ALAN RICKMAN

(Composes himself, then smiles)
Sweet Little Jesus.

YOU

I'm Charlie.

ALAN RICKMAN

(Frustrated)
Whatever. I'm here to provide you with a heavenly valuation.

YOU

A report card. You said.

ALAN RICKMAN

From birth to age fifteen. Technically fourteen. You haven't
entered your fifteenth year yet, but that's the way the cards
were drawn up, so …
Frustrated, your eyebrows furrow the way your earthly father's
eyebrows often furrow.

YOU

(Peeved)
What the fuck is this?

ALAN RICKMAN

It's not important. It's a requirement you see it, that's all.

YOU

Because?

ALAN RICKMAN

It's a guide. You wanted a sign, right?

YOU

Yeah, but, what the fuck, man?

ALAN RICKMAN

Language.

YOU

Sorry.

ALAN RICKMAN

The point is you have choices.

YOU
Yeah, so?

ALAN RICKMAN
To grow, to use your mind and your body, and to develop that adult brain that's currently going to waste. To read and write and take what the world offers into your heart and mind. You can use the valuation as a guide.

YOU
Hey, you know that pale kid? He bugged the shit out of me too. What's his name again? I can't remember it now.

ALAN RICKMAN
St. Patrick.

YOU
He really a saint? He was breaking my balls about reading too.

ALAN RICKMAN
And on that note, start with Salinger's *Nine Stories*. Start with "A Perfect Day for Bananafish".

YOU
The fuck you talking about?

ALAN RICKMAN
Language.

YOU
Sorry. What's a bananafish?

ALAN RICKMAN
You'll figure it out.

YOU
When? How?

ALAN RICKMAN
Trust yourself. Trust your heart.

Mr. Rickman begins to dissolve into a cloud of smoke.

YOU

Wait!

When the smoke clears, there's a report card the size of Mr. Rickman at the foot of the bed. It reads: *First Heavenly Valuation and ...*

You're still dreaming, but you see your eyes open wide as you take it all in. There is no explanation except what is on the valuation itself. The line for a parental signature confuses you. Then you see the footnote and are mortified. You blush and swallow hard, then read through the valuation and the commandments you've been taught *ad nausem* in Catholic school. You remember most of them, although some you know you haven't broken because you're still too young.

FIRST HEAVENLY VALUATION

Parent Signature	Age(s)				
Commandment	1-5	6-8	9-11	12-13	14-15
A = Very Good; B = Good; C = Average; D = Below Average; F = Failing; N/A = Not Applicable					
Thou shalt have no other gods before me.	N/A	A	A	A	B
Thou shalt not take the name of the Lord thy God in vain.	N/A	C	D	F	F
Remember to keep holy the LORD'S Day.	N/A	A	A	A	F
Honor thy father and thy mother.	A	A	A	A	C
Thou shalt not kill.	A	A	A	A	A
Thou shalt not commit adultery.	N/A	N/A	N/A	N/A	N/A
Thou shalt not steal.	A	B	B	C	B
Thou shalt not bear false witness against thy neighbor.	A	A	A	A	A
Thou shalt not covet thy neighbor's wife.	N/A	N/A	N/A	N/A	F*
Thou shall not covet thy neighbor's goods.	N/A	B*	A	A	C*

* Your neighbor's wife, Marion, is someone you've fantasized about when pleasuring yourself.

You blink and the report card is gone. Your sleep is deep again, and it lasts several more hours. It is one of the best sleeps of your life, one you don't want to awake from, but there you are the next morning, and it is exactly as Alan Rickman had said. Most of what you dreamed has fled your memory. What you do remember is a report card, not *the* report card, and that you'd have to have it signed by Monday or your ass is grass all over again. You remember how you told Mrs. Craig you were late for school, and how you slipped on a sewer cover and went sprawling across 94th Street, how all you could do was watch helplessly as your book with the missing signatures headed straight for the sewer opening.

It's *déjà vu* all over again.

The angst from your post-dream dilemma revolves around whether or not you ever had the book signed. You can't remember. Your adult brain is in turmoil.

Omerta ...

Although Thomas Rocco is still living with his family at 2186 Canarsie Road, which is now the only family home, he clearly isn't happy about it. The air inside is thick with tension and anxiety. Outside, things aren't so great either. Racial anxieties are heating up with the busing of minority kids from the East New York section of Brooklyn into Canarsie schools. Your sister has been kept home a few days because of rioting at the high school.

Your new home on Canarsie Road is as far away from the busing as possible, with a row of attached homes, the Belt Parkway, and Jamaica Bay its southeast border. The little time Thomas Rocco spends there has nothing to do with his family and much more to do with meeting a wiseguy from the Colombo team who spends some of his extracurricular time with his hot-looking *comare*, your next door neighbor. Her name is Marion—yes, the same Marion from your heavenly valuation—and she has two of her wiseguy boyfriend's extracurricular kids. She is also much younger than her wiseguy boyfriend and likes to share her other-woman angst with your mother. She knows some of what your father is up to, but keeps that to herself, lest she be cut off from her wiseguy boyfriend and have to work for a living.

When your mother asks Marion if she knows what's going on, the wiseguy's girlfriend, sticking to the laws of *omerta* she's obviously been schooled in, nods instead of answers.

One day, still sporting some of the bruises from a recent fight, you're asked by the wiseguy visiting his hot *comare* next door if you want to earn ten dollars. He and Thomas Rocco are sitting at a card table that has been moved into the middle of your empty living room. There are Chinese takeout containers and beer bottles on a separate folding table off to the side. It's during a break from the game, while your mother and Marion are next door gossiping, when the wiseguy offers you the job. You can see Thomas Rocco is grinning at the proposition.

"Sure," you say.

The wiseguy removes something from a brown paper bag on the floor. He hands you a license plate and a pair of metal cutters. He says, "Cut the plate into a dozen or so pieces and scatter them. You know what I mean? In different sewers and garbage pails, soon as you're done. Take a few out to the pier and toss them in the Bay."

"Sure," you say again, and his smile draws you in like the bait it's meant to be. It is your first dirty money and right before the wiseguy pays you, he points a finger and says, "Never tell anybody about this, kid. Never, ever. *Capisce?*"

You're nervous, but feel special having all this trust suddenly thrust your way. Not to mention your father is smiling and seems proud of you.

"Never," you say.

"Good boy," the wiseguy says, then winks, lightly slaps your face, and jams a ten dollar bill in your front pants pocket.

There will be plenty more dirty money in your future, but there's another dozen years of shit to go through first. You begin to understand the reason Thomas Rocco is still hanging around has everything to do with the wiseguy and little to do with you, your mother and sister. Thinking about it later, even his smiling made you suspicious. Was it for you or the wiseguy? Is the wiseguy using you or your father? And who is your father using? And for what?

You're beginning to hone some prerequisite street smarts, Little Jesus. It is the animal instinct essential to the life you'll pursue someday, and it will prove an ironic twist of fate that Thomas Rocco is the one who teaches you how to unmask him.

The Summer of Discontent ...

The way she misplays the shitty hand of cards she was dealt is this: Hope calls her husband's first cousin, disguises her voice and says, "You wanna know who your wife is fooling around with?"

"Yeah," he says.

"Okay, be outside your house in ten minutes. I'll pick you up."

Then she drives to where your father's first cousin lives, and when he opens the door to her Plymouth Valiant, he says, "Hope?"

Hope maintains eye contact, swallows hard and says, "Look, I hate to be the one telling you this, but right now my kids are suffering, and I told your wife they weren't going to be the only ones to suffer."

He's in shock. "I don't understand," he says.

"Look (*you dumb shit*), your wife and my husband are having an affair."

"My wife and cousin Tommy?"

"Yes, your wife and my husband."

He takes a few deep breaths before he recovers. It isn't the first time he's learned of his wife's supplementary love life, but this time it's a bit of a shocker. He spends the next several minutes telling your mother about other marital indiscretions his wife has engaged in, at least the ones he knew about.

Your mother tells him about a few of her husband's affairs as well, but that this time it's serious. She knows Gang Bang and Thomas Rocco are planning to take off, so he better take whatever money he has in the bank out before his wife gets her hands on it, something Hope doesn't bother doing for her own protection.

Why not?

Because deep down Hope still can't believe Thomas Rocco will leave his kids.

They spend an hour discussing how they've been made fools of, nailing down times and places when each one of their spouses had made an excuse not be home, like when you graduated from Catholic school and Thomas Rocco wasn't there. When they finally part, it is with mutual apologies, but they will never see or talk to each other again.

The fallout from Hope's vengeful blunder is immediate. The poor bastard tells his father, a family big mouth who acts as if he's a Don with one of the five families, except he's not. He's not even man enough to make the call himself, but instead has his wife, Poppa car Carmelo's sister, make the call to share the good news.

"Your son is screwing my son's wife," the wannabe Don's wife tells your namesake.

It is amazing to you, except it isn't, once you realize what a coward Thomas Rocco has been most of his life. Poppa car Carmelo never knew his son was about to leave his family. Was it that Thomas Rocco didn't have the balls to tell his own father, or was it an ingenious plan to let Hope destroy any chance she had for sympathy after being dumped in such a scandalous way?

As it turned out, the hand she played settled any questions about how she'd be treated in the future. Poppa car Carmelo was allegedly devastated. He'd have to live with the Sicilian sideshow that would ensue. Guilt by DNA requires him to defend an indefensible act, or turn his back on all his siblings, and there were nearly a dozen waiting for explanations.

How does someone run off with the wife of his first cousin?

It is a dilemma that doesn't trouble him for long. Poppa car Carmelo is a pragmatist at heart. When his wife lost her mind over the loss of her firstborn son in WWII, he put her in an asylum and found a new wife, another woman who left her kids. He never spoke of his dead son again and moved on. Thomas Rocco is his remaining son and the new family breadwinner. Hope is Neapolitan, not Sicilian, and someone he argued against his son marrying anyway. Her kids had always been expendable.

Sides are taken. Blood is thicker than water and to the Stella *famiglia*, money is thicker than blood.

One week to the day you cut up that license plate for a Colombo team wiseguy, Thomas Rocco makes his move and leaves the mess he's made of his family behind. Your mother's first reaction is a hysteria that sends you to the park looking for a fight you can't win. Taking a beating has become preferable to seeing your mother's pain.

When you return she's still crying in her bedroom. You put a hole in your bedroom wall with the fist you bruised getting your ass kicked in the park. You look for your sister, but she's not home.

Has she left too? Was she going to live with Thomas Rocco?

You head up to your room not caring if your sister is gone or not, but the sounds coming from your mother's bedroom are overwhelming. You do what you never do in public. You begin to cry equally as hard as your mother is crying and even after she hears you and comes to your rescue, you can't stop.

"It'll be okay, Charlie," she says. "Mommy will be okay in a few days. Don't cry. Your father still loves you."

"No, he doesn't. I hate him."

"Don't say that. He does love you and your sister. Just give it some time. It'll be okay."

"Bullshit."

"You're just hurting now."

"Is he coming back?"

"I don't know, honey. Maybe."

"Fuck him."

"Don't say that."

"I wish he were dead."

"No, you don't. You're just upset because I was crying. I stopped now.

I'm sorry. It'll be okay, I promise."

"No, it won't."

"You'll see. Just give it some time."

Your body heaves with the emotional spasms of loss and rejection, hate and desire, but your mother does what comes natural and tries her best to soothe your pain and protect you from hers. You'll appreciate a mother's love for the rest of your life. You'll owe her forever.

Tears will overwhelm you the same way at your sister's memorial almost forty years later, when pictures of her are flashed on a screen at the end of the ceremony. You are sitting next to your mother, trying your best to be hard and not cry, but when a baby picture of you and your sister flashes up on the screen, you collapse into your mother's lap and she holds you with both arms as you cry without restraint for what should have been.

The blowback from your mother having told your father's first cousin about his wife's affair with Thomas Rocco is fierce. If there was a spider web, your mother stepped onto it. Hope calls Thomas Rocco, but Gang Bang answers and a yelling match ensues. Gang Bang promises to see Hope broke and left with nothing, then hangs up. Hope is left shaking with fear from what she's unleashed. Would her husband really cut his family off? Would he turn his back and leave them to starve?

It isn't long before she learns. She and her kids are in fact cut off. Everything stops. The money first, so she's forced to use what remains in the bank until she finds a job working for a few dollars above minimum wage as a key punch operator for a local electronics company. Only then does she let everyone know she's about to do something about it and finally see a lawyer. The pragmatist, Poppa car Carmelo, convinces his son that he's better off giving her money for the mortgage, food and his kids, or her attorney might take him to the cleaners.

Years down the road, when you learn what Hope didn't do, it makes you crazy. She never called her first cousin, the connected dude with the West Side. Just the mention of his name would've scared the living shit out of Thomas Rocco and had him working two jobs to make sure he maintained the lifestyle to which his wife and kids were accustomed.

Later in life Thomas Rocco will tell you a story about your mother's first cousin and how he once asked Thomas Rocco to watch the door while Gazut hung some junkie thief by his ankles out a third-story window on Bleecker Street in the middle of the afternoon. The entire time he was telling you that story, all you could think was *too bad your mother didn't hate Thomas Rocco.*

The problem was Speranza Stephanie Marie Stella still held onto hope and an undying love for her piece of shit husband.

Divorce papers arrive the next week, delivered by one of Thomas Rocco's future brothers-in-law. Desperate from the realization she's given Thomas Rocco his get-out-of-jail-free card, Hope calls Poppa car Carmelo to apologize, but he hangs up as soon as he recognizes her voice. She calls her sister-in-law next and is told to stop bad-mouthing her brother to his kids. Hope denies she's said anything bad about Thomas Rocco to his kids, but Francis hasn't heard her because she's also hung up.

Hope is further distraught when her lawyer tells her she should stay out of the negotiations and let him handle her case. Her husband still earns enough of a salary from his job as a lithographer for her to keep the house. If she takes a job, she and the kids will be more than fine. The law is firmly on her side, especially with Thomas Rocco's recent arrest for moving booze off the Brooklyn docks.

The idea that Thomas Rocco will be out of her life once and for all is too definite an end. Hope fears that level of independence as much as she fears the loss of her husband. All will be too neat and tidy once the papers are signed.

He calls her a few minutes after speaking with her lawyer to complain the "Jew fuck" wants too much money for the divorce. "Where'd you get this bloodsucker from?" he says.

"Hey, you're the one who wants the divorce, Tommy," Hope says.

"But I can give you more money if you do it my way. We'll make a deal or something."

"I want it in writing."

"It'll be in the divorce papers, but what this guy is saying is crazy. What the hell am I supposed to do, work twenty-four hours a day the rest of my life?"

"What do you want to do, Tommy?"

"I don't know, Hope. We can come to some kind of understanding, for the kids' sake. We're still going to have to deal with each other. There's no reason we can't be friends. It's not like we don't have a history."

Thomas Rocco plays with Hope's vulnerability like a cat plays with a mouse. Still unable to accept that he no longer loves her or that he will stay away from his kids, she agrees to his terms of a divorce and accepts, against her attorney's advice, $85.00 a week for the rest of her life. And just like that, Thomas Rocco is legally excused from paying half the mortgage on the house while saving himself about $100.00 a week for the rest of his life. Hope's lawyer, a decent man trying to do the right thing for his client, could only shake his head.

The fact you, Little Jesus, will pick up the slack for Thomas Rocco a good ten years before he dies is one of life's little ironies. Like his father before him, Thomas Rocco went broke, and the same way he took over as the family money man, you became the family breadwinner. Like father, like son.

An extra dose of humiliation comes the day Thomas Rocco informs Hope they need to pay Poppa car Carmelo back for the money he lent them on the down payment for house number 1, and there goes any safety net for her and the kids. A week later she is so devastated by the reality of her situation, she has nothing but a mortgage she'll never be able to pay, she spends an entire weekend in bed, and is diagnosed as having suffered a nervous breakdown. The following Monday she is hospitalized for her troubles.

Two Times A Coward ...

Thomas Rocco disappears while your mother is dealing with her breakdown in a local nuthouse. Grandpa Pete, suffering from emphysema, has moved in to be with you and your sister in the interim. Your sister is already a junior in high school and has begun a life of her own. She's either in school, working at the library, or hiding in her room.

It is a weird time at house number two. No Mom translates to zero structure. Grandpa Pete does his best to hold down the fort, but you're not coming home early enough, and you're keeping him up later than he's used to staying awake. Then when you come home with a new shiner from a fight you actually won, he cries and you're crushed. You've never seen your grandfather cry before. He's tall and lanky in his old age, and his emphysema makes it dangerous for him to get excited, but somehow you've managed to make this man, who's been nothing but love to you, cry.

Every morning he brings a kitchen chair into the empty dining room where his television sits on a milk crate. A snack table for his ashtray, matches and cigarettes, is positioned alongside the chair. When you think of him sitting there, it is a surreal picture, an old man, his cigarettes and his television in a big empty room.

You promise to stop fighting, even though you only mean while he's living with you, and you spend the night wondering just how fucked-up you're making your life. You start to write it all down in a black composition notebook, the kind you used to draw pictures of Army tanks and soldiers in instead of doing your homework. It's a new form of escapism that will eventually save you. You promise your grandfather you'll change, and the next day a phone call from a friend presents an opportunity, an audition with a local band.

First, your mother comes home after ten days in a nuthouse. She looks thinner and pale, and has a bit of a glazed look in her eyes, but she seems happy to be home. She promises it won't happen it again, and it never does, but all you can feel is guilt for letting it happen in the first place. You tell her about the band coming to the house the next day, and she is excited for you, probably because she's thinking maybe it'll keep you from getting yourself killed in a fight.

Your sister isn't as happy about the band, but she is happy to have your mother home again. The three of you have a talk around the kitchen table about what happens next.

"I need you both to be more civil with each other," your mother says.

You're playing with the salt shaker, rotating it in your right hand over and over.

"Charlie?" your mother says.

"Yeah, no problem," you say, then look at your sister.

"Jerk," she says.

"Hey!" your mother says.

Your sister rolls her eyes. "Fine," she says.

"I mean it," your mother says. "It's going to be tough now. I don't know if I can hold onto the house. We may have to move. I need you two to be good. I need both of you to do good in school and stay out of trouble."

"She means you," your sister says.

You roll your eyes.

Your mother says, "I'm going to do as much overtime as I can, but I don't know how much they'll let me have. When it's busy I can work Saturdays, but I don't know if that'll be enough. You both need to save your money."

"She means you again," your sister says.

You flip her the bird.

"Charlie!" your mother says.

"Okay, fine," you say. "Where are we moving?"

"I don't know. Maybe we can stay here. I don't know yet."

You look at your sister. "Truce?"

She rolls her eyes again.

"Okay?" your mother says.

"Fine," she says. "I said fine."

You know it won't last, but you agree to try because you're feeling more than a little responsible for your mother's mental breakdown.

The next day the two members of the band you're auditioning for come to the house and set up in the basement. It's a semi-finished basement with wood-paneled walls. The 40 or so cases of Chivas Regal are gone.

There are curtains covering two small windows and two empty bottles of Boone's Farm Apple Wine and Mateus Rosé, the most popular booze amongst teenagers at the time, on the windowsills. There is no floor covering, so you each place rug remnants under your equipment. The basement is big enough to play in comfortably, and there are enough outlets for the amplifiers. Both the guys you're auditioning for are two years older than you and exceptionally good at guitar and bass. Both have long hair. You make a mental note to keep yours long, too.

The amplifiers are loud when they tune their instruments and then they ask if you know "Jumping Jack Flash".

The guitar starts it off, and you wait your turn to jump in and give it structure. You're playing Rogers drums, which you've saved for by working various jobs, including washing dishes at the catering hall weekends and unloading watermelons at the Foster Avenue market. The Rogers are your pride and joy. You chose a white finish with a chrome snare, because they remind you of the great Ed Shaughnessy, Doc Severinsen's drummer, you've often watched on the *Tonight Show* starring Johnny Carson.

The playlist moves to Grand Funk Railroad's "I'm Your Captain" ("Closer to Home"), Black Sabbath's "Electric Funeral", Led Zeppelin's "Dazed and Confused" and "Heartbreaker", Cream's "Spoonful", "Crossroads" and "I'm So Glad", and you're proving a natural once again in your Little Jesus life. The guys want to run through the playlist one more time, and it's even better the second time. A third pass is made, and the guys are smiling at one another. They tell you they'd like to come back the next week and do it again, maybe add another song or two.

"Sure," you say. "That sounds great."

Once they leave, your confidence is soaring. And it will soar again for another few weeks as the band, Arm & Hammer, practices in your basement every weekend. Anyone who hears the band suggests you play out somewhere. You can't wait for Thomas Rocco to see and hear you, and you don't even know he has connections all over Greenwich Village. Maybe Arm & Hammer could actually play at The Bitter End one day.

When you practice during the week, you do it to Cream's *Live at the Fillmore East* album. You imagine it's you that Jack Bruce and Eric Clapton are referring to when they say, "Ginger Baker, please." You're thinking this will all work out and maybe you can make Thomas Rocco proud of you after all, maybe he'll even love you some day, and how cool would that be?

Before anything that good can happen your sister starts a war with you and your band mates one afternoon, and your future as a rock star dissolves in embarrassment.

Your sister says, "My father knows you two only let him in your band because you need a place to practice."

"He tell you that?" you say.

"Yeah, but I knew it too."

"And you couldn't wait to say it, could you?"

"It's true."

"It isn't, Charlie," one of your bandmates says.

"Not at all," the other says.

"They're using you, Jerk," your sister says.

The messenger has performed her task well. Adding the work "Jerk" to the end of her message was just the right touch. Once your bandmates have gone, she waits until later in the evening to drive the nail home. She knows you've been sitting around thinking about what she's said. She knows that it has upset you and that self-doubt is eating away at your core.

"It's true," she says in a friendly tone. "You're not that good. They need a place to practice and we have a big basement."

"We sounded good, asshole," you tell her.

"Okay," she says, shrugging her shoulders and sighing as if she's done all she could for her loser brudthy.

And just like that, you know your drumming days are over.

A week passes and one of your bandmates calls to reschedule practice at a local studio, but you've already convinced yourself you can't do it anymore. You can't handle what might be true. You tell him you're going to give drumming a break for a while, and then you follow through with your dumbass decision. You don't even go down to the basement to practice afterwards. Your white Rogers with the chrome snare are stacked in one corner of the basement. The small tom-tom on top of the big tom-tom, on top of the chrome share, on top of the floor tom, on top of the bass. The cymbal stands, high-hat, floor tom legs and other hardware are stored in the closet.

If you don't see them, and it'll take an hour to set them up again, you won't miss them, except you do miss them. You miss them and resent what has happened, and eventually your resentment turns to anger, and all you want to do is hit somebody.

And it is the second time you stop doing something you love for all the wrong reasons.

Two times a coward. Your adult brain doesn't mince words.

Welcome to High School ...

It is nearly fall when the band is officially out of your life. The pounding on your drums that had probably served as a cathartic release from the anger you were carrying is no more. In need of a new way to release the negative energy, Little Jesus returns to fighting, and what better place to get your ass kicked than at your new school, Canarsie High School, where there are at least three grades of kids older than you?

Racial tensions are heating up with the new school year. School buses are blocked by white parents wielding baseball bats. Racial epithets are being spewed wherever you turn. Middle-class Jews and Italians are united in their prejudice. The people in your neighborhood are talking negative shit, and you wonder how long it'll be before you wind up in a fight with a black kid. In the meantime, there are more than enough white kids offering their services.

Like on your first day as a high school freshman, you get into it with a junior twice your size immediately after homeroom. The preferred method of getting into a fight without throwing a first punch is by bumping shoulders. It starts with making eye contact with someone headed in your direction, a challenge that often leads to a shoulder bump and then a fight, especially if you're intent on not yielding to the older, much bigger, shoulder.

So, there's the bump. Then you each stop to stare at each other. The junior says, "The fuck is your problem?"

"You," you say.

He takes the first swing and connects with your left eye. Enraged at the cheap shot, you fire one back, a body shot that moves him back, but then you're over-extended and he has you in a headlock. The fight is broken up, but you've got another shiner to bring home. You manage to avoid your mother, but the discoloring doesn't escape your sister, and it earns you a few sarcastic comments that lead to one more father-to-daughter-to-son/brother gut punch that will send you out trying to prove yourself all over again, and for a long-ass time to come.

"I see you got your ass kicked again," she says.

"He was older than me," you say.

"Sure he was."

"He was."

"So maybe you should try somebody younger."

"That wouldn't be fair."

"Or you're afraid of getting embarrassed."

"I win sometimes, too."

"Yeah, right."

"You'll see."

And then she delivers the blow: "Daddy said you can't fight."

"Daddy don't know shit," you say, but you're fighting back tears that never once welled while getting your ass kicked.

Day two you find the same junior who nailed you the day before. You bump shoulders with him in the hallway one more time, and when he wheels and smacks you off the back of your head, you spin and come up with an even better body shot than the day before, this one an uppercut to his solar plexus. Down to his knees he goes, and you're more than fine leaving it there, the junior sucking wind and you grinning a sweet revenge, but then one of his friends drops you with a haymaker you never saw coming. Now you have a welt on your right temple to go with the black eye. This time you manage to avoid everyone at home by staying in your room after school and sneaking down to eat when everyone is asleep.

You skip fighting day three and avoid everyone at home again, but you're right back at it day four, when you find the guy who delivered the cheap shot on day two. He's also considerably bigger than you, but since he broke the rules of fair fighting you abide by, there's no reason not to Pearl Harbor his ass right back, which is what you do, except your punch has a lot more rage behind it, and his nose breaks and blood splatters everywhere.

This time there's no escaping your mother because she's called up to school and notified you're being suspended for three days. At home your sister calls you an idiot, and your mother is frantic there will be some kind of retaliation, and she considers transferring you to another high school.

"No fuckin' way," you tell her. Now that you're the man of the house and tired of trying to be a decent human being to your loved ones, you feel it's your right to curse and talk smack whenever you want.

The next week when you return to school, you manage to get into a fight with one of the senior football players, and he kicks your ass six ways to Sunday. He's tall and muscular, and a lot bigger than you, but you accidentally bump into him coming out of the cafeteria, and he says, "Watch where the fuck you're going, asshole." It's easy enough to let go, except there are a few of his teammates there and they laugh.

"Fuck you," you say.

"Fuck me?" he says, stepping close enough to put his chest in your face.

"And your mother," you say, the magic words that lead to the beating.

You never get a punch in, but catch at least a half-dozen, including one to your left eye that keeps the rainbow your face has become alive with color. You're sent to the dean's office, but you both lie that it was just horsing around, and there's no way they want to fuck with a senior on the football team, so warnings are traded off for suspensions and another phone call home.

Once your mother sees your face, she about has a heart attack. She calls Thomas Rocco and you run downstairs to listen in on the phone in the den. It's a short conversation, during which Thomas Rocco sounds preoccupied, and it ends with him saying: "It's about time he learns how to fight."

"Stupid bastard," your mother says before hanging up on him.

A week or so passes and you're face is no longer discolored the next time you get into it, except this time it's at a battle of the bands performance you attend hoping to see your two former Arm & Hammer band mates. It is being held in the school cafeteria, and the bands set up to play about twenty yards apart from each other. The space between the bands is filled with stacked tables and chairs, the chairs being ammunition for a riot. There are three bands on each side of the cafeteria, but it isn't fifteen minutes old when a black band begins to play and a war breaks out.

This is the Canarsie you hate. This is the Canarsie where the prejudice of too many white parents has found its way down the DNA ladder, where young white kids too young to know how stupid they sound can't stop themselves from saying dumb shit about blacks and Hispanics. This is the Canarsie that firebombs a real estate agent for selling homes to blacks. This is the Canarsie that could just as easy be in Selma, Alabama, for all the fear and prejudice that permeates the air.

This is the Canarsie where white wannabe thugs jump the black band while they're playing. None of it makes sense, but when you see two white kids hitting on the black kid who was trying to sing just two minutes earlier, you tag one of the white kids with an overhand right and are jumped by a few of his friends for your trouble. None of the punches you catch land flush enough to hurt—that or you're getting used to getting hit. On your way out of the fracas finally broken up by the police, you see a black kid bleeding profusely from his forehead.

You don't tell your mother you were there when it is reported on the news the next day. You don't tell your sister either, but you try to engage in conversation with her about the black-white thing you're still trying to comprehend.

She is watching a news report of the incident in the sparsely furnished den. You sit on the steps leading up to the kitchen, mostly empty dining room, and still completely empty living room. "Why are they like that?" you ask.

"Because they're bigots," she says.

"How do they get that way?"

"Their parents probably."

"Mom doesn't talk like that."

"Dad does sometimes."

"But he doesn't mean it."

"Then he shouldn't say it. Nor should you. You're not like that, so don't become like that. You'd better not or you'll get killed. You can't even win against the white punks."

"Because I fight kids older than me."

"And you get your ass kicked. What's the point of that?"

How do you tell her you enjoy it? You don't tell her, but you defend yourself instead.

"Not all the time," you say. "I don't lose all the time."

She rolls her eyes.

Still, it was a moment of decency and good advice from a person you're almost positive hates you. You assure her you have no intention of going anywhere near the bigots, even the ones that jumped you at the battle of the bands, but as luck would have it, your first day back to school the following week, there are two of them in the school yard while you're outside for gym, and they recognize you.

After school there's a committee of them waiting for you. You, because you've already started to lose your mind, don't mind the odds. You'll lose the fight, but nobody can blame you if there are five of them. If anything, you'll earn street credit for having the balls to take them on. Even Thomas Rocco won't be able to ignore the stones it takes to fight a crowd. Nor is there anything his messenger, your sister, can say about it.

The poisonous rage you've come to embrace needs an outlet, and you see it when they form a gauntlet at the exit you use on Avenue K and 95th Street. You wait until you're a foot away and feign looking one way so you can nail the one closest to you with a right cross. Just like when you were Pearl-Harbored, the take-the-first-punch rule is out the window when you're outnumbered. The beating you take immediately after is short but brutal. This time you're on the ground getting kicked when the high school security guards pull them off. You're brought to the dean's office along with the one you hit first. You're surprised when you see his head is tilted back and he's holding a towel to his nose. You smile at the damage you've inflicted, and the result is that some of your pain is immediately alleviated, even though your face us back to having bruises and color, and your upper lip is swollen to gigantic.

You're not suspended this time, but your mother is called at work, and she has to leave early to pick you up. She's distraught again. She's also terrified you've become a target for bullies. She isn't aware it has nothing to do with being bullied. You're fucking nuts.

In the car on the way home, she is crying and you beg her to stop. You don't tell her how it all began at the battle of the bands, but you do mention that you don't like high school very much. Maybe you should be allowed to quit and get a job?

"No way," she says. "You don't have a skill, and you can't wash dishes the rest of your life. She's referring to the last job you had, washing dishes at the catering hall in Brooklyn. You have to go to school and you have to stay out of trouble. I'm calling your father again. He needs to know you were jumped. And if he won't do something, I'm calling someone else. Maybe you need to talk to a professional."

Once she says "jumped," your Little Jesus brain romanticizes the event, and you never hear her reference to a professional. Another epic daydream is born instead: Teary-eyed, Thomas Rocco arrives at Canarsie Road later the same night to see what they've done to his son. When he learns that six boys were involved in the attack, he becomes enraged and swears vengeance. You imagine him later bragging to his friends in the city how it took six punks to beat you.

What actually happens is your mother calls Thomas Rocco, and although you can't listen into this call, you can hear your mother yelling at him: "He needs you, Tommy. Take him out once in a while. Talk to him. You don't have to see me when you pick him up. Meet him someplace."

It goes on for a while before she hangs up and calls him a stupid bastard one more time.

Your adult brain is on overdrive. You're as confused as two of the Karamazov brothers you'll read about down the road, but you'll wish you could be the other Karamazov, Aloysha.

The Fall of Your Discontent ...

Little Jesus is warned: one more suspension from school and you're out, so you do the next best thing and start cutting classes. Why bother to show up when you know you'll be fighting again? Canarsie High School isn't for you. Half of your friends from St. Jude are attending Catholic high schools. Most of your new classmates are strangers. You weren't even seeing your sister at school. She's in her senior year and so advanced she only has four classes a day before she heads to work at the local library.

When Grandpa Pete moved in with Aunt Jo in Queens to help with her rent because her husband was out of work again, you became the man of the house and saw the opportunity for what it was. You stayed up all hours of the night into the morning either watching television or writing stories in the composition books meant for your schoolwork. You wrote dramas about a family coming apart at the seams where you saved the day, but you never really made it to that saving-the-day part before you started over and wrote something else.

You remembered *Pay or Die* and started writing crime stories, but you didn't know enough about crime or the Mob, so you were bored sooner than later and went back to the family stories you couldn't finish. When you were good and frustrated enough, you started watching the *Late, Late, Late Show* on Channel 9, and eventually you fell asleep an hour or two before you were supposed to get up for class.

You became a class-cutting fool.

One day when your mother wakes you for school, you go through the motions and get dressed, grab the books you aren't reading, then walk around the block until she leaves for work. It's a new tactic, and you get away with it for about two weeks before your mother is called at work. Then she comes home frantic about what you're doing to your future by staying home all day.

"You have to go to school," she says.

"I don't want to," you say.

"But you have to."

"Bullshit."

"I'll tell your father."

"Like he gives a shit."

"He will about this. Is that what you want? You want me to call him?"

"Knock yourself out."

She makes the call and Thomas Rocco asks why you're not going to school. You tell him you don't like it and once again he says you need to grow up or join the Army. You tell him you're too young to join the Army.

"Then get a job," he says.

You pass the phone to your mother. "Tommy?" she says into the phone, but he's already hung up.

Your mother gives you all kinds of grief, and you curse her out for not being your father. You give her grief until she breaks down crying, and then you feel guilty and resentful and angry for feeling anything. You punch another hole in your bedroom wall that features several similar holes. And when you can't take her crying anymore, you promise to go back to school and not get into any more fights. You tell her you'll try to hook up with your old band again for something to keep you out of trouble, but you know that isn't going to happen because you're still wondering if they were using you for the practice space.

"Please, or I don't know what else to do," your mother says.

"Alright, Ma, take it easy already. Stop fucking crying."

You're back in school a full week without a single fight, and you actually do a homework assignment that turns you on. You're assigned and read Albert Camus' *The Stranger*.

You are fascinated with the indifference of the opening lines: *Mother died today. Or maybe yesterday, I don't know.*

You can't imagine being so cavalier about your own mother's death. You'd be lost and you know it, but what makes a guy create a character like this, you wonder?

You ask your sister about the book you're reading, and she isn't horrible about explaining it. She tells you about existentialism, and although you're not fully grasping it, you remain interested in what she has to say. Your teacher also explains it in class over the next few days, and you have to write an essay about it. You somehow get an A, even though you're still not sure you understand. You can't wait to show your mother, but the same day you get the A, you also see your sister for the first time since you started high school. You hear her voice telling somebody to fuck off outside the school cafeteria. You see her flipping someone the bird and look to where she's looking, and you see a tall stocky kid at least her age laughing at her. You're instantly upset and investigate by following the stocky kid. Once both of you are in a stairway, you confront him.

"What happened back there?" you ask.

"Who are you?" he says, a look of scorn on his face.

"Her brother."

"Tank's brother?"

"Who?"

"Tank."

"The girl who told you to fuck off?"

He smiles. "Yeah, Tank. That's what I call her."

You won't throw the first punch, because it isn't fair, so you give him a two-hand shiver to the chest and he falls on his ass. Fully embarrassed, he gets up and proceeds to kick your ass. He's pulled off before teachers get involved, but you've got another shiner. You decide to keep this incident to yourself, especially because of what he called your sister; you don't want to have to repeat what he said when your sister questions you in front of your mother about your black eye. And when she does, you don't tell them what happened. It is the start of some extra sympathy for your sister, having to put up with hurtful comments from assholes because she's a little heavy. She's never been thin, but neither has she ever been obese. She's a stocky girl having to deal with the same shit at school she's felt from her own father, and you're more than sympathetic to her pain.

The next day the asshole who called her Tank is waiting for you outside the school and he threatens to kick your ass again. You flip him the finger, but he's restrained by two of his friends as school security appears in the doorway. You tell him you'll meet again someday, and you do in three more years, when he's twenty-one and you're eighteen, at which point he backs down from a fight, because he stopped growing and you didn't, you've lifted weights and are way stronger than three years earlier. Still, once your mother sees your latest shiner, it scares the shit out of her and she wants you to see a psychiatrist. You tell her to fuck off.

You're telling her to fuck off a lot since you've become the man of the house in that old-world style, assuming you're somehow the new boss with the privilege to curse everyone and everything. You want to know when the fuck she's coming home from work and what the fuck's for dinner. You want to know if she can drop you off at the fucking job washing fucking dishes you went back to, and if she can make sure your favorite fucking dungarees are cleaned before the start of fucking school next fucking week. You don't want to talk about why the fuck you're so angry all the fucking time, or if Thomas fucking Rocco's fucking girlfriend is there when you go to see him. All you want is to be left the fuck alone, except you really don't want that and are too fucking stubborn to admit it.

Nothing is going right, and you're more than aware of it. When you protected your sister by not telling her why you had the fight, she called you a loser. Your father saw you with a pair of black eyes and instead of being proud you stood up for yourself, he suggested you join the Army again. You want to protect your mother, but you have no idea how to do it, except to curse at her for all your frustration. You're taking it out on the one person who will love you no matter how fucking stupid or crazy or cruel you act.

You've become an animal, a time bomb about to explode, and everyone can see it except you, so your mother does the research and finds a child psychiatrist with an office in Prospect Park. It is an expensive endeavor she can't afford, but she's terrified you'll get into it with the wrong person one day and get yourself killed.

The day you're suspended from school for having a scuffle with two black kids does it. The racial tensions are too much for your mother to ignore. Mid-suspension you're off to Prospect Park, to Dr. Phillip Abegg's office.

Boy ... fucking ... interrupted.

PART II

"I love you, love me!" Dorothy Vallens *(Blue Velvet)*

Psychiatry 101 ...

"Why weights?" Dr. Philip Abegg asks. "Why not play the drums as well? Or baseball? Your mother tells me you were a pretty good baseball player. A switch hitter, in fact."

Abegg is a tall, gaunt, white-haired man. He reminds you of an undertaker. His office is a huge corner one, with windows facing President Street and Prospect Park. All the walls are cherrywood. Three of them are floor to ceiling bookcases. There's a big desk he sits behind, and a long black leather divan beneath the windows facing the park. There's even a silver nameplate on his desk, which seems silly, but the overall effect is one of intimidation.

You lie about growing bored with baseball, but admit how your sister ruined drumming for you. You want to build muscle, you tell him, that's why the weights.

"Maybe your sister was just being mean about the drums," he says.

"No, that's something Thomas Rocco would say, that the band was using me to practice."

"Maybe your father is jealous."

"Of what? He's the one with the money."

"What does money have to do with anything?"

"You'll have to ask him."

"I'm asking you. Do you believe money is a measure of your worth? Is that what bothers you?"

The fuck is he talking about, you're thinking. "I don't know. I don't care."

"Obviously you do care."

"I don't know. I'm too young to worry about money."

"Exactly."

You shrug. You can't tell if he's trying to con you, or if Thomas Rocco is whispering in your ear telling you he's trying to con you.

"All I'm saying is you shouldn't let your father, or your sister, stop you from doing something you obviously enjoy," he says. "No matter what they say or feel, it shouldn't stop you from moving forward. You can do anything you want, Charlie."

"Like be President some day?"

"You're being sarcastic, but the truth is, yes, why not? Anybody can be President. It would be up to you to pursue if it's what you want."

Almost 50 years later, the theory is proved correct when an incompetent con artist, in fact, becomes President of the United States. It is a presidency that will leave a stain on America forever.

Meantime, Dr. Abegg may mean well, but now you know he's conning you. "I don't know, okay?"

"Well, maybe your father was just being mean when he said that to your sister," Abegg says. "*If* he said it. You don't actually know that he did say it, do you?"

"No, that was him alright. And it was her job to deliver the message."

It's something you've come to believe in, a manipulative conspiracy theory. Thomas Rocco has your sister's number. He knows exactly what to say to her when he means it for you.

"Well, maybe they were both being mean," Abegg says.

Duh, you're thinking. "I'd rather lift weights," you say.

"So you can fight better?"

"I feel better knowing I'm building muscle. Building something."

Abegg suggests you write down your feelings each night and look them over before coming into his office the next week. "Sometimes keeping a journal helps us to see more clearly," he says.

You do as you're told, but the journal turns into another collection of starts to stories you never finish. You continue staying up late nights watching movies to get ideas for more starts to more stories you won't finish. And to some degree it works. Your mind's eye begins to work like a camera. The scenes develop as if on film:

> *He watched from a doorway across the street as his father left the restaurant with a much younger blonde woman. He watched them kiss before getting inside the family car. He watched them kiss again once they were inside the car, and he swore he'd wake up extra early the next morning to give the family car two flats before his father left for work.*

The problem is follow-through. It doesn't happen. Self-doubt turns to paranoia turns to anxiety, ruining each attempt to finish what you've started.

And forget about sleep. Your mind runs on all cylinders 24/7.

I can't write about the family without telling the truth because it's all I know and the truth is too ugly and painful and there's nothing I can do about it except to lie on the page and make believe everything is all right when it's not. My mother is in pain, my sister is hurtful, and my father doesn't give a shit about any of us, and it's all my fault because if I were someone he could be proud of, he wouldn't have left us. How the fuck do I tell that story?

You don't tell that story. You also don't go to school. You cut classes whenever you don't want to face what you're convinced is over your head anyway. The school calls home again and then you have to explain your latest problems to Dr. Abegg one more time. You're staying up late night writing stories you can't finish and can't get up for school in the morning, but you aren't bringing your journal because you're embarrassed you're writing stories instead of your personal tales of woe. Do you really want this guy looking that far inside your head? Does he have to know everything?

When will you have a girlfriend? Why didn't you ask Alena out? Or Jean? Or one of the twins that liked you in fourth grade? And what about the band? You need to play drums again. Girls like musicians. Or baseball. Why'd you quit? You can still play. He'll just say you aren't that good again. So will your sister and she hates you. Why? The hell you do to her? You should've helped that kid with his bike that day. You need to string together a series of wins in street fights, but they have to be older and bigger than you or it won't count. You could do something for your mother while you're at it. You need to show up your father, the prick. Get rich. Money is all he respects. But you don't care about money. You're a dreamer. Maybe start a business? Invent something. But what? Make them all proud. Make them all envious. Which is more important? You better join the fuckin' Army ...

Another few weeks pass and you're failing almost every class because you're not doing the work and you're still cutting classes. Even you know that this can't go on much longer, not if you want to be President one day.

The upside is you've begun to read again. You're reading what you enjoyed in that English class, everything Albert Camus wrote. You even learn a little bit about him visiting the library where you sister works during the times she's not there. You learn about André Gide and Jean Paul Sartre, because they've written existentialist works as well. You're starting to grasp this shit, but you want to grasp even more. Sartre's *No Exit* gets you to pen your own starts to plays, because that one has grabbed you, and for a lot longer than you can possibly realize.

For whatever reason, you begin to wonder about reincarnation and the justice inherent to your theory of it. Do we all get to be someone else, every other living thing, until we've lived and died as them all? It sometimes makes your head swim when you try and do the math, but you cling to the justice of not only being the human who squashes the bug for no other reason than seeing it on the floor, you'll also be the bug that gets squashed one day.

Justice is what counts. It can be pure, simple, and unavoidable, except it doesn't always work that way, does it? The fact that there are so many living things to become and then die seems overwhelming. Time marches on, and who is to say how long it has already been marching? How about until we've all lived and died all the lives possible before the true second coming arrives and everyone is sent one way or the other, to heaven or hell.

You're at the library one day and see *The Brothers Karamazov* on one of the tables. It's been left out by someone. It's a thick book, a lot thicker than the existentialist novels and plays you've read. The fact it's so thick makes it a challenge you can't pass on. You take it out and begin reading that night. It's going to be a chore you'll engage at least three more times in your more adult life, but you're glad you took the challenge. Although you can't pronounce any of the names, you figure out a way to shorten them so you can recognize each character. It is a wordy novel, but the story keeps you engaged, especially all the back and forth about religion.

Did God create man, or was it the other way around?

Little Jesus has become quite the philosopher, except this line of reasoning demands you take the religion you've abandoned seriously. Justice assumes a higher power. Or maybe injustice proves there isn't a higher power.

Take your pick.

It is what you often wonder about sitting in the chair directly across from Dr. Abegg. He no doubt lives a good life, but you wonder if he's ever lived life at the other end of the food chain? Was he ever truly poor?

You build a steady resentment for Dr. Abegg that you have to repress each time you're brought to his office, once a week at first, then twice a week, because you've become unbearable at home where your mother continues to catch the resentment you apparently have for Thomas Rocco. The office visits are supposed to be confidential, but your mother grills a chunk of your confidentiality from you after each visit to see if it meshes with what the good doctor has told her.

And it probably isn't helping that one of the Karamazov brothers, Dmitri, is often a violent whackadoo, and he's the one you're identifying with the most.

You've told Dr. Abegg how you feel about what has happened to your family, how you've become frustrated that your father doesn't seem to care. You've wondered if you're the reason they split up, because everyone else seems to have adjusted. Your sister has a girlfriend only you know about, and she's too preoccupied to care what else is going on. Although you know your mother is unhappy, she goes to work every day. Your weights are now the only distraction from the mess you've made of your life. The weights have taken the place of the drums you've stacked and pushed into a corner of the basement. The drums make you feel guilty when you see them.

The other thing you tell him is that you can no longer sleep without taking Nyquil. It's something you know your mother has mentioned to him because she's warned you about becoming addicted to the stuff. Most nights when you think you're ready to fall asleep your mind won't let you.

What if I was handsome? What if I was smart? What if I was a great boxer and I won the world championship? I like the way Joe Frazier fights. Maybe I could teach myself or join a boxing gym without telling Thomas Rocco and then I could fight and win the Golden Gloves, or maybe be a race car driver who wins the Indy 500, or a war hero that takes out a machine gun nest and saves the platoon, or maybe become President one day. Wouldn't that be neat? Go to a shrink on President Street and become President some day? What if I screwed Marion next door? What if she came on to me? What if I was a ghost and could go anywhere without people knowing I was there? What if I could walk into the vault of a bank and take all the money and give it to people who need it and nobody could see me do it? What if I could make Thomas Rocco fall back in love with Mom? What if I was whatever the fuck it is Thomas Rocco wants me to be?

It's insane shit when you think about it, but those are some of the thoughts that keep you awake nights until you take a dose and a half of Nyquil, until you're so half-cocked from the stuff, you can't think about anything and you're asleep before you know it.

And when you wake up the next day groggy from the Nyquil still in your system, it takes another few hours, usually several hours you're supposed to be in school, before you're awake enough to work out with the weights again, because you want to build something.

Your adult brain, which has been doing okay for being stuck inside your noggin, does NOT appreciate the Nyquil.

St. Patrick Part Deux ...

You're on your way to school one morning and decide to stop at
Ralston's on Avenue L for a Yoo-Hoo. When you turn the corner on 95th
Street, you see a bunch of bullies harassing a fair-haired, pale-skinned
kid about your age. He's fighting back, wildly swinging a heavy
backpack, but it's no use. They trip him to the sidewalk and start
spraying him with spit between kicks to his ribs. You recognize one of
them from a prior fight at the high school. He's one of the punks from
the battle of the bands, a group of local delinquents who have claimed
the avenue for themselves, except they usually hang out there after
hours. Watching them spit on the fair-haired, pale-skinned kid as he
protects his backpack is too much to watch. It affronts your sense of
justice.

You get involved, shoving the one you recognize away before a brief
exchange of fisticuffs. It ends when the hardware store owner comes out
with a baseball bat and tells the bullies to get lost. The leader of the gang
makes a few threats, and you yell out your home address in case he's
interested in continuing the fight some other time. The store owner tells
you and the fair-haired kid to come inside for a few minutes until the
cops arrive. He's already called them and it's just a matter of minutes
before they'll be there.

The last thing you need is for the police to bring you home. It'll upset
your mother no end. You and the fair-haired, pale-skinned kid take off.
Instead of going to school, you head in the opposite direction. Him
toward the projects where he lives and you toward home, both
destinations near the Canarsie Pier.

"Gave them your address, eh?" he says with the hint of a solid Irish
accent. "That was fookin' dumb."

Your eyebrows furrow.

"Perplexed?" he says.

"Excuse me?"

"You're not very smart, are you?"

"Hey, fuck-face, I wasn't the one getting spit on."

"Fuck face is it?"

"You heard me."

The fair-haired, pale-skinned kid smiles.

"What?" you say.

"You remind me of somebody," he says, "except you're an Eejit."

"And you're welcome," you say.

"I didn't ask for your help, did I?"

You roll your eyes.

He smacks you off the stomach and holds out his hand. "The name's Patrick. Patrick Cogan. Saint Patrick to you."

His name stops you. It's familiar, but you can't place it. Your brow furrows again. "St. Patrick?" you say.

"The one and only."

"And how's that?"

"I'll tell you some other time. When I can trust you. *If* I can trust you. What say we get something to eat in the meantime, then head down to the water?"

Half an hour later, instead of being in math class, you're both eating bagels on a bench on the Canarsie Pier. Jamaica Bay is calm. The sun bounces sparklers of light off the water, one of the miracles of nature that will always require your attention.

St. Patrick must not feel the same way. He says, "Hey, numb-nuts, the hell are you staring at?"

You motion with your head toward the water, but he obviously doesn't see what you're seeing. "Eejit," he says.

You ignore the insult and ask where he lives.

He motions behind him. "Bayview projects," he says. "Just moved there from the projects on Ralph Avenue."

"Why'd those clowns pick on you?"

He points to his backpack. "Books."

"Huh?"

"I had one out, checking the return date. The books are from the library. They must've seen I had books and figured I was an easy target."

"You were."

He flips you the bird.

"What books? Which ones?"

He unzips the backpack and spills the books onto the bench. You go through the titles and feel that *déjà vu* shit all over again. There's one small one, a paperback, called *Nine Stories*. There's a thick one called *The Grapes of Wrath*. There's one by the same author, *The Winter of Our Discontent*. That one rings a bell, but you don't know why. There are two you've already read, *The Stranger*, and the one that took you some time to finish, *The Brothers Karamazov*.

"Not impressed?" he says.

"I read a couple of those."

"Which?"

"None of your Irish mick business, is it?" you say, mocking his Irish accent.

He leans over and drags the back of his knuckles on the pavement a few inches.

"The hell is that supposed to be?"

"You and your kind, you Eejit, Dago."

You're confused.

"Knuckle-draggers," he said.

You can't help but smile. He does the same and you ask him which school he goes to.

"Tilden," he says.

"Why there?"

"We used to live on Linden Boulevard before Ralph Avenue. You a cop with all the questions?"

"You move a lot. What's up with that?"

"You're a fucking detective, eh?"

"Making conversation. How old are you?"

"Eejit. Fifteen."

"Me, too."

"And your name, you rude prick?"

You smile. "Charlie. Carmelo actually."

"I knew it, a guinea. Now it makes sense."

You flip him the bird again. He winks at you before flipping two back, and a friendship is born.

The Jesus Interview ...

Two weeks pass and you manage to stay out of fights. You and St. Patrick have become best friends. You trade insults like a long married couple. He's clever, a lot more than you are, and your insult repertoire expands because of it. You're picking up new insults, although your generation still calls them rank-outs, and he's learning there are people in the world who aren't scumbags. The two of you become inseparable, even though you each attend different high schools, which leads to a lot more class-cutting.

When you tell your mother you've made a friend, she's happy to hear it. "Invite him for dinner," she says. "I want to meet him."

"I'm not sure he'd go for that," you say. "He's kind of shy."

"Translation," you sister chirps in, "he's another loser. That or he's retarded."

"Why don't you go downstairs to the garage, make sure the doors are closed, start Mom's car and take a nap on the back seat?" you say, compliments of St. Patrick.

"Charlie!" your mother says.

Your sister looks shocked. Not only that, she doesn't recover as fast as she's used to recovering, and she has to take the cheap way out. "Why don't you?" she says. "And invite your new friend while you're at it."

You flash a big smile. You can imagine the confrontation between the two of them, St. Patrick and your sister, but you're afraid that once your sister learns your friend's situation, she'll go for blood. You don't want to witness that, so you avoid them meeting like you've avoided attending Mass since you graduated from St. Jude. You bring St. Patrick to the house after your sister leaves for school, and you get him out before she comes home from the library.

Over the next few weeks you and St. Patrick share family war stories. You learn a little more about him with each conversation. He'd spent most of his thirteenth year in the Spofford Juvenile Center in the Bronx before he was released and learned that his mother had taken off with her boyfriend. He'd since been living with his drunken, abusive, and all around dirt-bag father.

He'd also been in love with a redheaded, freckled, Jewish girl from Canarsie, which was why he knew the neighborhood so well. He was sure it was love until her alcoholic, single-mother, managed to set fire to their apartment, and the redheaded, freckled, Jewish girl was no more. You learn St. Patrick had walked in on his mother with other men more than once, and that he'd caught his father with a girl he recognized from a math class in high school. To round out the familial nightmare he described, St. Patrick's only other living relative, his paternal grandfather, was going to die in an upstate prison for killing a corrections officer while doing time for a bank robbery.

Learning about his father, big Jim Cogan, teaches you some perspective, little Jesus. St. Patrick has caught his father's wrath on more than one occasion, including fists to the face and boots to the ribs, and for nothing other than being more genetically linked to his fair-haired, pale-skinned, and slight-of-build mother than his black Irish, big-boned Dad. Thomas Rocco's slaps to your chops pale by comparison.

When St. Patrick shows you a picture of his mom, you can see the resemblance. St. Patrick is indeed his mother's son. You wonder if people see you as your mother's son.

"So why didn't you try and find your mother?" you ask.

He counts off his fingers: "First, you dumb wop, if she took off, it means she didn't want me. Two, you ignorant, knuckle-dragging Dago, because before she left my father for an even bigger scumbag, I almost killed him, her boyfriend. Why I got sent to a juvie joint."

"Spofford?"

"What I said, right? Maybe I should tattoo it on my forehead."

You smile.

His eyebrows furrow before he calls you an Eejit again.

You learn a lot more about St. Patrick over the next few days, including the fact he's incredibly well read. Reading has been his sanctuary, including spending most of his days in libraries, especially the one where your sister works at next to Canarsie High School. Does he know her? Does she know him? Her library was where he was heading instead of to school the day you first met him.

You want to discuss things with him, especially the Russian novel you've read, *The Brothers Karamazov*, but first you want to know about this St. Patrick business. The day you ask him, he tells you it has to do with a dream he's had, except he was certain it wasn't a dream. He claims he was diagnosed with mania before he went to Spofford, but he's damn sure the interview he'd had was the real deal.

The conversation takes place in your basement after a vigorous workout with your weights. Both of you are sweaty. St. Patrick is sipping a cold Coke. You're sitting on your drum throne, the only piece of your drum kit you haven't banished to the far corner.

"Explain," you say. "What's with the Saint bullshit?"

"It's no bullshit," he says. "Happened the morning after I was put in the calm room. I was there two days after I cracked one of Spofford's staff across the face with a table tennis racket. They shoved me in a jacket and put me in isolation. Was in the morning, about six or so, when I had the vision, except it wasn't a dream. It was real. I could even hear the monastery bells a couple blocks away. I knew it was real because I'd just woke up from a wet dream I had."

"Dream means you were asleep, putz," you say.

"Eejit," he says. "Was me and Bettie Page, her in black garters and heels, me in my Fruit-of-the-Looms, blotch-stained when she touched me and I came all over myself."

You recognize the name, but can't place it. "Who was she?"

"The most famous pin-up girl of all time. Why the shrinks at Spofford claim it's all a dream. She was, but the Jesus interview wasn't. That was for real."

"The Jesus what?"

"I'm just cleaning myself up from Bettie and suddenly I'm up on the ceiling watching myself on the bed down below. Not an easy task, since I'd been restrained the night before."

"Sounds like a dream to me," you say.

"Shut your pie hole and listen. I can't explain it, but I look up and can see myself watching down. I was embarrassed no end about the wet dream, even though it was only me watching myself."

He stops to take another sip of Coke. You're too familiar with the ceiling point of view to stop him. You're thinking about the funeral for yourself you've more than once daydreamed.

"Yeah, and?" you say.

"There's a voice calling, except I don't recognize it. Who's there, I say? I can see and hear myself say it, but I don't see anybody. My back is against the ceiling while I watch myself below. Again I ask, who's there? Who is it?"

He stopped to take another drink, after which he belched, and said, "Next thing there's a cloud at the end of my bed. The cloud takes the shape of a man, looks like a man, except I can't really tell." He flips you the bird while taking another sip of his soda, then belches and excuses himself. "This guy the end of the bed tells me I'm being interviewed for a Jesus job."

"A what?"

"The fuck, I'm speaking Chinese?" he says. "A Jesus job. The guy wants to ask me some questions, says it's a Jesus interview."

"Why you?"

"The fuck do I know, why me. Something about suffering. I'd passed the suffering test or some shit."

"Because of your parents?"

"And Kim. The girl I told you about. The one died in the fire."

"Red hair and freckles."

St. Patrick nods, coughs a few times, then swallows hard. The mention of the girl he'd loved has obviously jolted him. "Anyway," he says, "she was why they turned me down."

"I don't get it," you say.

"I loved her too much. They said I wasn't even a Job because of it."

"Who's they and who's Job?"

"You're one ignorant Dago, you know that? What you do in that Catholic school you attended, sleep through your religion classes? Job, you Eye-talian dipshit, was the guy God bet on against the Devil. God let the Devil take a series of shits on Job's head to see if he'd denounce God. You don't know that one, you're not Catholic."

"And you believe that bullshit?"

"Did I say that?"

You're curious about this bet and have to ask. "What happened with Job?"

St. Patrick is finishing off his Coke. "The fuck do I know?" he says before a long, loud, blast of a belch. "God won the bet, that's all I know.

Job didn't lose his faith after being fucked with by the Devil."

"So, what, they think because you loved this girl so much, they had to kill her to see if you'd love God more? That's some fucked-up shit."

"And I don't have a problem not passing their test, so fuck them anyway. Then I was asked a bunch of questions about my mother and father, and why didn't I kill the guy banging my mother when I had the chance, and so on."

"Why didn't you?"

"I did, you Eejit. A friend of his was there and stopped me. I had the knife and was going for his back, dead fuckin' center, but the friend grabbed my arm. Then ma's boyfriend kicked me square in the balls and that was the end of that."

"That when they put you away?"

"You catch on quick for a moron. Yeah, the same night. Never heard from her again, my mother. They contacted my father, and that asshole picked me up the day I was released. Never visited me once while I was inside, either, the prick."

"And the Saint bullshit, for the ten thousandth time, you arrogant, Mick cocksucker. Where'd that come from?"

"End of the interview, just before the guy was giving the interview turned back into a cloud. He said the Lord God was rejecting me for the Jesus job, but wanted me in the lineup. Called me a Saint and said that's what I was. So here I am, Saint Patrick."

There are too many similarities between your dream and his, but you can't remember most of them. Still, your adult brain is fighting the possibility of coincidence. Neither of you knew the other before you saved him from that spit bath on Avenue L. It suddenly strikes you to ask him, "When was this dream of yours?"

"Bettie Page? I still get that one. I'm St. Patrick two years now."

"When were you born? What day?"

"Another interrogation?"

"When, asshole?"

"June one."

"What time?"

"The fuck do I know?"

"You never asked?"

"The fuck would I care?"

"Moron."

"Eejit."

The back and forth insult-a-thon continues until your sister surprises you by coming home early. She comes down to the basement and obviously recognizes St. Patrick. You look to him and can see he recognizes her, yet neither says a word to the other.

"What is it?" you ask her.

"Mom will be late," she says. "She said to order pizza."

"Fine."

She turns and leaves. You look to St. Patrick. "She works at the library," he says.

You wait for more, but that's it, the conversation is over.

If your adult brain was already working overtime thinking that the brothers, Mitya and Ivan Karamazov, were spewing some confusing shit, your adult brain was in for some more overtime periods.

No Good Deed Goes Unpunished ...

St. Patrick sharing your birthday and the similarity in your dreams keeps you awake nights. What about his Kim? What about her red hair and freckles? Could it be the same girl who used to chase you around the schoolyard back in kindergarten? Is this all coincidence or something more profound? Had God the Father sent St. Patrick to teach you? Was he a sign of things to come? Is it possible you passed a Jesus interview you're unaware of and actually are the Second Coming?

It's a lot to contemplate along with the other questions you have for St. Patrick, including his take on the books you've both read. He clearly understands more than you. Will he think you a bigger fool than you must be to have to ask?

Before you get the chance to question your new friend about anything, Columbus Day comes and goes. The school contacts your mother. They're about to expel you for cutting and send you someplace else. She tries calling Thomas Rocco but there's no point. He reminds your mother that he never finished high school.

"Maybe it's time he gets a job," he tells her. "Or he can join the Army next year."

When you next hook up with St. Patrick, you notice he's wearing sunglasses. He takes them off before you can make fun of him. Both his eyes are black and swollen.

"My father," he says.

"That's fucked-up," you say.

"And he wasn't even drunk this time."

That night you ask your mother if it's okay if St. Patrick moves in with you. You didn't ask St. Patrick if he wants to or not, but you want to protect him. Your mother claims you can't, not so long as he has a father, but if you go to school and do your work, she'll talk to the father and see if he'll let the boy stay with you a few nights a week.

It's the best deal you're going to get. You agree to the terms, but your sister goes off the deep end. She's not living in the same house as you and one of your loser friends, she says. You remind her she already knows him because of the library. "What do you mean, loser?" you say. "He's a reader. He recognized you from the library. He goes there, like, five times a week."

She says if he's a friend of yours, he must be a loser.

You wonder if they've ever spoken to one another. Had St. Patrick given her lip? And which books had he taken home? Did she approve? Was she impressed before she learned he was your friend? Is she just being a bitch?

"He's a good kid," you say in frustration.

"Yeah, right," your sister says. "He's probably retarded."

And that does it. You go downstairs and punch a hole in her bedroom door. She follows you and hits you in the back of the head with the coffee cup she's been drinking tea from. You can feel blood and hot tea running down your neck. You step inside her room and punch a hole in her wall. She grabs a scissor and you warn her the next punch will be in her face. She doesn't put the scissors down, but she doesn't make a move either.

Your mother comes down, sees the door, the blood on your neck, the hole in the door, the hole in the wall, your sister holding the scissors, and your clenched fist, and that's more than enough for her. She runs for the phone. You think she's calling your father, but she's not. She's calling Dr. Abegg. He tells her he knows what needs to be done. She's terrified, but agrees to go along with the medical expert for the sake of your mental health.

You learn another of life's valuable lessons: no good deed goes unpunished, like trying to help a friend.

One Flew Into the Cuckoo's Nest ...

"Do you masturbate?" the young doctor asks.

Bad enough you're in an environment so sterile it's frightening. Everything is white, lime green, or powder fucking blue. The hallways are so barren you can hear the scuffling of slippers and the squeaking of shoe leather whenever someone is walking. The rooms are modern, hotel-like, and big enough for two beds with some distance between them, but the bars on the windows remind you this isn't a vacation. The thick glass partitions separating the nurse station from where they distribute the dope is another reminder you're amongst some crazy motherfuckers. This morning you were given a plastic cup with two pills, a yellow and a blue. You didn't know what they were, but were told to take them with one of the Dixie cups filled with water waiting on a tray alongside the dope booth.

And now this youngish-looking asshole doctor asks you something you have no clue about. Masturbation? The fuck is it? Sounds disgusting, that's all you're thinking, something you should never admit to, like cutting up the license plate. They didn't teach you anything about whatever it is in Catholic school, that's for sure. They didn't teach anything sexual ever, nor did your old man, or any other adult. Your sex education came from a possible pedophile in training and he never used that word.

"No," you say with a little attitude.

The youngish doctor smiles and says, "Do you know what masturbation is?"

"Yeah," you lie. "Big deal."

He smiles again, but you're pretty sure the smiles are smirks in disguise. He writes something in his chart and asks you about girls. Do you have a girlfriend? Did you ever have one? Is there some girl you like, but are too shy to ask out on a date? Is there some boy?

You're confused by his last question. You don't get it until a full four hours later and then you want to kick that doctor in the balls, mostly because he's reminded you of the pedophile in training, but you can't do that, you'll never get out of that place if you do. What you do is find a dictionary in the nuthouse library where you look up the word, masturbation, and then give him a nickname, Doctor Sexual-Stimulation-of-the-Genitals.

During the next examination later the same day, you notice he not only looks young for a doctor, he acts young with all his high and mighty smiling and smirking. Dr. Abegg hardly ever showed emotion. This change in authority and atmosphere, old to young, office to institution, confuses you. You won't remember what else Dr. Sexual-Stimulation-of-the-Genitals asks that day, but when you're through with him you're assigned a roommate, a man older than Thomas Rocco. You won't remember much about him, except that he wore pajamas a lot of the time and he was always very kind. After your initial night in observation, the nightmare *that* had been, you feel protected with your roommate, something you wish you could feel with Thomas Rocco.

You don't remember much else about day two of your stay at the somewhat famous, apparently all-purpose South Oaks Hospital, although you'd been reassured several times that your stay there has more to do with being emotionally disturbed than crazy. Apparently

South Oaks, among other things, had once served as a dry-out facility for famous drunks like Judy Garland.

You're not really sure. Those stories could've been rumors.

The night before, your first night, there weren't any beds available on the first floor where young adult observation was normally conducted. You were given a bed in post electric shock treatment recovery on the second floor instead. Whether it was someone's cruel joke or not, you'll never know, but you spent the entire night with your head under the covers, because one of the men in recovery had been strapped to his bed and was screaming as if he were being tortured, and it didn't take a fucking medical degree to know this place you were in had nothing to do with being emotionally disturbed.

You, little Jesus, were in a nuthouse.

And you were going to be there for at least ten days without visitors, not your mother or St. Patrick, no exceptions.

Day three you're at dinner in a cafeteria where you can see women, young and old, on the other side of a glass partition. A railing separates the two dining areas, but you're checking out the younger talent when two guys about your age sit across from you, blocking your view.

"Name?" the bigger of the two says.

"Charlie. You?"

"Mike," the smaller one says.

"Billy," the bigger one says. "Got any money?"

"Few bucks."

"We're gonna cop some weed."

"I don't smoke."

"We do."

"Good for you."

"You a wiseass?"

You smile. You know you can kick this one's ass. He's about your age.

"Hey!" he says, probably louder than he meant, but he also stands up and knocks the end of the table into your chest. No matter it's accidental, you see it as a challenge; the ghost of the nearly stolen bike still lingers. You nail the tall kid in the forehead with a straight right and the orderlies are there before you know it.

You spend the night in restraints. You assume the other kid does as well.

On day four Dr. Sexual-Stimulation-of-the-Genitals is back. He's heard about the fight at dinner last night. He wants you to tell him what was behind it and all the other fights you've had.

"It says here on your chart that you're an angry young man."

You shrug, this time with a lot more confidence, but you still don't have much to say.

"You can't fight the world, Charlie," he says. "You'll have to figure out a better way to handle your frustrations."

Yeah, no shit, you're thinking. You hope these geniuses didn't spend a lot of time and money earning their degrees.

"So, the question is, how do you want to handle it?" he says.

You're coming up with some clever St. Patrick lines about now and have to restrain yourself from spewing them.

How about you go fuck yourself while I take a cab back to Canarsie?

How about sticking your finger in an electric socket while drinking a glass of water?

How about I smack that dopey smirk off your face?

"Well?" he says.

You tell him what your mother told you Dr. Abegg had said: You don't know why you're pissed off, but you know Thomas Rocco is embarrassed by you, and that he wishes he had some other kid for a son.

"Somebody he could be proud of?" he says. "Or somebody you think he'd be proud of?"

The hint of smile on his face sets you off. Is he making fun of you? Is he rubbing it in?

You uppercut his chart and the metal end hits him in the forehead. You stop yourself from going further, suddenly realizing that you really are an angry young man.

You walk to the windows and watch the lunatics kicking a basketball instead of shooting hoops in the recreation yard. The young doctor attends to the small cut in his forehead, but after a minute or so, you hear movement behind you. When you turn around there are three orderlies: all big, all black, all watching you.

"Come wiff us," one of them says.

You look to Dr. Sexual-Stimulation-of-the-Genitals, but he's avoiding eye contact.

"Come on, kid," another of the orderlies says. "Le's go. Nice and easy."

Justo "Little Che" Espina ...

You spend the night in the equivalent to lockdown, strapped to a bed in a room with no furniture. They've given you a sedative, but you didn't mind, because you know it'll help you sleep. You were told to use the bathroom before being strapped down, but that was after the Dixie cup of water you used to down the sedative. Now that it's about three o'clock in the morning, you have to piss like a racehorse.

You know you won't make it and start to let it go when the door opens and an orderly pushes a youngish-looking dude in a wheelchair into the room. He's wearing a dark green beret with a star on the crown. He has thick black framed glasses and a peach fuzz mustache.

"Hey, you pissed yourself," he says with a slight Hispanic accent.

You don't respond but glare at him instead.

The orderly leaves him facing you, a few feet from the end of your bed.

"How long you in here?" he asks.

You continue to stare.

"You're going to blink sooner or later," he says.

You remain silent, but eventually blink. He's been waiting for it and smiles.

"The fuck is your problem?" you say.

"Me? No problem. You're the one pissed himself."

"Asshole, I'm tied down."

"Me too. You see any wet spots on me?"

You sigh.

"Hey, I'm just fucking with you, man. What you do to get locked up?"

"Smacked a clipboard. It hit a doctor and he bled a little."

He nods.

"And you?" you ask.

"Talked over my doctor. Recited *The Manifesto* while he tried to brainwash me."

"Recited what?"

"*The Communist Manifesto*."

"The fuck is that?"

"I figured you for short on intelligence."

"Say what?"

"You know who Karl Marx was? Friedrich Engels?"

"I know the Marx brothers. Groucho and Chico. Or the ones who make toys?"

"You're an idiot. Okay, conversation over."

"Hey, fuck-face. I get out of this, I'll break your jaw."

He yawns.

"The fuck is your problem?" you ask again.

He begins a spiel on communism, the manifesto he mentioned, and why he's been brought to South Oaks. His parents are legal immigrants from Cuba. They are also wealthy. His father is an international lawyer and his mother is a banker. They live in Sands Point, Long Island, but also own a condo in Manhattan where he goes to the prestigious Dalton private school. He's been asked to leave due to his inability to maintain the proper school etiquette.

"What's that mean?" you ask. "You fart in class or something?"

"I try to reeducate the mass of morons the school is turning into future capitalist pigs, many of which will one day continue the social stratification that suffocates the voice of the proletariat."

He waits to see if you've been following him, sees you can't, then adds, "The people."

"What about them?" you say.

"*Pendejo*," he says.

The two of you are stuck together for several more hours. Eventually you fall asleep from his reeducation attempts, but the truth is, you found yourself interested in some of the shit he was talking about. You decide you won't break his face if you get to see him again.

In the morning, after you've been shaken awake by a nurse carrying your medication, you notice he's no longer in the room. You ask the nurse about him and she claims she just started her shift and doesn't know where he is.

You're finally released from bondage and allowed to shower. When you return to your room, there's a thin booklet on your pillow, *The Communist Manifesto*. Inside the cover is a handwritten note. It reads: *Pendejo (asshole), it was good meeting you. Start with this and get a clue. Hope to see you again soon, but only if you've read this. Use a dictionary if you get lost. Call me in a month or so. Your comrade, Justo "Che" Espina.*

Asshole? You wonder if maybe you're better off punching him in the face.

There but for the grace of God ...

Your new friend aside, the research you did on masturbation, plus seeing some of the women at dinner the night before you got yourself into the shit, set you to wondering if you'll ever have a girlfriend. Outside of a few one-way, puppy-love crushes you had growing up, you're 0 for your life thus far.

Imagining a girl with freckles occupies most of your brain's energy. Jean from school liked you enough to let the other girls in your class know. This was back when the girls sent notes to boys they liked through a friend: *Jean said she likes you.*

Doofus that you were, you ducked the opportunity. That was in St. Jude's Catholic school, six months before Jean's family moved to New Jersey. The problem, of course, was you were too busy trying to impress

THE VOICES IN MY HEAD

Thomas Rocco with the more macho aspects of life in the 8th grade, like getting in fights.

And even after you managed to become at least one of the toughest kids in St. Jude, you were too afraid to ask Jean out. At South Oaks you wonder if she's found someone with more guts.

Or maybe there's a chance you can find her again once you're out of the nuthouse. Thoughts turn to daydreams so smooth and fast you forget where you are until you're confronted with the wood you're sprouting between your legs, except it isn't Jean you're thinking about. It's that wiseguy's *comare* again. Your mother had mentioned how Marion was frustrated because she's the other woman and she doesn't get to see her boyfriend enough. You, epic daydreamer, turn it into magic.

"Hey, Charlie, can you come over and help me with something?"

"Sure, Marion. What do you need?"

She walks you up to her bedroom, first checking on her daughters to make sure they're napping. A minute later, inside her bedroom, she says, "I need a favor."

"Sure."

"But you can't say anything to anybody. Not your friends or your mother. Especially not your mother."

"Sure."

She takes off her top and ...

The restraints of the open door policy and the dopey therapy sessions preclude you from taking care of business, and a new form of frustration is born.

Statistically, most people your age are already experimenting with sex, but it's been different for you. Your sex can't be accounted for, not with a possible pedophile. And now there's an erection you're too nervous to do anything about.

Until that Marion-inspired erection, it wasn't about sex. You wanted someone to like you. The girl-crazy images that you yearned for had more to do with holding hands, or walking with arms around each other's waist, or that special moment when a girl leans her head into a guy's shoulder. It's been kissing and hugging you longed for, not the stuff you thought you were supposed to fantasize about.

And that can't be Marion. That woman reeks of sex.

So maybe it's Jean after all.

"Hey, Jean. Do you remember back in St. Jude's when you had someone send me a note that you liked me?"

DOOOOOOOOOOOOOOOOOOOOOOOOOOFUS!

Okay, so you're not nearly ready yet, but aside from sex not being the thing you wanted most from women, you also want loyalty. You assume once you have a girlfriend, it'll have to be for life, that you'll marry and never stray, the exact opposite of what Thomas Rocco did. You've convinced yourself that there's no way you'll do to your family what he's done to his.

You can't imagine the end of a relationship. How does that happen once you fall in love? Is it possible Thomas Rocco never really loved your mother? Then why the fuck did he marry her? Why go through all that shit, marrying, having kids, buying a house, etc., if you don't love someone enough to stay with them? Can people fall out of love? If so, why?

These are questions that will long bounce around the inside of your skull, and sometimes turn your adult brain to mush. You'll eventually figure out there are no guarantees to anything in this life, except death, and you've already done that once. For now your overly romantic worldview precludes you from seeing the end of anything. You're still an insecure motherfucker, so you won't take chances once you find somebody willing to be your girlfriend. You're not nearly confident enough to have a clue how you'll someday become a guy who jumps from one woman and affair and marriage to another before becoming comfortable enough with yourself to fall in love with a woman who will change your life for the better.

But in 1971 you're less than a year from that first girlfriend you so crave, and girls have yet to prove an obsession. Truth be told, they aren't close to what Strat-O-Matic and drumming have been, or to what lifting weights has become. By day six, your mind is clear of concern about your lack of a love life.

The fight you had with the tall kid has left you with nuthouse credibility. Days four through six you sat in on a few morning group therapy sessions with him and some other kids around your age. You haven't seen the little shit who left you the book autographed with insults, but you haven't really looked for him either. Most of the kids in therapy are in a different ward than you and most of them come from money. They are in South Oaks because of addictions. There are eight of them in total: four drug addicts, two alcoholics, and two seriously fucked-up boys your age with addictions to both drugs and alcohol. You learn about them when they tell some of their stories in the bluntest language you've ever heard.

"I started drinking when I was nine," one says. "I do coke when I have money. When I don't have money, I steal or take the train into the city and suck dicks on Forty-Second Street for whatever I need. Sometimes I'll stay with a guy there that gives me board for sucking his dick."

"I started using my sister's Quaaludes in sixth grade," another says.

"I moved to heroin when I could afford it in high school. I was doing twenty bags a day when I was caught robbing a church. The priests there knew my parents, so they didn't press charges. Why I'm here instead of a juvie center."

"I hit my parents' cash stash one day and bought two cases of gin I hid in the garage. I drank half a bottle of gin before my parents came home from work every day until I drank too much one day and passed out," another says. "I moved to dope when they put me on that Antabuse shit."

The tall kid admits to being a doper, too, then rocks your world with an admission to having sex with his mother. She's in jail now, but she's the one who started him on dope.

And you, Little Jesus, thought your family was fucked-up?

When you're asked to speak, you have nothing nearly as dramatic to offer. You talk about your parents' divorce and a few fights you had, but you don't provide details. You're too embarrassed.

You get to spend some extra time with all eight of them during a second group therapy session before the last recreation hour, and you hear a few more horror stories. Then somebody points at you again, but you're speechless.

"What, you never get high?"

You shake your head no.

"Why not, man? You an athlete or something?"

"I don't like that shit," you finally say. "I have enough shit in my life without it."

"He's a fighter, man," another kid says.

You shrug, enjoying for the moment that little bit of celebrity. You wish there was something you could say to convince them they need to clean up their acts. Their situations are so much worse than yours. You want to tell them, but you're still too embarrassed and insecure to express your concerns for them.

That afternoon you take a short nap and are visited by a devil. You know it's a devil because you recognize him from *The Brothers Karamazov*. He sits across from you in your dream. He taunts you about the kids you were concerned about.

"Want to know what happens to them, those losers?" he says.

"No," you say.

"Too bad. They all die from their addictions. Or because of their addictions. One of them gets shot by the police. Another shoots himself in the head. Another hangs himself. Want to know which ones did what?"

"No, fuck off."

"No way. I'm here for the duration, my friend. You'll see."

You wake up when the loudspeaker announces medication time. It's the first time you're grateful for that shit.

Before dinner the same day the devil introduced himself to you, you're out in the exercise yard watching the chronics in another fenced off area. They obviously aren't seeing the same world as you and your new friends. You're told they can be dangerous, why they have their own area to exercise. All they seem to do is walk around the basketball court or stand in one place. They often just stare at nothing in particular, but they will occasionally kick or throw the ball against the fence rather than up at the basketball hoops.

You feel bad for them because they remind you of the Jerry Lewis Telethons and how your mother would always say, *"There but for the grace of God."* You still can't understand why God would do that to anyone, but you understood your mother's sentiment for what it was.

Bottom line? You've adjusted, little Jesus. You're still anxious to get the hell out of South Oaks, but you're no longer afraid of your environment. Hell, this will earn you some props back on the street. You can hear them talking about it in your Little Jesus daydreams.

Charlie was in a nuthouse, man. Don't fuck with him.

An idea comes to mind. Write a story about your stay there and call it: *There but for the grace of God.*

There's an uninformed portion of society that will think it's cool you're crazy. Juxtaposed to those people will be others who think you're damaged goods. Some might even feel sorry for you, the last thing you want. It's empirical knowledge gained the old fashioned way, by doing the time. You're learning about life in spite of yourself, and it reminds you of a few lines from a Joni Mitchell song you've heard playing from your sister's bedroom a hundred times: *I don't know who I am, but you know life is for learning.*

And it doesn't buzz by your soon to be mega-medicated little Jesus brain that that same song, "Woodstock", starts with this line: *I came upon a child of God.*

Cherchez la femme ...

You find Justo sitting on a bench in the recreation yard reading a book through Ray-Ban Aviator sunglasses instead of the thick framed glasses he was wearing when you first met him. It's a thick book in his lap, but you don't bother asking about it. Instead, you ask him why he called you an asshole in the inscription he wrote in *The Communist Manifesto* he left you.

"I was fucking with you, man," he says. "Having some fun. I'm a revolutionary, why I'm here. My parents are in on it, my political assassination."

You shake your head.

"I know, I know," he says. "You don't get it yet. You will if you do some reading. I'm a follower of Che Guevara, okay? You don't know who he is, but you should. I strive to have the same political determination and discipline. He's a hero. My hero. You probably like, who, Mickey Mantle?"

"Baseball? Joe Christopher."

"Who's he?"

"Now who's the asshole?"

Justo smiles as he points at you. "Good one, *pendejo*. You might have potential."

"What's with the sunglasses?"

He pulls them off his head and you see two blackened eyes.

"Who did that?"

"One of the bourgeois urchins here because he can't deal with a life of modest luxury, so he takes drugs to offset his inexcusable depression," he says.

"Asshole, why can't you say because so and so punched me in the face? Why the extra bullshit?"

"*Obiter dictum*, what you're trying to say."

You close your eyes in frustration.

"You're right," Justo says. "Some *pendejo* punched me in the face."

"Who? Which one?"

"Why, you gonna protect me?"

"Maybe, if you quit being such a smart ass."

He nods and you sit alongside him.

There's a bond forming you liken to that with your friend back in Canarsie, St. Patrick. Both your new friends are smartasses and apparently a thousand times smarter than you. It's an upside wherein you have nothing to lose and everything to gain.

At least you've figured that out.

One of the rich kid drug addicts approaches you with a pack of cigarettes and offers you one.

"No thanks," you say, but you notice he doesn't offer Justo. You ask him why not.

"Because he's a wiseass," the rich kid says.

"And you're what, a humanitarian?" Justo asks him. "You ever pay back the people you robbed to feed your habit?"

"See?" the rich kid says.

"He's got a point," you say. "Do you ever pay them back?"

"You weirding out or something?" the rich kid says to you.

"How about when you punched me in the face?" Justo says. "That something you're proud of?"

"You want, I can do it again?" the rich kid says.

"Not if you want to keep your teeth," you say.

And that ends that. The rich kid's brow furrows as he slinks away. He gives you a few looks over his shoulder as he leaves, and you're pretty sure he mouths "fuck you," but it's not loud enough for anyone to hear.

"You're welcome," you say to Justo.

"And so I appoint you Lieutenant *Comandante*," he says.

"Whatever that means," you say.

"Read," he says.

You take out the *Manifesto* book and read, but you skip the introduction and the several prefaces to the several foreign additions. When you finally get to where you think you're supposed to start you're immediately lost.

"That a French word?" you ask Justo.

"Bourgeoisie," he says without looking at you or where you're pointing to in the book. "It means middle class."

"Oh," you say, then try reading some more, but you give up after half a page.

"You'll have to do some background reading," he says, "but pay attention to newspapers, not just the sports pages. Read about workers and how our social structure is based on a few people earning off the backs of the many. From there you'll start to understand how America's national will is imposed on the undeveloped world, to exploit what America can for profit, and so on. It sounds harder than it is, but you need to get this shit down if you're going to be a revolutionary."

"How old are you?" you ask. "That's a lot of reading for someone looks about fourteen."

"Seventeen, *pendejo*. I just look young. I've been reading since I'm very young, the only thing my bourgeois parents did for me. Now they regret it."

"I'm not sure I will be a revolutionary," you say. "Sounds like a lot of fucking reading."

"Or you can go through life with your eyes closed and get fucked," he says.

"I wouldn't mind getting fucked about now?" you say. "You getting any?"

"*Cabrón*."

"And what's that mean?"

"Bastard."

"Well, have you been laid yet? I haven't."

"*Si*," he says, "but it was something my asshole father made me do when I turned sixteen. He brought me to an escort's apartment, probably the one he uses while my mother is off getting laid by one of her boyfriends."

"That's fucked-up, about your parents, I mean, but how was it?"

"I didn't last very long. I could last longer doing it myself."

The image freaks you out. "Did she laugh?"

"*Pendejo*. She probably made five hundred dollars. They're pros, they wait until you leave to laugh."

And that image freaks you out even more.

"What about at home? Any girlfriends?"

"There was one girl I thought I could like, maybe even love. Cute little thing, also Hispanic. Puerto Rican maybe. She went to Port Washington High School. We met at a carnival in town. We exchanged phone numbers and talked a few times, but then when we went on a date, I learned she was fucking with me for her friends' entertainment. They were watching us the entire time we were in the theatre and kept laughing from a few rows behind us. Once I caught her glancing their way I figured it out. They were all white, by the way. She wanted to be one of them so bad she used me to try and get closer to them. I left her there and walked out, but I was crying once I hit the street. That'll never happen again."

And it's that image that you find most upsetting, that people, especially young people, can be so cruel.

"And now?" you say.

"Now what? I told you, I'm dedicated to the revolution. I'm married to it. If a woman comes along someday, fine, but I won't go looking for one. Like Che, I'll eventually find the right one, even if I make mistakes beforehand. Are you that fucked-up over a girlfriend or something?"

"I don't have one, but, yeah. It bums me sometimes."

"Just remember, *pendejo, cherchez la femme*."

"Say what?"

"You want trouble in your life, look for a woman. That's not a literal translation, but it's close enough for jazz."

All you're thinking is you've been looking and can't find one.

"I think I've heard something like that before," you say. "Probably from my father, who fucked everything he could."

"He take off?"

"Oh, yeah. With his first cousin's wife. My mother calls her Gang Bang."

Justo chuckles. "That's a good one, *pendejo*. I like your mother."

"Yeah, except she suffered a nervous breakdown from it and it's probably why I'm in here."

"Me, I wish my parents would split up already. I'd rather live in foster care."

"We had some money for a little while, but my old man took most of it. We weren't rich or anything, but we're close to poor now."

"That sucks. They always do, you know, take whatever they can steal."

"Yeah, I guess."

"So, get your shit together when you get out of here and start over. No reason to let father-son issues keep you in the shit."

"Yeah. Maybe."

"What's maybe, *pendejo?*" He listed off his fingers. "One, do the reading. Two, avoid the shit with your old man. And three, avoid the bitches."

"Bitches?"

"Gender speak."

"Huh?"

"El imbécil."

"You call me what I think?"

You're tempted to slap the book off his lap, but he looks at you and smiles. You smile back and all is good again.

"You remind me of someone," you say.

"If you knew who Che was, it'd be him," Justo says.

You shake your head. You're thinking St. Patrick, a Hispanic version, but then there's a bell and it's time for a therapy session.

As you get up off the bench, Justo says, "Ever read Steinbeck?"

"Sounds familiar. The winter of something, right?"

"Our discontent," Justo says. "Well, start there. Read a few of his works. Reread them if you have to. Dickens, too. Then go back to *The Manifesto.*"

"You being serious or a jerk-off now?" you ask. "I know Dickens."

"The movie, no doubt. *A Christmas Carol?*"

"Yeah, that too."

"Good, but I'm serious. Start reading when you bust out of this shithole and don't stop."

"Okay."

He raises his free hand in a fist and says, *"Viva la revolución."*

You nod, then shrug and say, "Sure. Why not?"

You Go Down Swinging ...

Night six into day seven, while you consider this weird new friend of yours, sex and Marion quickly replace your focus. When you close your eyes you don't see Justo. You see Marion. She's in a yellow bikini, her arms reaching behind her head, her blonde hair splayed out, her eyes closed and her face expressing ecstasy. You see her body from a distance, but it's her facial expression that does the trick. You can't even make it to the bathroom. Before you know it, you've made a mess of your bed sheets.

The devil is back the same night, this time making fun of the chronics you observed in the yard.

"Want to know what happens to those silly bastards?" he says.

"No," you say.

"Yeah, you do. Even more than the loser addicts. It's intriguing, isn't it? What does society do with such people? Hitler had it right, you know. Just get rid of them. Or use them for experiments before getting rid of them. Learn what you can and lose the ballast."

"You're fucked-up," you say.

"I'm the devil, bro."

Day seven you get to talk to your mother on the phone. It's a short conversation during which you're choked up, because you can tell she's also emotional, and because you'd like nothing more than to be home with her.

"Are you okay?" she asks.

"Yeah, I guess."

"I mean it, Charlie. Are you okay?"

"I'd rather come home."

She starts to cry and tells you she loves you, and you have a hell of a job fighting back the tears you feel for her pain, but you have to do that because you're in a hallway and other people can see you. You ask her how much longer you have to be there, and she tells you just a few more days, she's signing you out. The relief is immediate.

A few minutes later there's a Q&A conducted by none other than Dr. Abegg himself. He's affiliated with South Oaks and this is his job two days a week, to come and chat with the poor bastards he's committed to this psycho hotel. Technically, you're a voluntary admission, signed in by your mother. Thomas Rocco wanted nothing to do with this nuthouse affront on his surname, but until you can see your mother, even though she's assured you she's taking you home, you're all theirs:

the orderlies, Doctors Sexual-Stimulation-of-the-Genitals, Dr. Abegg, the nurses, and all your fellow patients/inmates, including the group of chronics clearly on another planet.

Abegg says, "Charlie, why did you hit Doctor Mallory?"

The interview is conducted in the room you share with the older guy, but you're alone with the good doctor. You're sitting on the edge of your bed. Abegg is in a chair facing you the same way Dr. Sexual-Stimulation-of-the-Genitals/Mallory usually sits, but you aren't in a mood to talk.

"Charlie?"

"I didn't hit him," you say. "I hit his clip board. It was an accident he got cut."

Abegg smiles. "Okay. Why did you hit the clipboard?"

"Because it was in the way. I was aiming for his chin."

Abegg chuckles. "Okay, but you do know he's here to help, right?"

"He's an asshole."

"He's a good man and he's here to help."

You roll your eyes. It's a routine you've gone through in his private office on President Street dozens of times. Abegg repeats what he wants you to acknowledge, and you know the only way to get through this horseshit without screaming at the top of your lungs, or trying to strangle him, is to play along.

Abegg says, "He was asking you about the fight you had in here when you became angry, correct?"

You nod.

"The suspensions from school, the cutting classes, all the time missed, the fighting, that's why your mother is so concerned. Why we need to figure out what this is all about."

You say, "You already know what it's about. You said so yourself, what you told my mother. I'm trying to get my father's attention."

"And I wish she wouldn't discuss these things with you, but it's you who needs to understand, not her or me."

It suddenly dawns on you that Dr. Abegg doesn't know your mother intends to spring you from South Oaks. You aren't about to tell him. What you do instead is sigh, and it isn't complete acting. You get it, why you're all fucked-up. You want attention. You want Thomas Rocco's attention, and you know you're not going to get it, but that's not your fault, you shouldn't blame yourself. You repeat what you know.

"Saying it is one thing," Abegg says. "And it's good that you somewhat understand, but not blaming yourself is the more important issue. If you can accept that, really accept it, I suspect you won't be so angry anymore."

What you want to say is: *HOW THE FUCK IS IT NOT MY FAULT*

THAT THOMAS ROCCO WISHES HE HAD A DIFFERENT SON?

Okay, so you don't get it, but you're fifteen years old, and as has already been established, not the sharpest knife in the drawer. If you think you lost too many fist fights, your emotional record is even worse. Thomas Rocco and your sister have molded one oversensitive motherfucker.

What you say is, "I don't mind the fighting. I lose most of them anyway. To older kids usually, but sometimes I like the feeling of getting hit. I like that more than hitting them."

Dr. Abegg frowns. It was an honest answer, maybe put the wrong way, but it's what you felt. You'd gotten so used to being hit in the face, it became something you sometimes, probably too often, looked forward to.

"Do you think you deserve to get hit?" Abegg asks.

"What?" you say, completely thrown by the question.

He repeats his question and you're still taken aback. It's a good question, maybe a great question. You're feeling guilty about something, but aren't sure what or why. You're not good enough? At what, being a son? How does one become good at being a son? And what of your sister? How do you become good enough for her to accept you? She has the same father, so how come she's not in a nuthouse? Why isn't she a part of Dr. Abegg's discussion?

Because you haven't told Dr. Abegg much about her, nor were you willing to state aloud how you feel you do deserve to be hit. You're taking the pain of the world in your Little Jesus face, except you can't admit to it without sounding crazier than they already think you are.

Tell him that and they may never let you out.

Rationalizing it is easy enough, so you stick with that. Fathers hit their sons, it's as simple as that. Your friends were and are slapped around by their fathers, sometimes even their mothers. You know for a fact that some of your friends never deserved some of the beatings they caught. St. Patrick, for one. His father should be shot for what he does to his son. At least you can't remember Thomas Rocco physically abusing you. His quick slaps might've stung, but they weren't fists or kicks, and there was always a reason, even if it was a shitty one, like something based on a lie your sister told. As for the other hits you took in the streets, they were usually your own fault too, but even when they weren't, wasn't it part of growing up? Isn't getting hit a part of life? Doesn't it make you tougher?

It's what Thomas Rocco will tell you one day when you're adult enough and he's trying to justify having been a scumbag: "I was trying to prepare you for life is all. It's tough out there."

By day eight, you're no longer concerned with whether or not you deserve to get hit, because your mother has already told you it's just another few days and you'll be home. And just like a bad dream, one of the orderlies taunts you about going home.

And there's the devil on your fucking shoulder facilitating the storm.

"Watch out for this nigger, he gets off fucking with you weaklings," the devil says.

"Fuck off, racist," you respond in your head.

You are out in the recreation yard with some of the men that day. They are huddled into a few groups, most of them smoking cigarettes. Your nuthouse friends are in an addiction therapy session. You're shooting baskets and missing. The orderly is one of two out there to make sure nobody hops a fence and runs away.

"So, when you getting out?" he asks with a sarcastic smile.

"Not long," you say.

He chuckles. "Yeah, right. That's what you think."

"See?" the devil says.

"That's what I know," you say, giving away something you probably shouldn't. "My mother is gonna sign me out."

"If they don't commit you, sucker. They can do that, you know. Commit your ass. Then you not going anywhere."

"He loves this shit, bro."

You don't need the devil to read what he's going for, this down-on-his-luck, stuck-in-a-dead-end job, with nothing better in his life bully. You're about to tell him to fuck off when you think of St. Patrick and what he might say, then you say it: "Yeah, so what's your excuse, asshole?"

"Oh, snap."

The smile disappears from the orderly's face. "Say what?"

"Looks like you're the one's committed," you say. "This as good as it gets, working here the rest of your life?"

"You a smart ass, huh?"

You've learned how to be cruel, that's for sure. You flip him the bird.

"Nice."

He's been leaning against the fence. He uses a foot to push himself off. His hands come out of his pockets as he starts toward you. You accept the challenge, because you're crazy. You start toward him with the intent to go down swinging. When you're close enough and he's about to say something, you use both hands to fling the basketball at his face and break his nose.

"Score!"

"Motherfucker!" he yells, then covers his nose with both hands as blood spills through his fingers. You are chased by the other orderly and you make a game of it, trying white boy moves on a much more agile black man. Still, you fake him out once, and then he tackles you from behind. He proceeds to take a dozen or so cheap shots into your ribs while all the other patients stand around gawking, most of them numb from medications.

That night you're all strapped up again with nowhere to go, and guess who visits?

"You've got some balls, bro," the devil says. *"But maybe you fucked yourself with that basketball toss."*

"How's that?"

"You heard him. They can commit your ass. Or charge you with assault, land your ass in some Long Island juvie joint. Then what? No Saints there to help you. You think you're fucked now, wait until you get a taste of the American penal system."

You wonder whether or not they can do what the orderly said and keep you there, but the power of a mother's word enables you to convince yourself you'll be sprung soon no matter what happens. You have to sleep with the straps again, but this time they medicate you and you sleep like a dead man. Miraculously, the devil doesn't come along for the ride.

It'll take a few years, but once enough time passes, you realize you can adjust to anything, thanks to your time in a nuthouse.

A few years after South Oaks, *One Flew Over The Cuckoo's Nest* makes it to the big screen and R.P. McMurphy becomes your hero. By then you were reading lots of books, even *The Communist Manifesto* you still didn't much understand, but when you read Kesey's classic, it's after seeing the movie several times, and Ken Kesey becomes even more of a hero.

Your Guardian Angel ...

Days eight and nine are a blur. The threat you made against the orderly was reported and you're one medicated motherfucker. You sit in group therapy and hardly participate. You're numb in the brain. No thought can penetrate long enough to comprehend. Instead of your mind racing, everything inside and outside of your head seems to move in slow motion. Even when Justo crosses your path in the recreation room, you don't recognize him. He was staring at you as if you had a lobotomy.

Day ten arrives and your mother is there to spring you. You learn your ten days in the nuthouse were much more torturous for her than they were for you. She was as afraid for your life inside South Oaks as she was for it on the street.

"I never should've agreed to this," she tells you in the car. Her eyes are red from crying. "He wanted to give you shock treatments, that bastard. He told me you'd be with kids your age all the time. He lied to me."

"It wasn't that bad, Ma," you tell her. "I'm okay. And I'll go back to school. I promise."

You're almost home when she finally stops crying and tells you she has a surprise. You're the lunatic and she's the one who feels guilty. You want to know if Thomas Rocco asked about you, but you can't ask. You're in the house again when you hear the bark. It's a German shepherd pup you name Bruno after the Italian wrestling champion who Thomas Rocco HATES, Bruno Sammartino.

While you play with the pup there's a phone call and you overhear the conversation your mother is having with Thomas Rocco. She tells him that Dr. Abegg explained his diagnosis, "eighty percent rejection from father." He'd diagnosed your sudden outbursts of rage and violent conduct as symptomatic of intermittent explosive disorders—IEDs. She also told him about the shock therapy treatments she refused to authorize.

Even little Jesus had a guardian angel.

Their conversation isn't a long one. All you wonder about is how Thomas Rocco is taking what he's hearing. Is he embarrassed for not going to see you? For not calling? For not giving a flying fuck? Or is he even more embarrassed because now his son is a certifiable nut?

Never mind him forsaking you, Little Jesus. Why put your worth up for his judgment?

It will take another thirty rocky years to escape that mistake.

Menachem Begin ...

During the good periods with your sister, however brief they may have been, you changed hello and goodbye to the Israeli Prime Minister's name, Menachem Begin. It was your idea, and she liked it enough to keep it going. Instead of saying hello and/or goodbye, you and she would say, "Menachem Begin" or just "Begin" for short—pronounced *Bay-(hard g)-gin*.

When you return home from South Oaks, your sister greets you with the short version for hello, "Begin."

"Begin," you say.

"So how was it?"

"Scary at first, then it was okay."

"You get into fights?"

You ignore the question with a frown.

"Yeah, okay," she says, then smiles.

You've missed that smile.

She says, "Daddy see you?"

"No."

"He's a prick."

"Yeah."

"He didn't call?"

"No."

"He coming today? This weekend?"

"I doubt it."

There's a pause before she says, "I'm glad you're out of there."

This time you nod.

"You're still a jerk," she says, but it's with another reassuring smile that lets you know she doesn't mean it.

This is the better side of your sister, the one that seems to hide behind her anger at what's happened to the family. She isn't always nasty. She isn't always cruel. You wish she could stay this way. This is the sister you love, but it's also the one who always leaves you so fucking vulnerable.

So when the devil makes a return visit that night, he's anxious to make up for how decent your sister had been.

"You don't have to be nice to her, you know," he says. "Don't get fooled again by some momentary decency."

You think, *"I thought I was done with you."*

"You thought wrong."

You make the sign of the cross.

"You'd have to believe in that bullshit for it to work," he says. "Really believe in it."

"Sometimes I want to. I really want to."

And what you said is like magic, because the devil disappears.

You hit the library and take out some of the books and authors both Justo and St. Patrick suggested, but you start on *The Grapes of Wrath* when you get home. Early on you have to reread the paragraphs because you prefer reading dialogue to narrative, but soon enough your focus is steady enough to proceed without pause. You finish the book within a week and you know it is a special book, something you'll read again and treasure for having done so.

You try *The Manifesto* again, but wind up focusing on its most famous lines: *"Workers of the world, unite! You have nothing to lose but your chains!"*

You're too young to understand it the way Justo might, but it does make sense to you that workers should unite, or at least find solidarity. You're not sure what they're uniting against, not yet, but you will over time.

Thomas Rocco finally calls, but you're not comfortable speaking to him and thumb over your shoulder at your mother when she looks to you after answering the phone. She tells him you're not home and that she'll convey whatever message he's looking to pass along. She hangs up, looks to you again and says, "He wants you to call him."

"No thanks," you say.

"He sounded upset. He asked how you were."

"Too late."

"You don't understand him, Charlie. He has to do things his way sometimes. It's not that he doesn't—"

"See you later," you say and head out the door.

You want to catch up with St. Patrick and tell him about Justo. You want to tell him about the nuthouse and all that transpired there. You're anxious about sharing your tales from the crypt with someone, but you know it's not a safe subject to share with just anybody. Those who will view you as damaged goods will be quick to spread the news.

In a long walk around Seaview Park you come across the twins who were in your 4th grade class, Sarah and Sonia. One, Sarah, seems happy to see you. The other, Sonia, not so much. They are still dressed identically and you wonder how much longer that would go on. Do they coordinate their wardrobes while doing laundry or does their mother set out their outfits? Today they're wearing tight blue jeans with a white belt and tight white pullover blouses.

Even though they're twins, Sarah definitely looks better than Sonia.

"Mrs. Craig?" you say.

Sarah is smiling. She nods.

"I used to get in a lot of trouble back then."

"I remember. Are you going to Canarsie? I haven't seen you."

"We have to go," Sonia says.

"One minute," Sarah says.

"I was out for a few weeks," you say, but leave it there.

"What's your schedule?"

You don't remember all your classes or the times. "Regular," you say. "I get out at one-thirty."

Sarah's brow furrows. She's about to interrogate you when you say, "I used to like you."

"Really?"

You nod.

"You don't like me now?"

"Sarah, let's go," Sonia says.

"One minute," Sarah says.

"You look good," you tell her.

She smiles again.

"And me?" you say.

She nods. "You're okay."

"I'm going," Sonia says, then stomps off toward the avenue.

"You seeing anybody?" you ask.

"No. You?"

"No."

You smile, but she's lost hers. You don't understand the gimmicks utilized in flirting so your insecurity keeps you from asking the obvious question about going on a date to a movie or wherever. Your pause of silence lasts just long enough for her to feel her own frustration.

"Okay, I've have to get home. See you," Sarah says.

"Bye," you say.

You continue your walk around the half mile oval and daydream about rolling around with Sarah, but you know you've blown it. There's a good chance you won't see her again, especially at school, because you're still not sure you'll be there. Your prospects suck, especially if you don't finish school, but you still can't quite get Sarah out of your head.

The upside to being a hopeless romantic is the delusion that permits you to avoid the shit in your life, and so by the time you return home, you're back to fantasizing a make-out session with Sarah. You forget about St. Patrick and Justo and the fact you'll have to return to school. Life can wait. Life can be put on hold. Life is what you make it, Little Jesus, because otherwise it sucks.

So, sing it, Little Jesus:

Dreams can come true,
if you happen to be you,
and you're an epic daydreamer
with nothing else to do.

Let It Be Me ...

The good vibe you're feeling the next day changes when you attempt to find St. Patrick. You call his home phone, but there's no answer. The next morning you hang out around the library, but he doesn't show. In the afternoon you're off to see a Board of Education psychiatrist. He's the one who will decide whether you can return to school or not. This is the part of society that determines whether or not you're damaged goods, and although they let just about anybody attend their high schools, crazy white boys must be vetted, as the future will prove some 30 years later when a couple of crazy white boys massacre twelve fellow students and one teacher at a high school in Columbine, Colorado.

The Board of Education psychiatrist is no Dr. Abegg, or he'd be making Dr. Abegg coin. He wants to know if you feel you need to hurt yourself or anybody else.

"No," you tell him.

"Have you ever tried to hurt yourself or anybody else?"

"Just when I had a fight, but it was just to win a fight. I usually lost."

"But you never wanted to go back and do something violent, right?"

Now you're getting it, Little Jesus. This guy is giving you the out, probably because he wants this bullshit session over with as much as you do.

"Never," you tell him, even though it's a fact you've gone back to crack somebody more than once when you felt they took a cheap shot at you the day before.

"Okay, then," he says. "I'll get updates from your school from time to time. Good luck, Charlie."

And that's that.

You try St. Patrick's phone again when you're home but nobody is picking up. Losing St. Patrick so soon after the nuthouse can't be good. Did he move again?

For the first time since you were in Catholic school you say a prayer. Not on your knees in supplication, your hands folded and eyes shut tight, but in bed, hugging your pillow, determined to do something for your friend. It is a bedtime habit you will take long into your life, abandoning it from time to time, but always returning to it, even after you reject the Catholic Church. It is a prayer you make up as a final negotiation with an omnipotent being, if there is one, and since there's only one you kind of know, you hope to hell he/she is listening.

God, or whoever it is up there running things, please don't let anything bad happen to St. Patrick. Please don't let anything bad happen to my mother or sister. Please don't let anything bad happen to my dog. If anything bad has to happen, let it be me. Please, let it be me. Let it be me. Let it be me. Let it be me.

A few days of missing St. Patrick is all it takes for your sister to return to being nasty. You wonder if she shares the same cruel gene as Thomas Rocco. Seeing you without St. Patrick and knowing that Thomas Rocco hasn't bothered to call back to talk to you, she goes after the only affection you can find while your mother is at work, your dog, Bruno.

You love the dog, but your sister has gone out of her way to shower it with affection and make sure he's attached to her and not you. Whenever you look to play with Bruno, she's there first. Whenever you go to pet him, she puts on the high-pitched voice that goes right through you and sets Bruno's tail to wagging two hundred miles per hour. It's a conspiracy even you can figure out, and it's working. Eventually, you yell at the dog for no good reason. Within weeks you're ignoring Bruno as much as Thomas Rocco has been ignoring you, and that prick still hasn't called back.

The isolation you're feeling blows. Not only that, you're getting the urge to pound someone, or be pounded by someone. Remembering you've been cleared to return to school, you do the next best thing to fighting. You try to find your friend where he said he lived.

There are twenty-three, 8-story buildings on 34.02 acres of land that provide 1,610 apartments in the Bayview Houses, and you haven't a clue in which one of those 1,610 apartments your friend lives. He's never said, and you've never asked. You ask around the projects, but no dice. Maybe it's because he hasn't lived there all that long. Maybe because he never hung around where he lived.

You've returned to school and managed to do well enough not to be kicked out, but you're still lost without your friend. You don't fight, but you have to avoid a few temptations. The holidays come and go and still no word. St. Patrick has either moved while you were in the nuthouse or something worse has happened. The possibilities are endless and you're not feeling good about them.

The second semester begins and you're a new student all over again, except this time you're a dedicated student, just for the hell of it. You show up for all your classes, you do all the assignments, and whether it's in homage to your missing friend, or you're finally growing up, your new obsession is schoolwork, both reading and writing and researching. It's not just the reading lists from school, but other books by the same authors you're assigned, a practice you'll continue throughout your life.

More fascinated with politics than existentialism, you turn from foreign existentialists to American novelists and playwrights writing about the state of affairs before you were born. Steinbeck, Hemingway, Miller, and Williams overshadow the works of Camus, Jean-Paul Sartre, and André Gide. You jump from novels to plays and back. The theatre pieces spark an interest in dialogue, and you begin writing dialogue-driven scenes in a separate notebook, scenes loaded with guilt, curiosity, and accusations.

Charlie:	I didn't mean for you to die, Nani.
Nani:	God knows, Piccolo, *Gesù*.
Charlie:	I wanted to help my father.
Nani:	It's okay.
Charlie:	I'm sorry.
Nani:	Don't cry, *caro*. It's okay.

One with the uncle you never met, your father's brother.

Charlie:	How was my father as a kid?
Uncle:	He was pretty wild, my brother. Not a student, that's for sure.
Charlie:	Did your father love him?
Uncle:	I'm sure he did, but he didn't show it much. He was a hard man with his boys.

Charlie:	Did you love him, my father?
Uncle:	Sure.
Charlie:	Did my father hurt when you died?
Uncle:	I'm sure he did, and it's okay if he didn't.

And what you were saving for your sister's deathbed.

Charlie:	Why were you so fucking mean?
Adele:	I'm sorry, Charlie.
Charlie:	No, you're not.
Adele:	I am. I mean it.
Charlie:	I can't forgive you.
Adele:	I'm sorry for that, too.
Charlie:	I want to, but I'm still so mad.
Adele:	I understand.
Charlie:	Why couldn't you ...
Adele:	It's okay.

The message is clear, to let it all go, but you can't. You don't want to. Not yet.

The conversations haunt your sleep and sometimes interfere with your ability to focus while reading. You read a passage in a book or a play and immediately return to the incomplete dialogues and scenes you've started and stopped writing. When you lay your head on a pillow, there they are. When you daydream, they become the focus on your musings. Like the moon's pull on the tides, this drive from somewhere deep in your soul will never let you escape its pull. It will come and go, over and over, until the force of its energy is too great to ignore and it spills out on a page.

In 1972, at age 16, as much as you're enjoying reading and writing, you want someone to discuss your new fascinations with, but St. Patrick has remained MIA, and your sister is no longer saying Menachem Begin when she sees you. Starved for St. Patrick's company, you ask her if she's seen him at the library.

"Not in a while," she says.

"I think something happened to him," you say.

She doesn't answer. You can tell she doesn't want to go there. Maybe she's feeling guilty for calling him a loser.

Maybe.

The upside is that you aren't thinking about pleasing Thomas Rocco. Although he never called or asked you a single question about the nuthouse, he put you to work in the city rolling posters. You're working where Bob Dylan and Jimi Hendrix once played for their meals. It's called The Night Owl, and your father's friend from childhood owns it. He's turned it into a headshop and you're earning $.02 a poster, which translates to $10.00 a day when you can work a few hours during the school week and weekends. It's a deal he's recently made with you, maybe one from guilt for not visiting you in the nuthouse. If you do well in school, he'll keep you employed in Greenwich Village.

The renovated coffee house gets a ton of traffic, mostly hippies and hippy wannabes attending NYU. You slip one end of a poster into a groove on a long metal bar, step on the pedal beneath the table, and keep your hands over the bar so the poster rolls nice and neat. Then you pull a plastic sleeve onto the poster with one hand until the length of the poster is covered, then let go of the poster, slide it off the roller, tap in both ends so their even, and drop the poster in a barrel.

Those pennies continue to add up, and it gets you a ton of attention. The hippies and hippy wannabes are stopping to watch how fast you can work, and you can work pretty damn fast.

You're suddenly flush with coin, but you're more concerned about your friend and what might've happened to him. You continue your new prayers before sleep. *God, or whoever it is up there running things ... Let it be me.*

Sex Education 201 ...

She's every bit as shy as you, but she's also clearly attracted to you.
Her name is Tammy and she's thin, pretty, one year older than you, and
she lives in Queens, one exit from Canarsie on the Belt Parkway. You
meet her at your cousin's house. They are friends, and for whatever
reason, there's an immediate chemistry. Her smile and your smile have
connected across a small room.

Somehow you find the nerve to speak to her.

"You like music?"

"Sure," she says.

"Wanna go to a concert?"

"Sure. Who?"

"Sly and the Family Stone?"

"Wow, yeah. Where at?"

"The garden. My old man can get me tickets."

"Sure, that'll be nice."

You knew about the concert because of your job at the head shop
Thomas Rocco lives above, the same Greenwich Village iconic Night
Owl.

The concert date takes place on a Saturday night and you have to take
two trains to meet Tammy where she lives, then another two trains to
Madison Square Garden. You've already spent time on the phone
together so there isn't much more to discuss. Midway through the
concert, you ask her if she's enjoying the show and she says, "Yeah,
thanks for taking me."

Then comes an unexpected kiss, and you can't believe it's happened.
You can't wait for the concert to end so she can thank you again, but you
know you'll have to ride all the way back to Queens before that can
happen. When it finally does, the thank you kiss comes at the foot of the
subway stairs on Liberty Avenue, and it lasts a long time before you
start to walk her home.

"I wish we had a few more minutes alone," you say.

"You can come in if you want," she says. "My parents will be asleep."

"You sure?"

"Yeah. We can hang out in the basement."

Tammy knows enough from prior boyfriends to guide you through
your awkwardness, like making sure when she lies on top of you while
making out, your erection is positioned in exactly the right spot, so she
can grind against it through the pants you're both still wearing and

reach orgasm.

That first date night you stay until four o'clock in the morning before one final kiss that lasts another few minutes before you ask her if she'll go steady with you. You're already fearful of losing what you've just found. After she says yes, you're on your way back to the train station with a joy in your heart that is overwhelming. There's still no word about St. Patrick, but the universe has provided you with someone to replace your best friend.

You'll have to wait until the next weekend before you can be together again, so all communication is over the phone. You don't notice her lack of interest in education or anything else, because she's pretty and you FINALLY have a girlfriend. You FINALLY know what it's like to kiss a girl the right way, and soon you'll do all the other stuff you've been fantasizing about, but before that you'll meet her family and be overwhelmed one more time.

A family not at war with itself, eating dinner together, shocks you. There are aromas from a home cooked meal that startle your senses of smell and sight. It is a table loaded with food, most of it fresh. Corn and carrots and spinach and squash and turnips and potatoes and two different meats, one with brown gravy. There's bread and butter and salad and three different brand name sodas. Even when the money was flowing, and/or when Thomas Rocco was still around, dinners this big only occurred during holidays, and they never featured anything like the colorful settings featured nightly at Tammy's home.

It's the first thing you tell your mother after a third dinner at Tammy's house, how everybody sits around the table at dinner time and everybody gets along.

"That's nice, Charlie, but you and your sister can do that too."

"No, I mean her mother *and* father are there. And her sister and brother. And there's always so much food. Stuff we never have, Ma. Turnips and green beans and mashed potatoes and carrots and stuffing and two different kinds of meat."

You're telling her this in the kitchen of the home you won't be living in much longer. The refrigerator is bare, except for a few leftovers and bread your mother doesn't want to spoil. Money is tight and getting tighter, but you're too excited about having a girlfriend and seeing a family act like a family. It never dawns on you how your newfound faith in family must be killing your mother.

"They do that every night, Ma," you say. "During the week and on weekends."

You mother smiles as best she can without crying, then tells you to invite your girlfriend over for dinner one night. "I'll cook lasagna or stuffed shells," she says.

You can't even hear her offer to cook dinner.

"Ma, the best thing, they do stuff together," you say. "They go on vacation together. They have a place in Maryland where they go every weekend in the summer."

Suddenly you can see the disappointment in her eyes. You ask her what's wrong, but she doesn't tell you. Ignorance is indeed bliss and there's no bliss like falling in love.

Over the next few weeks you fall further in love from one kissing exchange to the next. You're an insecure kid so grateful for a girlfriend, you can't imagine you'll ever need more than what Tammy represents. The honeymoon that ensues, especially because you live far enough apart to keep from growing bored with one another, helps to seal the deal. Telephone calls during the week facilitate weekend yearnings for *amore*. The girlfriend will stunt some social growth, but also save you from some of the bad shit going on in Canarsie. Many of your friends and former teammates, some of them great athletes, have become addicted to the drugs of the day. Few will recover. Some will die.

Your newfound love gets so intense so fast, you take a job closer to home rather than rolling posters at the Night Owl. Thomas Rocco's fatherly advice includes the following: "Make sure you wear something, Mister. You get her pregnant, it's your headache. And don't piss your money away on her. There'll be plenty more where she came from."

Fuck him. How could you not want to take part in dinners with Tammy's family with an asshole like that for a father?

The reception Tammy receives at your home is somewhat different. Mothers are inherently suspicious, but polite. Your sister is another story.

Adele sees Tammy as one more way to batter you, and her pursuit in doing so is relentless.

"She quit high school? What is she retarded?"

Fortunately for you, Little Jesus, first loves are all consuming. You and your girlfriend are too in love to permit your sister access to your emotions, at least at first.

In the meantime, your conversations with Tammy become a form of worship for her family.

"I think it's great that your family eats together," you say.

"We always do that."

"We did when my father was still around, but he's gone now."

"Do you see him much?"

"Once in a while. Like I said, he got me the tickets, but he lives in the city. My mother works and can only cook small dinners for us, me and my sister."

"Doesn't your sister help?"

"Never, unless it's for herself. You know how to cook like your parents?"

"My father made us learn from him. My mother doesn't cook so much anymore. My father picks her up at her job on the way home from his job and then he likes to cook."

"We'll be like them once we're married."

She smiles at the suggestion, the kissing starts, and the world is right.

The first month is devoted to kissing, getting it right. Learning how to position your mouth and use your tongue and making Tammy want to kiss you as much as you want to kiss her.

Once you figure out how you're used like a vibrator that doesn't vibrate, you naively feel a sense of accomplishment from all the panting she does, along with the extra hard kissing she engages in right before her body tenses and shakes and she tells you how much she loves you.

Usually you perform the motionless vibrator trick on daybeds in your basements, safely out of sight. Eventually you both grow bold and find the nerve to unbutton each other's clothes. The triangle of hair you've been fantasizing about is as magical as you've imagined, and although you'll experiment with oral sex for several weeks before you find the courage to go all the way, you never take notice at how goddamned skilled she is on her end of the oral bargain.

You wonder: *Has she done this before?*

It's a thought that briefly crosses your mind and vanishes, because you're so grateful you FINALLY have a girlfriend, and because she's letting you be the first to go all the way. The fact that she's a virgin doesn't discount all the sexual knowledge she brought to the table, and you will wonder about that from time to time, but she clearly loves you or you wouldn't have been the one. And in your world, having grown up in Canarsie, even a Queen's girl apparently expert at the art of a blow job, so long as she held out where it counts, is the one you're supposed to marry.

At least it's what you'll believe until you trick her into a confession six months before you do marry her, sealing the fate of that marriage, and two others, before they begin.

You will learn that life has a way of fucking with romantics and that you're no exception, Little Jesus or not. Among many of your faults is the ability to believe what you want to believe with the determination of a gambler standing at a craps table down to his last dime. The fact there's a sucker born every minute doesn't alter just because you may, or may not be, the second coming. The signs were there all along, your girlfriend has been around the block, but you were too grateful for finding love and sex to pay attention.

In the meantime, you and the first of a few loves of your life screw like the world is about to end. You teach each other stuff you've only read about until she liberates her father's eight millimeter camera and his porn flicks while her parents are away on vacation, and then you're both screwing like porn stars.

The sex you're having every weekend dominates your life. Nothing else seems to matter, not even missing St. Patrick. You have entered a world of ignorance is extreme bliss until one day Tammy calls to tell you she's missed her period for the second straight month, and you each get the scare of your lives.

You're both sure you're in love with each other and that you'll marry someday, but there's no way either of you want a kid, not yet. Fortunately, your mother is cool about this stuff, and she finds you a doctor in Queens where you can find out if Tammy is pregnant. The doctor is an off-the-boat Italian with pictures of the Pope hanging everywhere inside his office. You're both extremely nervous while telling him what you need to learn, and then he says, in a very heavy accent, "Please don't'a ask'a me to take'a the life of this'a baby if she is'a pregnant."

"No, of course not," you say, but you're already planning on quitting school and working two jobs to pay for the abortion you know is a must if Tammy is with child.

A week later you learn you're safe and that it's okay to keep pulling out, that's how naive you both are. Your sexual routine returns to normal, you and your girlfriend go back to screwing at every opportunity. Life can't be better. Your mother is still working overtime whenever she can to try and hang on to the house she really can't afford, so you pretty much have the place to yourself. Your sister is either in school, working or hiding in her room. You, Little Jesus, are king of the castle.

You've even managed to get your old job back. Three nights a week you're washing dishes at that catering hall on McDonald Avenue. Things are going great until the day you have to ask your sister a question and you walk into her room without knocking.

Catch 22 ...

You ask if she took the dog out, but what you heard through her bedroom door you've just knocked on is a lot of giggling, and it isn't just your sister's giggling. You knock again, louder this time, and the giggling begins anew. So you open the door and there's your sister and her girlfriend under the sheets.

"Knuckleheads," you say. "You walk the dog or not?" you ask your sister.

"No," she says through a laugh.

"The hell is so funny?"

"Get out," she says.

"Pair of fruits," you say, then shake your head, step out, and close the door behind you.

You move to the den and watch television from the love seat. The girl she was with leaves a few minutes later. Your sister walks her out, both of them still giggling as they head up the short flight of stairs. When she returns, your sister stops at the bottom step and folds her arms.

"What did you call us before?" she says.

"A pair of fruits."

"What's that?"

"Queers."

"What's that?"

"Lesbians."

"You know what that means?"

"You think I'm an idiot?" you say. "I know you're gay."

"Yeah, you're an idiot," she says, "but that's beside the point. What does gay mean?"

"It means you like being under the sheets with another girl."

She smiles. "You gonna tell Mom?"

"Why would I?"

"Dad?"

"No."

"I'm thinking it's time he knows."

"So tell him."

"I will. Next time I see him."

She squints. You ask what her problem is, and she says, "How'd you get back in the house without us hearing?"

"Maybe you were busy doing something else."

"Something else what? Do you know what we do?"

"You giggle a lot. I know that much."

"Jerk. I'm being serious. Do you know?"

You're not sure if she's trying to educate or mock you, but you go along with it. "Yeah," you say. "I know what you do, but you didn't invent it."

"Invent what?"

"Sex, moron."

"I meant specifically."

She clearly wants to tell you, even if it is in her own special way.

"Like I said, you didn't invent it," you say.

"It's different for us."

"How's it different? Everybody does it."

"How would you know that?"

"Third time. You didn't invent it."

"I don't know how to take that. Did you ever—"

"Me and Tammy, you idiot."

"Oh, gross," she says, then mocks sticking a finger in her throat. "Yuck."

You shake your head.

She says, "Do you think Daddy'll be upset?"

"Of course."

"Why?"

"Because he's a dinosaur. The only thing worse'd be if I told him I was gay. Then he might kill himself, but it wouldn't be for my sake. He'd just be embarrassed."

"What do you think he'll say?"

"He'll probably choke is what he'll do. It won't be easy for him to hear his daughter is a lesbian. He's probably got other ideas for you."

"Yeah, well, now he'll have a real excuse for being embarrassed about me."

You're shocked. You can't believe she feels the same way you do. She's his favorite. She's been his ambassador to making you feel like shit since you can remember. You say, "Embarrassed about you? You're the special one. He thinks I'm a moron."

"You are a moron."

You flip her the bird. She calls you an idiot. You call her a queer. She laughs, and sucker that you are, you smile.

"Asshole," she says, angry this time.

Now you're fed up. "What are you breaking my balls for? Go back in your room and play with yourself."

"I do, you know. Women do that, too."

"Good for you and good for them."

"You know what else we do?"

"Break balls."

She flips you the bird. "And we use our mouths," she says.

"Yeah, you eat each other. No shit? I already said, so do we."

She chuckles. "Is that what you call it?"

"Eating, yeah. Big deal."

"That's so crude."

"As opposed to using our mouths? It's the same thing, imbecile."

"You're an imbecile," she says, scowling this time. "Men are assholes."

"Maybe because you can't get any."

Her eyes narrow. She's hurt. "Fuck you," she says.

You immediately feel guilty. "I was joking," you say. "Take it easy."

"No, you weren't. That's what you think because you're a moron. Dad'll think the same thing."

"I said I'm sorry."

"How dare that prick be disappointed in me."

You swallow hard. "He's a lot more disappointed in me. At least you do good in school."

"You're a fuckup. He's disappointed in me because I'm not beautiful."

Your feel her hurt in your soul. "He's an asshole with stuff like that. You should hear the shit he tells me. He can't help himself. He likes to put us down."

She's almost crying. "He is an asshole."

"Yeah, he is, so forget about it. Don't let him piss you off. Look at his wife. Mom says she's a slut and a gold digger. She calls her Gang Bang."

"He loves her."

"Who cares?"

"I hate her."

"Me, too, but I don't think about her like Mom does. Gang Bang won the battle. Big fucking deal. She got him. What a prize."

"He fucks with your head, too, so stop trying to blow it off."

"I just said he does, didn't I? I'm trying to keep you from crying, asshole."

"I'm not crying now, jerk. I'm done crying over him."

"Good. It's about time."

"And you're still a jerk for saying that before. I can so get a man."

"Great. Run for President."

"Loser," she says. "You are, you know. He's right about that."

"Here we go," you say. "Got anything else on your mind?"

"Yeah, why'd he have us if he's so disappointed?"

You do a double take. You know her pain is real. You want to help, but you need to be careful, your sister is a master of deception.

"I don't know," you say.

"First he had us and then he was disappointed. He left us and now he's with that cunt he tried to have more kids with. I'm glad she lost the baby."

Ouch. You didn't know about a pregnancy. It hurts to learn it like this, but you make believe you knew. "Me, too," you lie.

"I hate her and I hate him."

You're still somewhat rocked. "Huh?"

"I said I hate them."

"Oh," you say.

"I can't wait to tell him I'm queer."

You're still thinking about Thomas Rocco holding a new baby Jesus.

"First chance I get," she says. "When he's with all his dumb fuck friends in the city, all those losers he hangs out with, I'm going to say, 'Daddy, didn't you know I was gay?'"

"Sounds like a plan," you say.

She wipes her nose with the sleeve of her shirt and gets up to use the bathroom. You remain in the den, unsure of whether you should leave. You hear her blowing her nose through the bathroom door and then she comes back out, looks at you and says, "Don't spy on us anymore."

You're there, but you're not there. "I wasn't spying."

She's staring at you, her eyebrows furrowed. You look up and say, "What?"

"You didn't know she was pregnant."

You swallow hard again. You shake your head. No, you didn't, but you can't speak.

Voi sogno di St. Patrick ...

That night St. Patrick returns in a dream, except he's the fair-haired, pale-skinned kid again, the one without the name you remember. The two of you are walking around the Canarsie pier. It's a bright sunny day, the waters are as calm as they were the first time you sat with him there. The smell of brine is refreshing and you're sure you can sense it, even in your dream. You're looking out at the familiar sparklers of light on the water while St. Patrick eats a knish smothered with mustard.

He says, "So, what now, you ignorant Dago? You're gonna let Gang Bang get to you, too? If she was pregnant, there's a good chance she aborted it. It probably wouldn't be her first and she'd about done the same with the ones she had, putting them in a foster home."

You smile. "Where the hell you been?"

"Moved."

"You could've told me," you say. "What about ... you think he'd treat a kid with her the same way he treated us?"

"No, but he's probably just as relieved it's not gonna happen."

"You think she did it on purpose?"

"Get pregnant? The fuck would I know, you knuckle-dragging wop? And who cares? You're finally getting some of your own, something I never had the chance to do. You're in love now, why concern yourself with a half-

brother or sister you almost had? You can turn the page on Gang Bang and your father. You've got a world to save, you dumb guinea. You can't be wasting time losing sleep over the likes of those two."

You stop near the end of the pier and turn to him. He's got mustard smeared around his mouth. You can almost taste it. You hand him a napkin and point to his chin. He takes a couple of wipes and you nod when his face is clean.

"So, I met this kid, about sixteen or so, in the nuthouse."

"Justo."

"Yeah, how'd you know his name?"

"Eejit, I'm a fookin' Saint, yeah?"

"He's a lot like you, a real ball breaker, but he's smart too. At least I think he is. He certainly reads a lot of shit."

"He's a wannabe."

"Excuse me?"

"A Che wannabe. There are loads of them up here. Loads down there, too."

"The fuck are you talking about?"

"Hold your horses, a minute, yeah?"

"Fine," you say, and then wait a few too many seconds for your patience to handle. "Well?"

"The old man was drunker than usual," he says. "Caught me a good one on the side of my face when I wasn't ready for it. Surprised more than hurt me, but I hauled off and punched him one in the chops, gave him a bloody lip. Made me smile when I saw that blood, I'll tell ya."

He stops to take another bite from his knish and suddenly it's gone. Time is jumping ahead and you're both walking on a path in Seaview Park.

"I couldn't get away fast enough," he says. "Dopey drunk grabbed the nearest thing, a fungo bat he'd filled with metal he usually kept in his car. Clonked me on the noggin, busted me open. Cracked my skull."

"Then what?" you ask.

"Coward bastard ran to the bedroom, grabbed his revolver from the night table drawer, made a sign of the cross, and asked forgiveness before he offed himself. Put one through the roof of his mouth."

"You feel bad?"

"What do you think, you smelly greaseball? I'd've felt a lot better he shot himself before he hit me with the bat."

"You see him where you are now?"

"Sometimes, but he makes like he don't know me, the fookin' coward."

"What's he doing up there?"

"Up there, huh? You're a naive bastard."

"Down there?"

"Shut your pie hole."

You stare at him, but he knows the question you're asking in your head.

"Yeah, yours'll do the same thing," he says. "It's what all the cowards do, hide from their shame. But in your case, once you're there, the cowards'll be dispatched. That's one form of saving the world."

"Saving what? Dispatched how?"

St. Patrick points a thumb down.

"Okay, there's some justice in that."

"You think so? I'd prefer doling out the justice myself. I wouldn't've mind using the fungo bat on his dull cranium."

You smile at one another. He calls you an Eejit and you call him a potato head.

Then he's gone along with your dream, which you forget until one week later, after a long jog you take around Seaview Park. Flashes of the dream interrupt your usual runner's high. When you return home, there's a newspaper on the stoop. You pick it up, glance at the sports headline first, something about Earl Monroe and the Knicks, then you turn to the other headline as you reach for the door. It stops you before you can take another step: *Father beats son to death, kills himself.*

One of the two pictures under the headline is of a black-bagged body on a gurney. The other picture is a mug shot of big man, Jim Cogan it says, something the police had from prior arrests. Your knees go weak as you stare at the body bag and wonder if it's your friend. At first you can't read the article, because you don't want to see his name. They won't publish his real name, St. Patrick. They'll use the proper form of his name, the one you're privileged to ignore because he trusted you.

You let go a string of curses before you finally read the article. You want to cry, but won't, because you know St. Patrick would prefer you curse instead. You read the article once more before you can no longer hold back the tears, and then you grab a hammer and nails from the garage. You nail the article and cover page of the newspaper to your sister's bedroom door.

"Happy now?" you say, but nobody is there to hear you.

Smokin' Joe ...

A month passes and you're still angry about what has happened to your friend. Sex has become a blasé routine and you're finding out that you and your girlfriend have little to no use for each other after being intimate.

The scribbling you do into notebooks has become more violent and vengeance based. Dialogues have turned to condemnations and persecutions. The force driving your writing is an angry one, the adrenaline like poison, and it spills out one day in ranting suicide notes.

Dear Thomas Rocco: I don't know what the hell I did besides being born, but I'm sick of trying to figure it out. If you didn't want me, you shouldn't have had me. You should've punched Mom in the stomach when she was pregnant. It would've been less painful for all of us. I know my dying won't bother you. It's more likely to relieve you and that cunt you knocked up. As for the kid she lost, aborted probably, it caught a lucky break. Thanks for nothing.

Dear Adele: Sometimes I love you. Sometimes I wanted to love you so bad it hurt, but you never let me, not for long. You always reminded me it's a huge waste of time and effort to get anywhere close to you. I don't know what the hell that was about, but I no longer care. You need to give Mom a break, no matter what your issue is with her. She doesn't deserve your shit either. Nobody does. Menachem Begin.

Dear Mom: I'm so sorry for everything. Know that I love you. Know that I wish with all my heart you didn't have to go through the shit you've been put through this life. Know that with all my heart I'm sorry for this last bit of pain and if there's a way to pay that motherfucker you married back, I'll find it the next go. Your son.

That bit of bile expunged from your soul, at least temporarily, you come to realize there's something missing from your life. Having sex with your girlfriend has become nothing more than a distraction. Trying to figure out what you need from this world leaves you poking at the bad shit instead of looking for what's good. Even reading isn't doing it for you. You're no St. Patrick or Justo. The revolution will have to wait.

It's springtime in Canarsie and now that St. Patrick is gone, except for what has become of your girlfriend's singular purpose, you don't have any close friends. You see a few former classmates from St. Jude, and they ask you where you've been. You tell them a nuthouse, and they shy away. Writing has become your new solace, but you continue to crave a good old fashioned fistfight.

One spring day you see your chance to exorcise some demons and get into it with a bully shaking down freshmen in the high school schoolyard. You don't notice the football team across the yard doing calisthenics. You're more focused on the bully, itching for him to approach you. This is another chance to avenge the time you froze when a kid on your block was fighting for his bicycle.

It's a win-win. If you get your ass kicked, it's a red badge of courage. If you win, your reputation and self-esteem are enhanced tenfold.

You've been lifting weights religiously and have a muscular chest and arms. You see the bully shove a kid, and your fist is cocked and ready to go. Several months of little Jesus' wrath is about to uncoil. He's a six-footer, at least three years older than you. You see him coming and purposely avoid eye contact to lend him some confidence, because you want to be fair, and you know he's going to need it.

"You got money?" he asks.

"You got money?" you ask.

"You a funny man?" he says.

"Your mother thinks so," you say.

He slaps your face with a quick backhand and it is the spark that sets off the explosion. You nail his forehead with a right, backing him up several steps. He's pissed-off now, embarrassed too, so he fires a series of hard jabs, and they nail you one after another. One you can actually feel and it is comforting, his knuckles pressed against your eye socket. Another couple of jabs bounce off your forehead, which doesn't hurt, because you're overloaded with adrenalin. You feel juiced, because you're still one sick puppy and this is exactly what you've wanted and needed.

There's euphoria in the sick smile you're showing as each of you have squared off like boxers in a make-believe ring. He circles as you crouch down low. You worship Joe Frazier and have taken to his style of fighting. In a few years you will cry when George Foreman knocks Frazier down six times in two rounds, but you've practiced Frazier's stance and his famous left hook a thousand times in your basement while working out. You've improved the punch Thomas Rocco once taught you. You've floored many an imaginary foe in that basement and a few real ones on the streets with a left hook.

A crowd of students along with the bully's hangers-on flock to the scene. The hangers-on are yelling for Renlo, apparently his name, to beat you down. The rest are silently hoping you'll get lucky and land at least one good punch before he kicks your ass. He manages to catch you across the nose and it stings just enough to trigger the bomb you've become. Lightning-like adrenaline surges through your body as you come up from down low with that left hook you've been waiting months to let fly … and there's his jaw.

The crack is loud, everyone hears it. Renlo doesn't go down, but he's stunned and he turns away, both hands covering his mouth. Blood pours out one side of his mouth as he tries to shield the mess you've made of his face. He's trying to say something, but he can't speak.

The bully is completely vulnerable. You can go up to him and smack him like a child, pull his ears, trip his feet, call him names, whatever you want, but you don't. Little Jesus isn't a bully. Not yet. Little Jesus is cognizant enough to realize he's killed two birds with one stone. You've satisfied a desire to feel some physical pain AND delivered some justice unto the world, at least unto one schoolyard bully.

You go from victim to hero with one punch. You're a temporary legend, the David who slew the schoolyard's Goliath. The crowd that has gathered is now large, most of them congratulating you or hurling insults at Renlo, even some of his hangers-on.

White boy kicked your ass!

Renlo a pussy!

White boy broke his jaw!

It's a miracle of sorts, because you know, and probably so does everybody else in that schoolyard, that nine out of ten times Renlo would probably kill you, and that the white boy was one lucky fuck.

But today Renlo didn't kill you. Today you broke his jaw and you feel great about it.

Word spreads fast and the next day you're convinced to go and try your hands and head at playing football. One of the football players' fathers witnessed the schoolyard fight that was going on while his son was practicing with the team in the same schoolyard. He examines your eye and says, "You trying out for the team?"

You nod.

"You the one who beat up Renlo?"

You nod again.

"He's not even in school anymore. That jerk, his real name is Doug Simmons. He's out of school two years now."

You shrug, but a smile has formed on your face full of bruises and color.

He brings you to meet one of the coaches and explains why your face is a mess. You smile and nod. The coach frowns. He's wishing you wouldn't smile. He's wishing you weren't as crazy as you clearly must be to have fought someone obviously a lot older and stronger than you. He's wishing he didn't have to deal with kids with blackened eyes who smile about having fights. He's wishing they'd pay him enough so he could teach six hours a day and not have to coach football another two hours a day for what amounts to less than minimum wage, which in 1972 is something like $1.60 an hour. He's a good man with good intentions. You don't know if he's been beaten down by the system, but he still longs for signs there remains some good in this world, even though you're clearly not one of them.

He continues frowning and says, "Be in the gym tomorrow at four o'clock for practice."

Welcome to Queens ...

Before your senior year playing football, you'll have to move to Queens and watch your mother go through yet another depression. She can no longer hold onto the house. It's finally sold and you all three have to move to an apartment in a neighborhood on the border of Brooklyn and Queens called Ozone Park. Technically, you should be attending John Adams High School, but strings are pulled and you get to continue at Canarsie, a commute that takes two trains and a bus.

But for one more year you're condemned to Queens, and as close as you now live to your girlfriend, about a mile walk under the El, and for all the extra screwing you'll get in while you live there, your mother is distraught at going from a homeowner to a double homeowner to a renter in less than two years.

And then there's Bruno, your dog. He hasn't adjusted to the move from a big house to a tiny apartment and he's biting anyone who comes to the door he doesn't recognize, including the landlord. He has to go, and when he does, to some junkyard a friend of your mother's suggests, your sister blames you.

"This is your fault, jerk," she says. "She had to go and buy you a dog because you're crazy."

"It's my fault your father let us go broke? Why don't you blame him for this? He's the one let us lose the house."

"Fuck you."

"That's right, keep defending him. He's the hero here, not Mom. Why don't you go live with him?"

It's a question that pierces her soul. Her eyes well with tears and you know why, because Thomas Rocco would never let her live with him. He may feel closer to his daughter than his son, but he doesn't want her interfering in his life with Gang Bang any more than he wants you interfering in his life with Gang Bang.

Your mother catches a break when one of her friends talks her into joining Parents Without Partners, and she gets to go out dancing. She meets a few guys who do their best to get down her pants, but strikeout because she's somehow still carrying that torch for the piece of shit she married and since divorced. At least she's getting out is how you see it, but your sister doesn't see it the same way. She refuses to say hello or goodbye to anybody your mother brings home, embarrassing her no end. It's a shame because some of the PWP guys aren't too bad, and although one or two are assholes, your Mom is no moron and can figure it out for herself.

The one guy who pisses you off most is a retired firefighter who makes a point of telling you how he never walked around in his underwear in front of his mother, something you do without giving a second thought, and even though you know he's right, you don't like his telling you jack shit. You want to tell him, "Look, asshole, I'm glad my mother met somebody, even you, but don't think for a second you're welcome to any part of my life."

What you do instead is bite your tongue for your mother's sake, and the asshole is only around for a couple of more weeks before your mother ignores his phone calls.

The day you ask your sister what she thinks of your mother dating, she tells you, "Who cares what she does? I'm out of here soon as I can find someplace else to live. You two losers can do whatever you want."

And when your mother dates a weasel, you put up with him because you know he's harmless. He brings her stolen miniature bottles of booze he clips from the airport where he works as a baggage handler. "He's a good dancer," your mother claims, but you don't like that she always cooks for him and all he ever brings her are dopey miniature bottles of booze.

Your sister nicknames the airport thief Twinkle Toes just to upset your mother. She says it all the time, the same way she's taken to calling your girlfriend Tam-tam. It is humiliating to your mother that her friend, especially when he comes to pick her up, has to suffer your sister's constant indignities. One day she calls him Twinkle Toes to his face and your mother is mortified. The argument that ensues after Mr. Toes leaves is revealing.

"Why can't you be nice just once?" your mother asks your sister.

"Why don't you fuck off?" your sister says.

"Why is it you hate me? What have I done to make you so mean? Maybe I should've knocked the shit out of you the way your father did to your brother."

Any comparison to you, Little Jesus, is an extra insult to your sister. "Oh, shut up," she tells your mother. "You're an idiot."

"Because I didn't go to college? Do you talk to your father like this?

Do you treat Gang Bang the way you treat my friends?"

One again, your sister has no answer, probably because admitting the truth is too painful. She wouldn't dare treat Thomas Rocco or Gang Bang with anywhere near the same level of disrespect, at least not at that point in her life.

Watching the exchange between your mother and sister is painful, and when you see your mother has tears in her eyes, you can only hope your sister sheds similar tears when she returns to her room.

At least you treat your mother's friends with respect. You know Twinkle Toes is a dork and that he gets over with the free meals your mother cooks, and even if she's sleeping with him, you know it's her choice, and to that end it's none of your business. If he were to harm her, you wouldn't think twice about killing him, but there's no need. The guy is her friend and her life has been shit for so long she deserves a little attention from someone other than a shrink, especially now, after having to move into a shit apartment in Queens.

You award yourself points for being a decent little shit, but the frustration you're feeling from your sister's cruelty toward your mother is stirring up some reserve anger, and anger is the last thing you're in short supply of.

Big Balls ...

Your sister attends Queens College in Jamaica, a really bad neighborhood, and is paying for it herself. Once again Thomas Rocco hasn't delivered on a promise. He was supposed to pay for her college and books so she could continue to save the pittance she was earning at the library, but he never came through with the money. You don't know the dynamics between them anymore, except she's seeing him even less than you see him, and he's certainly not sharing their relationship with you.

"How's your sister doing?" he'll ask during one of your monthly visits with him, during which South Oaks is never mentioned.

"Okay," you'll say.

"She dating anybody?"

You can't tell him the truth because it isn't your place to do so. You tell him you don't think so and he nods, the end of that discourse.

When you tell your sister that Thomas Rocco is asking for her, she tells you to mind your own business.

"He wants to know if you're dating," you say.

"Did you tell him, jerk?"

"You just said it's none of my business, asshole."

"Why don't you and Tam-tam run off together?"

You think about St. Patrick, what he would say. "That would be none of your business," you tell her, then flip her the bird.

"Get out of my face!" she says, but you know you've won that round, so you wink at her to piss her off even more.

The summer comes and goes and you're anxious for your last football season. Your mother can only look forward to an occasional night out dancing. Your sister is pissed off at the world, it seems, and when you learn the reason why, because her girlfriend of a few years has broken off with her, you don't say anything half as nasty as she says about your girlfriend, who has become the extra special object of your sister's scorn.

"How's Tam-tam?" she asks at every opportunity.

"Why do you have to do that?" you say.

"Do what?"

"Make fun of her."

"Because she's a ditz."

"Because she's not as smart as you?"

"She's an idiot."

"Can't you be nice?"

"No, I can't. She's a dope and so are you."

It never dawns on Little Jesus that his sister might be jealous of Tam-tam, or that some of the hurtful things she spews has to do with her own insecurities. Maybe Tam-tam is someone she picks on not so much because Tammy isn't smart, but because she's a thin, attractive girl, the kind her shallow fucking father would rather his daughter had been, someone with better looks than brains.

When Thomas Rocco gets around to meeting Tammy, he's clearly not impressed, although at least he doesn't call her Tam-tam. He calls her honey and swoons her with kindness until he's alone with you long enough to make a disapproving face about your choice for a girlfriend.

"She's flat," he says.

You're completely caught off guard. "What?"

"No tits."

You're still confused.

"What?" he says.

"The fuck is wrong with you?" you say.

Now *he's* pissed off. "Excuse me?"

"Everybody says your wife is a hole, but I wouldn't think to say that to your face."

You catch a quick, hard, slap. This time, not only do you not flinch, you smile immediately afterward. "Feel better?" you say.

He tries his best to stare you down, but it isn't going to work. As soon as he realizes it, he gets up and leaves. You know he's rattled and that was worth a dozen slaps.

Little Jesus has grown himself some big balls.

Football Americano ...

What you get from football is discipline, confidence, and the opportunity to release your aggressions without getting into fights. This new form of physical contact is a Godsend. There is nothing quite like the sweet spot of a good stick, the feel of your facemask in the chest of a ball carrier. It is the equivalent of the knuckles of a fist in your eye socket, except now your face is the fist and the ball carrier's chest is the eye socket.

Praise be to Allah for the preparation of your new *jihad*. Helmet to helmet warfare is your new *justum bellum*, and it's as good as sex. You up the ante on the time you put into building muscle and speed for the battles that lay ahead. It is a new form of dedication that precludes you from being lazy.

"Charlie, where are you going so early?" your mother asks.

"Running," you tell her.

"It's six o'clock in the morning."

"I can tell time, Ma. I'll be back by seven."

You do as you said you would and are back in time to take the shower you feel you've earned. So look at you, little Horatio Alger of a sudden. You even get dressed and go to school. You're awake for class and enjoy English most.

After *Of Mice and Men* is assigned, your interest in the author sends you back to his masterpiece, *The Grapes of Wrath*. You're nowhere near sophisticated or steeped enough in your own country's miserable history to grasp the background to the novel, but you become instantly sympathetic to the Joad family and its plight, and you want to learn more about the Depression your parents suffered through as kids.

More importantly, *The Grapes of Wrath* stirs a fire inside you. Tom Joad is a working class hero you root for from the time you first meet him, fresh out of prison for committing a homicide. A guy down on his luck who has to fight, even kill, to survive. The stirring in your soul doesn't fade, and so the stories you write begin to take some shape. This time it's the thinking you do between workouts, sometimes during workouts. You create scenes in your head and then stay up late nights and write them out at the kitchen table. You write about working class heroes you're more familiar with, each fighting a just war of their own.

Because Thomas Rocco was a lithographer, you start with a story about a pressman told to do something illegal by a greedy boss.

"It's that or your job," the greedy boss says to the pressman.

"Fine, but I'll tell you this much, Joe. You cost me my job, my family can't eat, I can't find another job fast enough, I'm coming after you."

"If that's a threat, you're fired," the greedy boss says.

"Fine, then I'm fired ... and now you can pick up your teeth," the pressman said before he punched the greedy boss in the mouth.

It's silly shit you write, but it is writing and you want to keep doing it, especially with the working man in mind. At the least, this thirst for knowledge has enlightened a sense of camaraderie with the poor. You'll take a few twists and turns along the way, but you'll take to the socialist paradigm once your political wheels move in the same direction.

One night after a particularly good practice during which you stung one of the hotshot running backs on the varsity with a helmet to his chest, you fall asleep with a smile on your face and are visited by the friend you met in the nuthouse, Justo, but there's a hole in his forehead and you can feel your brow furrow in your sleep as you reach a hand up to point at the hole.

"What's that about?" you ask.

"Suicide is painless," he says.

The realization of what he's said strikes home. *"What the fuck, Justo. Why?"*

"Because my father was going to have me committed to that place, South Oaks. Fuck that shit."

"Couldn't you run away again?"

"Couldn't you?" he says, and then is gone, leaving you to wonder about what he last said. Run away from what? From who? Yourself?

Your brow furrows and you wake up to a game day. It's against a local rival and it'll be one of your better games in your short-lived high school football career. There's an extra dose of inexplicable anger inside you when you take the field and it has something to do with being huge underdogs to a team that has been undefeated and unscored on. The talk in town is your team will be crushed, but it is a game that will end in a 6-6 tie.

After the game, and after you screw your girlfriend, you wonder what the hell Justo meant in that dream. Since when was running away an answer?

Or was he suggesting you should kill yourself too?

You're a confused young man again. You won and lost something today, but you can't figure out what you won or lost. The confusion unsettles you through the night.

What you didn't know, what you couldn't possibly know or understand, especially at that point in your life, was how football and writing would ultimately wage their own war, one against the other, for your ultimate attention.

In the meantime, what football does is earn you some respect and confidence, because in a prior year you won an award, and in your senior year you were one of the captains of the team. You will have a short-lived senior football season because you break an arm after just four games, but you perform well enough to catch the attention of a few small college programs. One will lead you to a school in North Dakota, where you'll meet a man who will forever change your life.

The progression is ironic. Thomas Rocco humiliated you when he taught you how to box. You had sissy arms you needed to strengthen enough to throw the left hook that would lead you to football, and it is football that will lead you to college and a burning desire to write.

In the meantime, you're becoming strong as a bull lifting weights, another ironic twist of fate for a kid with sissy arms.

The 300 Club ...

You've been weightlifting for a few years and at seventeen, you're as strong as most men. On days you work construction, upon returning home, you've been taking two buses to the YMCA on Flatbush Avenue three times a week. You've been running sprints and distance at Seaview Park the other four days. It is a routine you rarely vary during the months before you'll leave for your first college football training camp.

In the meantime, breaking the news to Thomas Rocco that you have a scholarship to play football for a small school in North Dakota is something you can't wait to do. You've already forgotten what you should know better, to avoid the cocksucker, but you see each accomplishment as something to put in his face, and you're about to hit a new goal, one even he can't knock.

It's at the YMCA where a few of the powerlifters there have taken a liking to your work ethic in the gym. The captain of the powerlifting team, a black man named Phil, has been giving you advice and encouragement, something that's been so foreign to your being, you've welcomed it like a starving infant reaching for its mother's teat. You're attempting your second 300 pound bench-press. You missed 300 a few months before, but you weren't ready. Today you are.

The Olympic bar is loaded with four forty-five pound plates and two thirty-five pound plates. The bar itself weighs forty-five pounds. The collars weigh five pounds each, bringing the total to 305 pounds. Phil is spotting you from behind the bench. He asks if you want a lift-off, but you decide to take it yourself. You grip the bar at the markers to keep the proper spacing, inhale a few times, then arch your back and grunt loud as you push the weight off the rack. It feels good, not heavy the way it did when you missed it.

You bring the bar down in a smooth motion, not too fast and not too slow. You let it touch your chest and hold it there until Phil claps his hands, the signal used in powerlifting meets to press the weight back up. Upon hearing the clap, you explode the weight off your chest, growling from the depths of your soul.

"Push it!" Phil yells. "Push it! That's it!"

You push the weight past your sticking point and lock your arms. Phil helps guide the bar back onto the rack and there is applause from the rest of Phil's powerlifting team.

It is a milestone, and it feels better than being named captain or winning lineman of the year, or getting the football scholarship. It is something you accomplished solo, something that can never be taken away. Phil hands you a T-shirt with a picture of a loaded barbell bending across the racks of a bench. It reads: 300 Club. It is something you'll treasure the rest of your life.

Like most kids thrilled with themselves, you wear that T-shirt until it reeks and you're forced to take it off because even you can't take the smell. When your sister sees you wearing the T-shirt, she makes believe she doesn't read it, but you know she did. Like her father, there's no way she's going to acknowledge what you're obviously proud of. Bench pressing three hundred pounds at a body weight of 198, at age 17, the way it's done in meets, with a pause before pressing the weight, is an accomplishment, whether your father and sister acknowledge it or not.

Your suspicions are confirmed the next time you visit with Thomas Rocco. It's at Miteras, a diner on Sullivan Street in Greenwich Village. It is the day your sister is going to tell him that she's gay. You both sit

at a table and are surprised as Thomas Rocco tells a gay joke to the
owner of the restaurant near the cash register. They both laugh. You look
to your sister and can tell she's fuming.

When he joins you and your sister at the table, he's about to tell you
both the same stupid joke, but your sister cuts him off.

"Daddy, didn't you know I was gay?"

The gut punch is instant. He swallows so hard his throat actually
makes a gulping sound. There is a long moment of silence during
which you could hear his spoon stirring his coffee over and over, and it
reminds you of the way he crushes out his cigarettes.

"I have to get a Times," your sister says. "I'll be right back."

She leaves you and Thomas Rocco alone while she heads to the
newsstand around the corner. She won't be long, so whatever has to be
said, has to be said right away. There is no way you're going to mention
your football scholarship now. This is too big a deal. Your sister has just
come out to your father and he's been rocked by the news.

Then he says, "That was like a kick in the balls."

You know he's upset, but you also know why. He's embarrassed, and
it pisses you off.

"She's your daughter," you say.

He shakes his head. "You don't understand," he says. "It's not easy for
those people."

You can't believe he just disowned his daughter, but in some way he
has. What the hell does *those people* mean?

Deep down you know what it means. He's embarrassed. He really is
embarrassed.

He's looks down at his coffee. You're pissed off and want to hurt him.
It is then you remember your T-shirt and notice Thomas Rocco is also
wearing a T-shirt. You see how some of his chest hairs have turned gray.
It's an awkward moment for you. Here's the guy you've feared most of
your life, the man you've tried to impress since you were a kid, and now
he looks old and defeated.

Defeated by his own insecurity.

You point to your 300 Club T-shirt and it gets the same response from
him as it did from your sister, which is no response.

Angry for his lack of acknowledgment, but also anxious to put
something in his face, you tell him about the football scholarship.

He frowns, then nods.

"And a few weeks ago I benched three-hundred-five pounds," you say.
"That's what this shirt is about, the three-hundred club."

He nods again.

"Some guy who gave a shit, a black guy named Phil? He gave me the shirt."

Not a nod nor a frown, and you should've known better, but no longer willing to be a coward with this motherfucker, you say, "Fuck you, too," then get up and leave.

"Hey!" he yells, but you don't acknowledge it, except to raise both hands up, giving him a double dose of the finger.

And this time there's nothing to cry about. If Thomas Rocco was looking to turn you to stone, he's somewhat succeeded. You return home more determined than ever to beat the son-of-a-bitch at every fucking thing there is possible to beat somebody at, including making money, being a criminal, and fucking up your family.

You're A Natural ...

While you're becoming a strong little fucker, you're also falling into a funk you don't understand. When you aren't screwing your girlfriend, you're finding faults with her and acting a lot more like a frustrated husband than a decent human being. You yell at her a lot, constantly re-establishing your dominance in the relationship, if only in your mind, but it is ugly and degrading, and often much worse than what Thomas Rocco and your sister do to you.

"What are you, an idiot?" you say when she leaves you a note with words missing from a sentence. "Did you read what you wrote here?"

After watching a movie together and asking her what she thought of it, it wasn't enough that she said she liked or didn't like it. You suddenly required a discussion she isn't interested in having. "What the fuck, Tammy? Are you dumb or what?"

Or after having sex and cleaning yourself off with a shower and returning to the living room where she's watching television, you want her to leave. "Don't you have to get home?" you say. "It's not like you're going to do anything different here than you do there. Go home and watch television."

And once she's gone, and you're alone with the monster you're becoming, you hate yourself a little more.

When the frustrated husband routine spills into your relationship with your mother yet again, you overhear her reaching out to Thomas Rocco one more time for help.

"Please, Tommy, I can't handle him anymore. Do something with him."

But there's no way Thomas Rocco is going anywhere near you, not after what you said to his face. If anything, he's using that as just cause to keep his distance.

And neither is your sister anywhere to be found of late. She's preparing to take a trip to England to study Renaissance English for school and will be gone from summer until the Christmas holidays. It dawns on you that come the fall your mother will be alone for the first time in her life. Her parents are long dead, her husband is gone, and now you and your sister will be leaving the nest as well.

You can't imagine the relief it will be for her not to have to deal with you and your sister, but only because you're still too young and too stupid to understand how much of a pain in the ass you've become.

"Ma, you sure you're gonna be alright once I go to school?"

It's then you learn that your mother has balls every bit as big as yours. She may have been badly wounded by Thomas Rocco, and her emotions may have betrayed her better judgment, but make no mistake, she's been the strongest one in the family all along.

"Are you kidding me?" she says. "Between you and your sister, this will be a vacation."

You smile. "Ma, but we're your kids. You're supposed to miss us."

"Please, you're a pair of pains in the ass, the both of you. Just don't get in trouble while you're away, and I told your sister the same thing, so don't give me any shit about saying that."

You try and lay on the guilt, but she's not biting. "Ma, but I'm your sonny boy."

"You're a lunatic. Go play football and get it out of your system. I can't put up with it anymore."

"And Adele? What about her?"

"A bitch. There, I said it. Happy now?"

You can't stop laughing.

There's still the summer to get through, so you apply for a second job at the McDonald's on Rockaway Parkway across the street from Holy Family Church. You're trained days, but with the understanding you'll work nights. It is at that McDonald's where you learn firsthand the indignity of working for a rich kid. His father owns three of the local McDonald's gold mines in and around Canarsie. The rich kid likes to correct every fucking thing you do, until one day his father sees you flipping burgers, points at you and says, "He's a natural."

In the past you might've wondered whether or not his comment was a condemnation of your future, something Thomas Rocco might've suggested, but now you know it was a compliment. You no longer doubt yourself the way you have in the past. You know you were the best grill kid in that particular gold mine.

The night before you leave for North Dakota, St. Patrick is back in a dream. He is seated in the armchair in your living room. You are in the couch-bed you still use because your sister hasn't left for England yet. Your girlfriend is asleep beside you. St. Patrick is smoking a joint, something you've never seen him do before.

"Since when do you smoke?" you say.

"None of your business. You're finally wetting your noodle and now you wanna bang your noggin some more? Gonna fly across the country to do it?"

"Where the fuck you been, you arrogant Mick?"

"As if you don't know."

"Seriously, what's with the joint? You a head now?"

"Pay attention, you knuckle-dragger. I don't have time to dick around."

"Where the fuck'm I going? You're the dream."

St. Patrick takes a drag from the joint, holds the smoke in his lungs a long moment, during which he squints. "There's a devil back on your shoulder," he says after exhaling. "A master of deception. A shape bender. He'll haunt as often as you allow."

Your eyebrows furrow at St. Patrick. "The fuck are you now, the Riddler?"

"He's relentless."

"The fuck is this?"

"A master of deception. A shape bender."

"Oh, asshole. You said. So?"

"There are two ways to expel him. Just two."

"One is to wake up, I know that much."

St. Patrick raises the thumb of his free hand. "An exorcism, and I don't mean that bullshit in the movie, priests waving crucifixes and sprinkling holy water. I'm talking exorcism by self. Exorcism by you, Dago."

"You're being a real jerk-off now."

He raises the index finger of the same hand. "Two, a woman," he says, then motions at your girlfriend with his head. "Not her."

You're offended. "I love her."

"Is that what it is when you call her an idiot?"

"Fuck you, Hojo. I have a temper."

"Yeah, you're a natural with that too."

"Say what?"

"Never mind, wop. You'll have plenty of time to figure it out, but it'll be someone with freckles, the woman."

"How do you know all this?"

"How'd you think, you ignorant fuck?"

Fuck yourself, you're about to say, when your sister walks into the dream. You see them exchange glances the same way they did the first *time she walked in on the two of you in the basement a few years back. You always suspected they knew each other.*

"Mom will be late," she tells you. "She said to order pizza."

She leaves you two alone again and you look to St. Patrick for an answer.

"She patched me up once," he says. "After the old man opened my forehead with a coffee mug. I used gauze and tape, but it didn't hold and she saw I was bleeding in the library. Took me to Brookdale Hospital for stitches."

You're shocked. "My sister? She did that for you?"

"Bought me a sandwich too. And a soda. Went back to work, then came back to the hospital to check on me. Drove me home after."

"Why didn't you say something? Why didn't ..."

"She asked me not to."

You try and picture everything he's just said, but can't. You're confused no end. Why wouldn't she tell you? Why wouldn't he say something?

"I don't know what it's about," he says, "but she'll treat most others with respect and kindness. She'll have a loyal following, very loyal. She'll get a library named after her where she teaches English as a Second Language someday, but for whatever reasons, you and your mother ... I don't know. I think she loved you both, but couldn't show it the way you needed it. Don't ask me why."

You think about it for a moment, but anger gets the best of you. "Fuck her," you say.

"He'll hide from her, too," St. Patrick says, "for whatever it's worth."

You're confused about what he's said until you realize he means Thomas Rocco will hide from your sister after they're dead.

You wake up to see if it's possible it wasn't a dream. You sit up on the couch-bed and stare at the armchair. You can still see him if you close your eyes. You can smell the joint he was smoking in the dream, if it was a dream.

Your girlfriend stirs besides you. She mumbles something you can't make out. There's a pause and she mumbles it again. You lean in closer to hear what she says and swallow hard at the mention of a name.

"No," she says, a slight smile on her face. "Nick, don't. Not now. He's inssssss."

You spend the rest of the night into the morning drinking coffee at the kitchen table. Your flight leaves at 10:30 a.m. and you can't stop wondering whether or not you should stay home and find out who the fuck Nick is.

A New Frontier...

North Dakota will prove the greatest learning experience of your life, both on and off the football field. In North Dakota you meet new people so foreign to your Brooklyn existence, your world can't help but change for the better. In North Dakota, although it'll take more than one semester, during which you fuck up and almost fail off the team, you'll eventually realize education isn't your enemy. In North Dakota several seeds of confidence take root and your world begins to bloom.

You make the traveling team, tie for the lead in tackles on kick-offs, and you get to play the fourth quarter in almost every game the team wins.

In one game you get to play the entire fourth quarter in a 34-0 blowout win. On your very first play, you're in the zone and can envision the move you're about to make a split second before it happens. The ball is snapped and you use your best skills, quickness and strength, in a grab and pull move to blow past their starting center so fast you're in the quarterback's chest before he can plant his back foot to throw a pass. It's your first official college sack.

That night, after you've called your mother drunk out of your mind to tell her about your sack, St. Patrick is back to visit you in a drunken dream.

"Proud of yourself, eh, numb-nuts," he says.

"You're fuckin-A right I am."

"You're doing okay, I suppose, with the football anyway."

"It's what I'm here for."

"Is it now? You expect you'll be jumping to the NFL after playing in this little pond?"

"I didn't say that, asshole. I said it's what I'm here for, to play football."

"And education be damned. That's a Dago for you."

"Hey, you know what? Blow me."

"Blow yourself, you ignorant goombah. You're blowing a free education sleeping through your morning classes. You're about to fail history. Why not grow the fuck up already and take this stuff serious?"

"I'm passing three classes, moron."

"Out of five, and one of those you're passing is athletics, because you get an A for being on the football team. Eejit!"

"Hey, fuck-face, don't ruin my night, okay?"

"You've got more inside you than you think, you dope. You're not just a head-banger."

"Right, I'm a fuckin' poet."

"You still want to know something about The Stranger, *Eejit? I'll tell you something. It caught your interest for a reason, you moron. You can do more than one thing at a time. You won't be playing in the NFL someday, so maybe you should take advantage of this place, you dumb shit."*

St. Patrick is gone when your roommate comes back from another party and wakes you up. The two of you talk about the game and drink another few beers before you both fall asleep. When you wake up the next morning, you head to the Student Union for breakfast and spot a book someone left on a table. You pick it up, *The Stranger*, then sit and begin to read it again.

The novel sparks an idea. Since you can't imagine having the same thoughts as Camus' Meursault about his mother, you try to write something from Thomas Rocco's point of view.

You try a number of opening sentences in an attempt to draw a reader in the way *The Stranger's* opening hooked you, but your efforts prove fruitless. What you come up with are openings for a sociopath, a scumbag, and a coward.

When Thomas Rocco found the suitcase full of money, instead of bringing it home to his family, he hopped a flight to Mexico and started a new life.

Thomas Rocco was bored watching his son playing football, but he was all smiles when Gang Bang pulled up at the curb and beeped the horn.

When Thomas Rocco spotted his daughter holding hands with another girl, he stepped inside a shoe store to avoid her seeing him.

Eventually you're too critical of what you're writing and stop in time to watch *Kojak* in the student lounge, but you can't focus on the show and have no idea what it's about. Your mind is still writing.

By morning your focus has returned to football, your education be damned, and it remains damned until the spring semester, when you need to make up some D's and an F to be eligible for next football season. You take a required English class from the man who will make all the difference in your life. A professor who graduated from the famous Iowa Writer's Workshop, and was taught by Kurt Vonnegut Jr., and another writer who will become one of your favorite authors, Richard Yates. Both Vonnegut Jr. and Yates, in fact, had signed your professor's MFA thesis.

His requirements for the introductory class include reading *Newsweek* cover to cover and writing a rebuttal or confirmation essay with one of the four featured columnists week to week. There is also a reading list, and all of it interests you. The work you hand in is always sloppy and loaded with grammatical and spelling errors. He often grades you with an A or a B over an F, a content and structure grade over a grammatical grade, and it works. You progress as a wannabe writer, learning a little punctuation and spelling along the way.

One day he hands you a few books he thinks you should read. You take them back to the dorm and begin reading a collection of short stories by Kurt Vonnegut, Jr. By the time you've finished reading one story, "Harrison Bergeron", you want to write again, even more than you want to read.

North Dakota is indeed a new frontier.

You meet a girl there two years your senior. She teaches ballet, is thin as a rail, but she's cute and she's taken an interest in the weirdo from New York. The two of you do a lot of talking. You want in with her, but learn she's got a boyfriend in Montana she sees from time to time, and he's two years older than her. Your odds aren't very good, but she's hanging around you and letting you hang around her. It's the off-season and one day she meets you at the gym where your work-study job is to watch the weight room. You're finishing up a series of sit-ups on an inclined board and she sits on your stomach with a big smile on her face.

"What's up?" you say.

She wiggles on your stomach, but slides a bit further down and is covering your waist. You do what comes natural. She feels it, opens her eyes wide, and says, "Uh-oh."

"Uh-oh bad or uh-oh good?" you say.

"I'll wait for you in my car," she says.

You can't believe it. You look at the clock and see you only have 20 minutes left before you punch out for the day.

And you still have wood.

This could be it, your first non-Tammy sex, your first collegiate action, your first ballet instructor, and so on.

When you sit inside her car, she's still smiling, but you aren't sure if she's going to drive someplace or try to sneak inside your dorm.

"Where we going?" you say.

She shrugs.

You lean into her for a kiss. She allows it, but not your tongue. Then she giggles and you couldn't feel more foolish.

And your wood is gone.

"What's the deal?" you say.

"Deal?" she says.

"I don't get it."

"Get what?"

You huff.

"Whaaaaaat?" she says, drawing it out like a child, and that's it, you've had enough.

You get out of the car and head back to your dorm. She beeps the horn but you don't bother to turn around. This time you know it isn't your fault. You don't know what her problem is, but you have no intention of being the brunt of her joke.

The next day you meet a girl you know has been eyeing you, a junior with a little more meat on her bones than you're usually attracted to. She's got a hell of a body and a cherry ass, which is but one of the misogynistic adjectives you begin to use to describe a woman's anatomy. She also wears glasses, something else you're attracted to. You strike up a conversation at the student union, and later walk her to her dorm. You agree to meet later the same night back at the student union for the meal plan dinner.

Her name is Pamela and it's clear she's into you. This time when you walk back toward her dorm, you stop and kiss. It's a good kiss. A really good kiss, the kind you've been missing and desperate for. She lets you grab her ass and she teases your cock through your pants, but that's as far as it goes. You return to your dorm horny as hell and have to take care of business the usual way.

It's a storyline that repeats itself for two weeks before you can't take her refusal to go any further. You tell her it's over but she wants to talk about it at breakfast the next morning.

"Sure," you say, but I'm drinking tonight with a few other guys so you'll have to come get me at my dorm in the morning. Wake me up and we'll go to a diner for breakfast or lunch.

You don't get to bed until close to dawn, and when you do, you purposely remain naked. Sometime after the sun has risen, you feel someone tugging at your arm. You wake up and it's Pamela. You lightly pull at her to join you in bed, but she tells you, "No, not like this."

"Fine," you say, and turn over, pulling a sheet over your ass and legs.

"You coming or not?" she says.

You don't answer, but you can hear her leave and the door slam shut.

That's it, Little Jesus. That's as far as your attempts to cheat on Tammy goes in college. At least you think so. Two rebukes. One from the ballet dancer who laughed at you and Pamela's decent attempt to know you better. You give up on the process and remain focused on your studies for a change.

The new frontier is officially closed. At least for getting laid it is.

Playing House ...

"Ma, how you doing?" you ask over the phone.

"I'm doing fine. You okay?"

"I love it, Ma. I'm worried about you."

"I can take care of myself, Charlie."

"Twinkle been around?"

"Yes, Tony is here right now, in fact."

You roll your eyes and wish you didn't call. The thought of your mother rolling around on a bed with Twinkle Toes makes you cringe, but you decide to turn it into a joke.

"Make sure he uses something?"

"You're a sick son-of-a-bitch, you know that?"

"I love you, Ma."

"I love you, too, but you're still crazy. Don't get into any trouble out there."

You forgot to ask about your sister, but she probably hasn't asked about you either.

Neither do you speak to Thomas Rocco while you're in college. He does send a ten-dollar money order every three weeks or so, but you figure that's a combination of guilt and an attempt to make you frugal, or he'd send you what he could afford and you wouldn't have to go to an all-you-can-eat buffet every Sunday and pack your pockets with however many rolls and Danish you can steal.

Tammy is another story. During the football season you spoke to her at least once a week and usually for fifteen minutes to a half hour at a time, but during spring semester things change. There are long breaks between phone calls, sometimes as long as three or four weeks. You've become busy reading and trying to write, and you know Tammy is working full time in the city. She's probably going out with girlfriends on the weekends and is waiting for you to call her.

You aren't jealous of what she might be doing weekends until you hear about a kid on the team who has left school because he found out his girlfriend had a new boyfriend back in Florida. It is then you begin calling Tammy every weekend, sometimes catching her home, but mostly she's not around.

After not hearing from her for two weeks, she finally answers the phone, but you can tell she wasn't expecting to hear your voice.

"Sorry, I was in the shower. I'll be down in a few minutes. Can you pick me up on the corner?"

You're so caught off guard, you don't speak, and then when you're about to speak she says, "Joe?"

You hang up before you say anything, then feel your stomach twist and turn until you're nauseated enough to hurl, except there's nothing inside you to vomit, and you're stuck with ten minutes of painful dry heaves. Emotionally, it's worse, a feeling of betrayal you can't shake. Not that you wanted to, but you remained loyal while at college, doing nothing more than kissing and groping. Somehow your warped sense of morality lets you off the hook, so you're not sure you can trust Tammy to be as loyal. Yours is a noble notion born of hang-ups and insecurity, but when it comes to amore, Little Jesus, you're still quite the child, way too insecure to let nature take its course.

When the spring semester ends, you make a point of getting your driver's license before you leave North Dakota. You buy a car on the cheap and make the drive back to New York. You intend to return to school early and work at a local furniture warehouse before training camp and you intend to bring Tammy with you, because you no longer trust her. You still can't imagine losing her.

First, though, you need to interrogate her about the phone call you made from school.

"Who the fuck is Joe?" you ask the day you return to New York.

"What?" she says, but you can see she's blushing.

"Joe?" you say. "The guy's name you asked a few weeks ago when I called from school. "You didn't know it was me, but you asked if it was Joe."

She tries resentment for your accusation, but it isn't working.

"Just tell me who it is," you say. "Unless he's your new boyfriend and you want me to leave. That's up to you."

For whatever reason, she doesn't tell you to take a hike. She chooses to make up a bullshit story instead. This one about a friend from work who was driving a few of her co-workers to a concert at Jones Beach. You, because you're still afraid of having no one, force yourself to believe it. You get her to commit to making the trip back to school with you, so maybe she was telling the truth, you convince yourself.

That summer you work six weeks of construction before packing your stuff, including Tammy, and returning to North Dakota mid-July. You rent a basement apartment in the Minot valley from a sweet old lady, where you and Tammy play house just like adults. A teammate gets you a job at a local furniture warehouse, and you're the husband you thought you wanted to be, a man earning enough to pay the freight for two.

The bonus of having Tammy there for you is obvious. Now you can

THE VOICES IN MY HEAD

have sex after practice, school, and work. Now you can have home-cooked meals instead of the cafeteria crap. Now you can be the man of the house for real, never concerning yourself with the boredom Tammy is going through, the nights and days without anything to do except watch television or go for long walks, or maybe meet a guy who isn't such a Neanderthal.

The football season comes and your mother flies out to North Dakota after recovering from pneumonia at home. She attends the first two games of the season, one home and one away game, both of them wins. She gets to see you start at outside linebacker for a college football team, and she's ecstatic that you seem to be much more normal than you were at home. She asks if Thomas Rocco plans to come out to see a game, and you smirk at the idea. "The prick sends me a ten-dollar money order every three or four weeks," you say. "Fuck him."

She asks about Tammy, genuinely concerned for her lack of anything to do in a place without any friends.

"She's made a few friends," you tell her. "Where she is now. And she's thinking of taking a waitressing job nearby."

"Did she really want to come?"

"She's here, Ma."

"Don't do anything stupid out here. Don't get married without telling anybody, and don't get her pregnant."

"She's on the pill, Ma. Nobody is getting pregnant. And we're not getting married out here, that's for sure."

She asks you about school in her own special way. "How are you doing with classes, and don't bullshit me."

You chuckle. "I like a couple classes this semester, but the one I told you about, that teacher, that class I love. I get up for his class. I do the work."

"And the rest of your classes?"

"They're okay, but nothing like his class. I think I like writing."

"Good," she says. "I was hoping you'd meet somebody out here to get you interested in more than just football."

"I am, Ma. I mean it."

Your mother returns home the morning after your second game. A few games later, after a pair of overtime losses, Tammy isn't home when you get back from a game in Jamestown. You wonder if she's taken off for home until she shows up close to midnight. She's been drinking and is sick before she falls asleep. In the morning you don't dare ask her where she's been from fear she'll tell you.

The team runs the table from that point on, blowing out the three remaining schools on the schedule. The final record is 7-2. It has been a sweet season, but you know it was the end of your football career. You've accomplished what you wanted, to start during your sophomore season. You can come back and play two more seasons, but something is calling you home, and it has everything to do with your girlfriend. She's told you she won't stay after the semester ends, and that she won't come back next fall. A rumor you heard about who she was with while you were playing that game in Jamestown haunts you. You can tell she's been depressed, and you fear what she might do when you're not around.

You learn another of life's lessons, Little Jesus: Playing house isn't all it's been cranked up to be.

The Friends of Eddie Coyle ...

You return to school for the spring semester with one goal in mind, to focus on schoolwork and the two English classes you'll be taking from that special professor. One is a creative writing class, the other another English requirement.

When he reads the first few pages from the crime novel, *The Friends of Eddie Coyle*, by George V. Higgins, it is nothing short of an epiphany. You are hooked for life. The dialogue you are confronted with in that book is a dialogue you've heard most of your life growing up in Brooklyn. You can't believe there are books published with that kind of dialogue, something you have an ear for, street talk.

You read through to the end of the novel by the end of the day and begin writing one of your own after dinner. It is a raw, dialogue driven effort that will never be finished, but there are clear signs of an ability beyond what you've ever thought possible. You return to the Higgins book, reread the first few pages, and sit down and write again. The creative juices flow. You can't stop yourself. Although you won't use a single page of what you write through the night, your production is substantial, half a spiral notebook; both sides of each page.

A few weeks later, your professor tells the class about a writer's conference in Grand Forks. Truman Capote and Ken Kesey will be there. You sign up for the conference and take the two-day trip with a few of the others in your class, all driven by the professor in one of the school vans. You're intimidated once you're there and don't dare ask a question when there's a Q&A after the authors panel, but you are inspired to write all over again.

Later in the semester, you learn that a short story you submitted was given an honorable mention in the college magazine. Your professor did that for you. When he hands you a copy, he says, "Once you see your name in print, you'll always want to see it."

Teachers, from an early age on, have been your blessing. Are they guardian angels sent from the heavenly father? Maybe, because whether they came in the form of coaches or instructors, you're life has been saved a few times already because of them. Their influence will ultimately save you over the long haul, because like Augie March, you're one clueless motherfucker when it comes to any formalized game plan. Unlike Augie, there is a force working at you from somewhere inside, at first speaking to you through daydreaming, and now through a camera in your mind's eye. Life has become snapshots you need to transfer from your head to a page. You will think in terms of scenes from this day forward, whether consciously or subconsciously, organizing scenes to stories in your head, one after another. Often they will be with you first thing in the morning when you wake up, and almost always the last thing in your head before you fall asleep.

No matter what has gone on back home with your family and/or Tammy, this last semester has proved a blessing. So when St. Patrick visits your dreams a few weeks before you leave for summer break, it's after you've reneged on your promise and spent an hour kissing Pamela again. She's still a very good kisser and she still lets you grope her, but that's it. She lets your hands go everywhere but inside her clothes. When you leave her at her dorm this time, your frustration has returned and you don't even say goodbye. She stopped your hand from reaching down the back of her pants and that did it. Later in life you'll come to appreciate her strength in fending you off, but on campus you're still an entitled motherfucker. You think: *If she wants somebody to kiss, there are plenty of other suckers on campus.*

When St. Patrick visits, it's while you're touching yourself in the middle of a really good Pamela dream, one in which she lets your hand inside her pants.

"*You're a piece of work, Dago,*" he says. "*As if that girl needs you in her life, needs you rating her body or anything else.*"

"*Well, why'd she get so involved just to stop short?*"

"*Why, you think she owes you something? If I didn't know you, I'd punch you in the mouth.*"

"*You know what I mean, Mick fuck.*"

"*I'd punch you in the mouth.*"

You huff.

"*At least you're finally seeing you have choices,*" he says.

"*You mean Pamela?*" you say. "*That girl can kiss.*"

"*Eejit!*" St. Patrick yells. "*I mean choices in life, you dopey wop. School, reading, writing, things you can do for yourself, because you like them. Things other than lifting weights and banging your brain-dead head on a football field to impress your old man."*

"And, what, Pamela isn't something different?"

"A fuckin' intellectual you are, boyo. Yeah, even Pamela. Choices, eh?"

"Yeah, so? I'm doing good in school. I'm not fucking off anymore."

"How the fuck did MENSA miss you?"

"The fuck is MENSA, potato head?"

"Look it up, genius. Just remember there's more to life than what you've limited yourself to so far. Especially when you get back home. Don't let the gravity of familiarity pull you in."

"Seriously, you Leprechaun, bog trotter, motherfucker. Where do you get this shit from, gravity of familiarity? What the fuck?"

"Just don't get yourself in trouble, should Pamela dear let you nuzzle her muff with your wee Johnson, boyo. Protect yourself. You won't do well living out here amongst farmers."

And it is Pamela you're dreaming about at eight o'clock in the morning when she shakes you awake a second time in your dorm room. She's snuck into your room again, but you're not sure why. Still, the wee Johnson has awoken, and it and you are ready to rock and roll.

You try to convince her to join you in bed, making sure she sees you've got wood again, but she's still not budging.

"Why'd you come here?" you say.

"I want to talk to you," she says.

"What about?"

"Us. About us."

"What about us. There is no us."

"That's not true. You're the first boy I've let go this far in a long time."

"I'm not a boy."

"Fine. You're the first man I've let go this far in a long time. A very long time."

You wonder what that means, a long time, a very long time. You say, "You're two years older than me. The fuck are you waiting for? I was fucking at fifteen and I was late to the game."

"I don't want to fuck, Charlie. I want more than that."

"Based on some kissing and ass grabbing? Are you serious?"

"I'm not having sex until I know it's a real relationship."

You sit up and cover yourself. You want to make some ground with her, but this time it has nothing to do with sex. You want to know why she thinks the way she does. It's too foreign from what you know, even though there's something about her stubbornness you admire.

"You've never had sex?"

"Not fully, no. Not intercourse."

This throws you. "Then what?"

She squirms a bit. "I'm not comfortable saying."

"Oral sex?"

"No," she says emphatically. "Never."

"You say it like it's a curse."

"No."

"Masturbation?"

She shrugs. You take it for a yes.

"Anything else."

She holds out her hand.

"A hand job?"

Now she blushes. "I guess that's what they call it."

"Jesus, Pamela, so what the hell is the big deal with me? I'm not looking to get you pregnant."

"I'm afraid you're not looking for anything."

She has you by the short hairs and you couldn't feel worse about it.

You shoot for honesty. "I'm not looking for anything like marriage, if that's what you mean. Not now."

"Because you have a girlfriend back in New York."

"Yeah, I do."

"So what are you doing with me?"

It's a pair of smacks to your head in a row. You look at the ground and shake your head. Are you that fucking shallow? Are you supposed to be? Isn't this what college kids do, try and fuck one another?

"Look," you say, "I like you, Pamela, but I do have a girlfriend back home and I'm not looking to get over-involved here. It's like you can have a girlfriend for a friend, right? Or a boyfriend. You can have sex, however you do it, but it's just intimate moments between friends. It doesn't have to mean marriage. People have sex and they don't have to be in love."

And the one man chorus in your head says: *Too bad you can't apply the same formula to your girlfriend back home, you Eejit!*

"That's bullshit and you know it," she says.

"No, I mean it. I'm not trying to deny I want down your pants, don't get me wrong. I want to wrap your legs around my head and eat your pussy until you have five orgasms, but all I'm saying ... what?"

Her head is slowly moving back as she squints at you.

"What?" you say again.

"You really do that?"

"Everybody does it. Almost everybody. It's good. Women love it."

"Women, plural? As if you know," you can hear St. Patrick saying.

"It sounds disgusting," Pamela says.

"Oh, come on. You're not gonna tell me that hasn't crossed your path. You have to know about oral sex."

"Yeah, but the way you said it. Eat my pussy?"

You can't help yourself now and go one further. "Hey," you say, "I'll tongue your asshole if it turns you on."

She's visibly disgusted. "Yick!" she says, pissed off now. "Stop it, please. Don't talk like ... what was I thinking?"

And just like that you're shamed, because no matter her insecurities, you're a fucking pig and what you said just proved it.

The both of you will have to help yourselves, if either of you ever can, but the smart money is on her doing a better job of it.

"Why don't we just pass on this?" you say. "We both meant well. It's not good, okay? You and me, I mean."

She'd been sniffling. Not anymore. She's up and out, leaving you alone.

And you no longer have wood.

And it isn't five minutes after you're back asleep before you recognize the voice in your head taking one shot after another.

"Not a boy, huh? With that wee Johnson, you're more a fookin' toddler, boyo."

"Girlfriend back home, huh? More like an albatross you're afraid to let fly the fuck away."

"People might have sex, but you sure aren't. Not without your albatross."

"So, you want to wrap her legs around your head, eat her pussy and tongue her asshole? Way to charm them, Eejit. Mr. fookin' romance, you are."

And no sooner than St. Patrick's voice is out of your head, then the ghost of Tammy begins to haunt anew. You call her at home, but she's not there. You call her again on the weekend, but she's not there. You call her a few more times during the week, but she's not there. Your panic meter registers high, and you decide it's time to know what the fuck is going on. You ask permission from your professors to take your finals early, and then plan a sneak attack on your girlfriend once the permission is granted. If she's fooling around behind your back, you intend to catch her.

Pick up the Pieces ...

You and your roommate leave North Dakota shortly after taking your last final on a Friday afternoon in late April, ten days before the official end of the semester. You have sandwiches one of the sororities packed for the trip. The plan being to spend as little money as possible, because neither of you have much money to spare. You do the driving the first ten hours, passing the twin cities of Minneapolis-St. Paul and the rest of I-94 Minnesota on pure adrenaline. You're headed for Eau Claire, Wisconsin, a city both of you call Egg Claire, because neither of you are sure how to pronounce Eau. It's the first planned stop along the 1,704 mile trip home, but a white cross pill you popped two hours ago keeps you going through to Milwaukee where your roommate takes the wheel.

The light blue, 1965 Oldsmobile F-85 you bought from a kid on the wrestling team last year is holding up like a champ. It had a crack in the windshield the state of North Dakota didn't require you to fix, an aluminum block engine, whatever that means, light blue carpeting, and a speaker system front and back. All you know is when you turn the key, the engine starts, and when you step on the gas, the car moves. It is all you will ever desire to know about cars.

Included in the deal was an 8-track tape player that hangs just under the middle of the dashboard. The Average White Band tape you found under the front passenger seat was a bonus. It will provide the entertainment for the thirty-hour trip you make in just under twenty-one hours. You will hear the hit instrumental, "Pick Up the Pieces", in your head for weeks afterward, and reflexively sing the Spartan lyrics:

> *Pick up the pieces, uh, huh*
> *Pick up the pieces, alright*

Your roommate drives through Chicago doing 80 miles-per-hour when you've finally closed your eyes. He makes it through Indiana across the Ohio border before he needs to sleep. You're behind the wheel again, but you're still tired and want to save your last white cross for home. You make it across the Ohio-Pennsylvania border before you begin guessing how long you can drive with your eyes closed. When you nearly drive off the road and have to whip the wheel hard right to keep from crashing into a ravine, your roommate makes you pull over. He uses his last white cross to handle the long stretch of Pennsylvania interstate. "Pick Up the Pieces" is now so embedded in both your heads, neither of you even hear it.

You get some sleep, but your roommate wakes you after pulling into a gas station outside of Stroudsburg, Pennsylvania. He's out of money. You fill-up, pay with your next to last twenty, pop your last white cross, and take the wheel again.

It is dawn when you take the exit for the Brooklyn Bridge off the FDR drive. After circling the entrance ramp, the sun's brightness forces you to pull down your visor. Looking straight ahead, the spires of the bridge form a perfect V through the cracked windshield, a martini glass with a golden olive.

Your roommate has been snoring alongside you on the front seat, but the sun's glare wakes him somewhere on Flatbush Avenue. He covers his eyes with one hand and turns to you.

"Where are we?" he says.

"God's country," you say.

St. Patrick visits your thoughts as you navigate the circle at Grand Army Plaza. The conversation takes place in your mind.

"Aren't you grand in your new used car?" St. Patrick says. "Stupid fuckin' Dago, you almost killed the two of you playing that dopey sleep driving game."

"Now you show up?" you respond without speaking. "You could've helped me stay awake, you ignorant Mick."

"Help you why?" he says. "Who am I, Santa Claus? And do you really think you're foolin' anybody racing home like this? You don't trust the girl, let her go."

"You could help me out with that too, moron."

"I'm no snitch, goombah. You'll have to do your own dirty work when it comes to that. As if it'd make a difference. You're still too scared to leave her. Which is another thing I don't get, you knuckle-dragging wop. How the hell can you be around all those women in school and still be afraid of losing the one you have home?"

"Fuck yourself, potato head."

"Ah, sore spot, isn't it?"

"Blow me."

"I'd die again first."

"Maybe I don't wanna be with anyone else. Ever consider that, you freckled-faced imbecile?"

"Oh, yeah? So why can't you have a discussion with her once you're finished screwing? Why do you get so pissed off with her?"

"Fuck off, already. I'm busy now."

"You call this busy, you moronic guinea? You're looking to hurt yourself again."

"Fuck you," you say, this time for real.

"What?" Your roommate says. You've woken him.

"Huh?" you say.

"Fuck you, too," he says, then closes his eyes again.

Your mind is racing, this time without the benefit of St. Patrick's counsel. His allusion to you having to do your own dirty work haunts you.

Tammy has made you crazy. You're still suspicious of some of the missed phone calls and her being unaccounted for so often. You're wondering if she cheated on you with her ex-boyfriend, if they used her basement the way you and she had in the past. Did she grind against his hard-on the way she did against yours? Did she get off that way? Did she blow him? Did she let him fuck her?

That last image is too much to ignore. You speed passed a police car parked on Eastern Parkway. Fortunately, it doesn't give chase.

Your roommate is awake when you stop at a light at Kingston Avenue. A group of Hasidic men are crossing the street on their way to morning prayers. They are all dressed alike, each one carrying his own book. Another group of younger Hasidic men, boys really, walk along the tree-lined pathway separating the service road and parkway proper. You look for signs of individuality amidst the uniform dress code and spot a tall, lanky kid carrying a prayer book like a football. He could be any one of the kids you grew up with.

Your roommate says, "You really think they fuck through sheets?"

Your roommate's question reminds you of the Italyener in the Malamud novel, *The Assistant*, you read. You can't remember if Frank Alpine had thought the same thing, but he wound up raping the grocer's daughter, Helen Bober, and later was forgiven by her. At the end, Alpine became a Jew, but you never understood whether it was an act of love for Helen or an attempt at redemption for what he'd done.

Or maybe it was both.

"No," you answer, but your roommate has already forgotten his question.

"Huh?" he says.

You drop him off in front of his house in Canarsie. It is a few minutes after seven. You live two blocks away, where your mother moved once she could afford to leave the shithole apartment in Queens, but you have no intention of going home. You head for the Belt Parkway, then to Queens where your girlfriend lives. It's another fifteen minutes in the car, a few more listens to "Pick Up the Pieces", before you can get your rocks. It's been five months and you're more than anxious to get busy, except there's more to it than getting laid.

Finding Tammy with another guy is definitely on your mind. You're convinced you'll catch her with somebody. You can see them asleep in her bed together. You're grinding your teeth as you apply pressure to the gas pedal and miss the Cross Bay Boulevard exit.

You don't have a clue, but if you find her with somebody, somebody is going to die. Your adult brain is lost.

Fools for Love ...

Her confession is the result of trickery. She's alone when you surprise
her. Her parents have gone away for the weekend, but her reaction is
way too nervous for comfort. You take a shower while she puts up a pot
of coffee, but then you sneak out of the bathroom and halfway down the
stairs to listen to her end of a telephone conversation.

"He just came home," she says. There's a pause before she's pleading.
"I'm sorry, I can't. I'll call you tomorrow."

She breaks your heart, but now you want something from her,
something cheap. You finish your shower and wait to see if she mentions
the phone call when she comes back upstairs with your coffee. She
doesn't.

You avoid asking her too many questions and talk about the trip home
instead. You need to be cautious. She's not the brightest girl in the world,
but she's obviously street smart enough to make a fool out of you.

Your eyes grow tired before you know it. No amount of caffeine will
keep you awake much longer. You decide to get what you can while
you're still awake and interrogate her later. You guide her to the bed,
lay on your back, then tell her how you missed her and that you love
her, and then you cover your face with a pillow while she gives you a
blowjob.

When you wake up, it's late in the afternoon. Tammy is watching
television downstairs. You make a fresh pot of coffee and finish two cups
before joining her. You apologize for passing out. You let a minute of
silence pass, during which you figure out exactly how to start.

"We have to talk," you say.

"Uh-oh," she says and straightens up on the couch faster than you've
ever seen her move before. She uses the remote to turn the television
off. The room is dark except for a single light in the dining room. You
move to the edge of the couch.

"I have a confession," you say. "It's not as bad as you think. It was just
a few times, and I'm not in love with anybody."

"You bastard," she says, and you can see she's clearly shaken.

"Oh, come on," you say. "I didn't expect you to stay home all this time
without going out yourself. I'm only telling you this because I want us
to be honest with one another. We're going to get married someday,
Tammy. I don't want to have secrets."

She's watching you for a hint of deception.

"Besides, it's what happens in college," you say. "Everybody screws around. There were always parties after the games, you remember that. People get drunk and do shit, that's all. It was never about love."

She frowns, but her head turns away for a moment and you know she has something to say, something she wants to say. Now it's just a matter of pushing the right button.

"It was only three times," you say. "Twice with one girl and once with another. That one was horrible."

This time she's looking at you with accusatory eyes. "What did you do?"

Here's where you need to be extra careful and not exaggerate too much. You shrug to stall for time.

"You fuck them?" she asks, making it easy.

"Just the one," you say. "The bad one. The other one, you know ..."

"You prick," she says.

"Come on, Tammy. You're not gonna try and bullshit me about this. Please."

"What else did you do?"

"What else what? I told you. Just three times."

"You went down on her?"

You know she's close to breaking. You shrug again. "What's the difference? If you did the same thing, if some guy went down on you, or you blew him, how could I hold that against you? I didn't expect you to stay home every night, every weekend. You went away, you said. The weekend after I left, you and your friends went to Peekskill, right? The dude ranch. I just assumed you went with guys."

"We didn't go with guys," she says. Your heart begins to race. It's the way she said it, "go with guys."

"So, even if you met somebody there, big deal," you say. "Unless you fell in love with somebody, started dating him, it's nothing I have a right to get pissed off about, not while I was screwing Judy."

"Judy?" she says, her eyes glaring then.

It was a stroke of genius making up a name. Within a few minutes she tells you the truth, except the truth will do anything but set you free.

First there's this one: "It's just a guy I met at my friend's bachelorette party. He was at the bar, and he asked me if I wanted to smoke."

"Smoke what, a joint?"

"Yeah."

"And?"

"Nothing. All we did was make out. Kiss, that's all."

"And he didn't take your number? He didn't call you? He just smoked a joint, kissed you and that was it? Do I look like a moron?"

"I gave him a hand job in the car, that's it."

You nearly punch her, but hit the wall instead. "The truth, God damn it!"

"Alright, alright," she says. "I gave him a blow job, but all he did was feel me up, I swear."

She's crying, and you let her get over it before you start in again and learn about the next one, somebody from work, another blow job, she swears.

"So, what? Nobody bothered fucking you? Is that what you're telling me?"

And then comes the one she admits to fucking, some guy she met at that dude ranch, but you wonder if it's the guy she once mentioned in her sleep, Nick.

"It was just once, and he didn't even come," she says. "Not inside me. He came on my stomach."

All you can see is some guy's sperm shooting across your girlfriend's stomach and you literally go blind from a rage you can no longer control. Your head breaks the sheetrock wall, forehead first, the perfect tackle. There's blood spilling down your forehead into your eyes and then your mouth. You taste the blood, but do nothing to stop the bleeding. You leave that to her, your frantic girlfriend, the woman you'll marry someday.

You spend the next two days having sex or torturing her with non-stop interrogations about her several trysts. You don't let her out of your sight. Your territory has been taken and you're determined to reclaim it. You give her an ultimatum: either she gives you the names of the guys she's been with, writing out the specific details of what happened, or you're out of there and she can forget she ever knew you.

And how fucking sick is that?

St. Patrick lets you know, but you shut him down.

"You're a fookin' tyrant, boyo."

"Go fuck your mother," you say without saying it.

You become a caveman. You rant and rave and threaten and bully, but the reality is you're the one who won't let go, you're the one condemning himself to his temper along with a woman he can't trust, and who can blame her? The reality is she has no more self-esteem than you, and will say and do anything to keep you in her life. You're both fools for love and the eventual outcome will leave lifelong scars.

Going to the Chapel ...

Window washing is described to you as the greatest job in the world. You can start work early in the morning and be home before noon. You can work private jobs for off-the-books extra money, or a second job for another paycheck. You can go to school or hang out in bars. It is a union job and there is nothing to worry about once you're a member. Your future father-in-law is a longtime boss with the biggest outfit in Manhattan and just about every male member of his and his wife's family are window cleaners.

The enticement is obvious, and the freedom the income will afford makes the job too good to turn down. All you need do is announce you're getting married. It's easy enough, but there's still something tugging at your insides. You want more from this life. Instead of jumping into the opportunity, you have a discussion with Thomas Rocco about what you should do.

It's been a while since you've seen him. The relationship has remained strained. You travel to see him in the new store he's opened in the New Rochelle mall, a head shop that will be closed down by anti-drug crusaders over time for selling drug paraphernalia. He looks very much at home behind the counter. You feel awkward in his presence.

"What's it about?" he says.

"I have two options," you say. "I can get married or keep going to school."

"School for what?"

"I've been writing. I also like history and politics."

He frowns.

"But Tammy's father can get me in the window cleaning union. It's good money and short hours. I can work two jobs or go to school nights."

"But you have to get married?"

"I don't have to, but I think it's what everyone expects."

"She's your first girlfriend, right? You fuck around out there in college?" You shake your head.

"Why not? You should first. Get it out of your system. Never marry the first girl you screw. That never works out."

"I do love her," you say defiantly.

He frowns again. "What about her? She with anybody else before you? While you were away?"

The motherfucker can read your mind, but you can't admit it.

"No," you say.

"I'm not for getting married, not at your age. I say try and take the job with her old man, but don't get married. Put it off. Live together for a while if you have to, but don't get married until you're sure. Even then, there's no guarantee it'll work long term."

It's sound advice, but because it came from Thomas Rocco you feel a need to buck it.

"What about this school?" he says. "It expensive?"

"Yes."

"You really want to waste all that money on school? You were never a student, Charlie."

And with that remark, the deal is sealed. You'll attend Hofstra and put off window cleaning, but not because it's the smartest choice. It's because you need to prove you can do it.

And when you do attend Hofstra University, at five thousand dollars a semester, it proves much easier academically than that small college in Minot, North Dakota. You bankrupt your savings to live at the dorms, but the lure of that window cleaning job is hanging over your head.

You take a Bible as Literature course, a creative writing course, and a few requirements. You do well, winning a fiction writing contest outright and making the honor role. Is it possible you're getting smarter or is this Hofstra University a jip joint for suckers who can pay the freight for a diploma?

The ghost of Thomas Rocco continues to haunt you after all. If you did something well, there has to be an excuse.

Tammy returns to work in Manhattan and isn't always available to see you on weekends at the dorm. It is an unsettling feeling that keeps you on your toes. You ignore several passes from a short-haired blonde on the same floor and take to doing term papers for coin. A rich kid on your floor whose father is an executive with North American Van Lines pays one-hundred per B paper and you spend a few weekends at the library earning some extra scratch.

The rich kid has an oil painting in his room and a recliner to sit and observe it from. You wonder why he's there, except you can't yet look a gift horse in the mouth. One hundred per B is a challenge you enjoy. Getting him two B+ grades and two As, four hundred in cash for no more than ten hours work, is a piece of cake.

The morning you pick up Tammy a little earlier than she was expecting you, she's on the phone smiling when you walk into her kitchen. She sees you and says, "Oh, shit." Her face turns pale and she says into the phone, "I'll call you back."

As quick as you're filled with rage, your mind is made up. First you'll let her blow you, then you'll lie and tell her you think they should get married. There's no reason to ask her, because she'll do whatever you say, right?

You fall into a deep sleep and when you wake up, Tammy tells you she's through being grilled and won't discuss it anymore. Either you both bury the past or you quit being a couple. You think about your options and realize you don't have enough confidence to do the right thing. Not yet.

Soon you'll be going to the chapel. For better or worse, you're going to get married.

Fuck You Too ...

You've already talked to Thomas Rocco, but now you want to talk to your sister. She doesn't like Tammy any more now than she ever did, but she's also moved on in her life and is living with a new partner in Manhattan. As it turns out, she has something to tell you as well when you meet at Cafe Reggio in Greenwich Village, her choice of location.

"I'm going to work for Daddy," she says.

"What?" you say, your eyes wide.

"I'm going to work at the store. Manage it. I also do taxes for gay businesses some of my friends run, so I'll have enough money to save for a house someday."

"What about Gang Bang? Isn't she there all the time?"

"Just nights, and usually when it's time for me to leave. It'll be me and him running the place. He tried one of our cousins, but that didn't work out. Daddy has to go to the city for merchandise and he needs someone at the store."

"That's twice you called him Daddy?"

"Don't be a jerk."

"Hey, knock yourself out. I think you're crazy, but if that's what you want, go for it."

"He can use you on weekends. He told me to tell you that, in case you need extra money."

And you're instantly suspicious. "Yeah? What else he tell you?"

"That you're going to marry that moron girlfriend of yours."

At this point, you've had enough. "What's he think of *your* moron girlfriend? He say?"

"He hasn't met her yet. He will."

"Good. He won't like her either."

She switches gears on you and asks why you wasted all that money on Hofstra if you were going to become a window cleaner and marry a moron.

"It was a challenge," you tell her. "I wanted to know I could do it and I did. I won a fiction contest, by the way. I'm still writing."

She gives you the frown she's perfected over time, Thomas Rocco's frown.

"Why does that bother you so much?" you ask. "When I mention something good that happened to me? I won a fiction contest. Why can't you acknowledge that? You're just like the old man. Exactly like him. You'll probably be happy together in that store."

No response.

"Fuck you, too," you say, then leave.

It is an angry walk to the subway on Sixth Avenue. What goes through your mind is how stupid it was to even attempt to explain yourself. The lesson still hasn't been learned. Neither your sister nor Thomas Rocco will ever accept anything about you. It has become a personal vendetta, fuel that will keep you preoccupied to do what you want, but for all the wrong reasons.

At home that night you tell your mother you're going to get married. She asks if you're sure. It is a measured acceptance of your decision, but one you respect. It is in her facial expressions and tone of voice you see and hear the truth, that you shouldn't do this yet, but it is also time to step out of her life to try and make one for yourself.

"Yeah, Ma, I'm sure," you tell her.

Her eyes grow wet and she reaches out for a hug. Neither of you really want to let go.

In the Presence of the Lord ...

You're just a few months from your wedding day and an urge to speak with a priest is overwhelming. It stems from the silly classes Tammy's had to take in order to be married in a Catholic church, something your mother has begged you to do. You've been a doubter since before you left Catholic grade school, but suddenly you want to believe.

There has to be a meaning to this life or why save it? Why leave a mother's womb? Why leave a mother's arms, except to find the arms of another? But what if the new set of arms can't be trusted?

Your world has proven too callous and unjust for something like marriage to make things right of a sudden. In your heart you know marriage is no way to take away the sins of the world. Nor is a sudden crucifixion the way to absolve sin. Maybe the crucifixion was meant to be slow, to last the length of your Little Jesus life, to maximize the pain and suffering for the sake of salvation.

It's a romantic thought, all that pain, but you know it's a crock of shit. People born with horrible diseases suffer. People living in poverty suffer. People incarcerated for speaking their minds suffer. People incarcerated for anything suffer. You, you little shit, have it made.

For all your best intentions, you've been a complete scumbag when it comes to the woman you're about to marry. You may not trust her, but you can't for a second blame her for wanting to be with someone else. You haven't advanced beyond a Neanderthal when it comes to your relationship with Tammy. If anybody should be paying the piper, it's you.

You return to the church of your youth, where you once served as an altar boy knowing full well none of the priests of your past will be there. And they aren't there. Instead you arrange a meeting with a father Akwasi. This priest is tall and thin and extremely dark, and the whites of his teeth and eyes are brighter because of his skin color. He has a vivid smile and large green eyes. His voice is as deep as Geoffrey Holder's voice was when he did those funny 7-Up commercials way back in the day. And like the actor, Father Akwasi is also from Trinidad and Tobago.

You meet on the steps outside the front doors to the church. He has a few minutes before he begins taking confessions, and you want to make sure he understands your situation before you make a decision about snitching on yourself.

It's a sunny August afternoon. You shake hands with him and are eased by his smile.

"I have a brother named Charles," he says.

You nod while thinking of what to say. "Here in the States?"

"Trinidad. Also a priest."

His smile is infectious. You can't help but return it.

"You mentioned you're getting married," he says.

"Yes, Father. In October."

His smile somehow brightens. "You were part of the first graduating class of our school," he says. "I looked it up."

"That was a long time ago."

"And you were an altar boy."

You nod.

"Are you're having doubts?"

"I'm not sure, Father. I've had them before. For a long time actually."

Someone passing calls to him and the priest acknowledges the passerby with a wave.

"It's understandable," he says to you without skipping a beat. "You're still a young man."

You shake your head. "I'm not sure it's about getting married, Father."

"Oh?"

"I don't know."

He gestures toward the church front door. "Would you like to make confession?"

"I'm not sure. That's what I mean."

"You can tell me what you're feeling, my son."

"I'm not sure I deserve confession, Father. I haven't believed in a long time."

"I see. And you blamed God for the bad times. It's what many people do in frustration, blame God for the troubles that befall them."

"I don't want it to be that easy."

"How do you mean?"

"Confession. I'm supposed to suffer, no?"

The priest looked confused then.

"What?" you say.

"But you are suffering," he says. "If you're here and you're struggling, in your mind and in your heart, then surely you are suffering."

You pause for a moment and remember what Dr. Abegg had asked you back in the nuthouse. *Do you think you deserve to get hit?*

"It should be more," you say. "Just feeling guilty is too easy. It isn't enough."

The priest looks even more interested now. The front door to the church opens and someone reminds Father Akwasi about confessions. He glances at his watch, shakes your hand and asks you to come inside and wait until the confessions are finished, unless you wish to say one yourself.

"It's been forever since I've been inside a church, Father."

"Are you afraid?"

You don't answer.

"I have to go now, but I'd like very much to continue our conversation."

"I'll see, Father."

"Well, I hope you do," he says. "Excuse me for now."

He shakes your hand again, the infectious smile fading as he pulls away and heads inside the church of St. Jude. You wait a few minutes, during which you stare at the front doors, but you can't go inside. You turn away instead.

"He's right, you know," St. Patrick says.

The conversation goes on in your head as you walk to your car.

"About what?"

"Everything."

"Everything what?"

"You really are an ignorant Dago, you know that?"

"Right about what? Everything what?"

"You believe."

You're at your car, but continue walking.

"What do I believe?" you say. *"That you're an asshole?"*

"If you suffer, you believe. It doesn't have to be Jesus you believe in, or

any other God or religion. Let your conscience be your guide. Ever hear that before?"

You have, but you can't be sure where and are too embarrassed to admit it. You re-cross Seaview Avenue and head into the park. The smell of fresh cut lawns fills the air. You take it in with deep breaths, filling your lungs to capacity before closing your eyes and exhaling. The smell is a memory from a time when running while training for football was the best part of your day.

"If you suffer, you believe," St. Patrick says again.

"Oh, parrot, give it a fuckin' break."

A full court basketball game is being played by black teens inside the playground where swings, seesaws, and monkey bars are also located. You watch the game as you walk and think: *"It used to be white kids. This is good it's like this now."*

"You're going to ignore me now, is that it?" St. Patrick says.

"What are you breaking my balls for? I'm trying to clear my head here."

"You want to clear that thick cranium of yours, you'd be in confession."

"Oh, Christ, you're a pain in the ass."

"Here's the thing, you ignorant wop, you can't force love. You may be adding another demon with this wedding. One that'll cost you down the road."

"Can't you find somebody else to haunt?"

"Talk to the priest again, Dago. Save yourself some suffering. Save the poor woman you're about to torture by marrying her."

You sit on the bench, your head tilted back and your eyes closed. You imagine a family with Tammy and how it can all fall to pieces: You're yelling at her across the dinner table. Your kids are frightened from the volume and tone of your voice. You slam the table with a fist and storm off to the bathroom where you can have a moment's peace. You look at yourself in the mirror and see Thomas Rocco over one shoulder, your sister over the other. They look to one another and smile. To the victors go the spoils of satisfaction.

You open your eyes, make the sign of the cross, and whisper The Lord's Prayer.

"Amen, wop," St. Patrick says when you're finished.

"Amen," you say.

In the Presence of the Little White Elephants ...

"Look," your best man says, "he's got elephants on his shirt."

You look up and can see the priest's shirtsleeves poking out of his vestments, little white elephants patterned like polka dots on a light green background.

You suppress a laugh. Your best man does the same. The priest takes a quick look your way as the wedding march begins and your bride is walked down the aisle by her father. You jab your best man with an elbow. He jabs you back, and you both have to suppress another laugh.

You turn and face the aisle, but you're really looking to see if Thomas Rocco has arrived yet. The last you looked on your family's side of the church, he wasn't there. It is a bittersweet moment. If he doesn't show, it's another act of betrayal, maybe the final you'll put up with, a father not showing up in time for his son's wedding. On the other hand, if he doesn't show in time, the embarrassment will be overwhelming.

You can't imagine being late for your son's wedding, although you'll go one worse and not show up for one of your own sons down the road, because of a petty insult, one he learned from you.

Still, it's how you perceive Thomas Rocco on the morning of your wedding, not having the balls to tell Gang Bang to move her ass. You can see her being the last one out of the house, making everyone else wait, and nobody accounting for traffic on the Belt Parkway or for parking near the church.

The last image you see is Thomas Rocco sweating profusely behind the wheel as he searches for a parking spot. He knows it was his wife that caused him to be late. He'll know that you and everybody else will know what happened, but before you can envision any more of that fiasco, your bride is standing alongside you at the altar, and the priest begins the ceremony.

"Friends," he says, "we are gathered here today …"

At no point do you look back at the rows of pews on either side of the church. Instead, what you do is focus on Tammy and the ceremony. You're going with traditional vows to keep it short and sweet, and it's over before you know it.

Finally, the priest says, "What God has joined together, let no one separate."

"Amen," you say.

"Amen," all those behind you say.

There's the proud walk back down the aisle to the church doors, and there's no way to avoid not seeing Thomas Rocco. He isn't there. You wonder if he'll make the reception, but it's no longer important. He's already failed you.

It's an ironic role reversal, him having to please you for a change.

You can see your mother crying, but those are happy tears. Even your sister is smiling. The rest of the crowd on your side of the aisle are maternal family and friends.

And then you're at the door, literally on your way outside, when there he is, just stepping inside. His face is bright red.

"I'm sorry," Thomas Rocco says.

"It was the traffic," Gang Bang says.

You don't acknowledge her, but nod at your father, never stopping to kiss hello or even shake his hand. You're outside the church and notice a few of your paternal cousins, the ones who have been leeching off Thomas Rocco since before he left his wife and kids. The rice shower saves you from having to be polite and smile at them.

By the time of the reception, everyone has found their way and the festivities keep the clock moving. At your mother's table are her sisters and their husbands, your sister and Twinkle Toes, because your mother really wants to show off dancing that night.

And she does a good job of it, dancing with Twinkle Toes at every opportunity. Thomas Rocco's table is farther from the dance floor, and except for the wedding song you and Tammy have picked, "I Only Have Eyes For You", he and Gang Bang don't move from their table.

Later you'll hear how he broke up crying when you and your mother set most of the place to crying during your dance with her, but you figure his tears were for effect, he was doing what he was expected to do, especially after missing the actual wedding ceremony.

At one point before it's over, Thomas Rocco finally meets one of your high school football coaches, a man he never once bothered to meet while you played. The coach, going for humor, says, "Well, we did it."

The look on Thomas Rocco's face is pure resentment. He can't believe someone had the nerve to joke that way, except it was no joke to you, the coach was around a lot more than Thomas Rocco while you went through high school. That coach was a major influence on you.

And he made it to the church on time.

At home later the same night, you go through envelopes to assess the damage. The total cost of the wedding was five thousand dollars. By the last of the envelopes, you've recovered nicely. Almost six grand, thanks mostly to the thirty or so window cleaners invited by your father-in-law. Thomas Rocco's gift was the biggest, a clean grand, but you didn't expect anything less. You're sure he did *at least* the same for your cousins and Gang Bang's kids, and there was no way he was late to their weddings.

Both you and your bride are pretty exhausted by midnight. The following morning you'll be on your way to Holland for a three week honeymoon, so it's off to bed on your wedding night. It's not like you haven't been intimate yet.

You dream a lot that night. The tiny redhead with the freckles who chased you all around PS 115's schoolyard is back. So are the Jewish twins and the woman who used to live next door to you at house number two, the gangster's *comare*, Marion. And then comes St. Patrick, but this time it isn't the usual back and forth insult-a-thon.

"The next twenty plus will be rocky, boyo. Your doubts will win out. It'll get pretty dark."

"You believe he didn't show up on time?"

St. Patrick shrugs.

You turn to your wife asleep at your side. "She's beautiful," you say, then reach for your wife, but St. Patrick stops you.

"Let her sleep," he says. "You'll have a busy day tomorrow."

You want the world to be right again, at least for tonight and throughout your honeymoon. You want the coziness of a life without familial discord. You want a return to a life when it wasn't so full of disappointments and internal turbulence.

Cozy was how you wanted to feel most nights, some days too. Cozy the way you once snuggled in bed, the comforter wrapped tight around your body as you clutched a pillow on bitter cold nights. The colder the night, the tighter you snuggled. When you needed something to fall asleep to, some thought, some storyline, it was usually a battle imagined out in the streets. When you were younger, it was a civil war battle with rebel skirmishers poking and prodding at the homes on your block as you waited for them to get close enough to shoot from your window. You imagined your family loading and reloading the Enfield rifles placed strategically around the house, two or three near every window, and you couldn't do it alone, so there were anonymous men with you, all dressed in northern blue.

And when you fell asleep there was no dreaming about the battle, but you were still comfortable clutching that pillow tight against your body, the feeling under the covers similar to being back in your mother's womb, and wasn't that what you always wanted, to feel the protection of your mother? It's what you sometimes did dream about, being back inside the womb, a living thinking being too afraid to leave, but when you had to do so, you grabbed onto whatever you could and ripped apart the insides of your mother's womb, nearly killing her for expelling you.

There's no going back, Little Jesus.

Don't ruin it by trying.

And it didn't have to be sleep or a nap when you craved coziness. Sometimes it could be an extremely cold day and you took to the couch with a comforter and hoodie sweatshirt, and you cuddled there with a pillow you could lay on your lap, but you always made sure the comforter

THE VOICES IN MY HEAD

covered your feet because if they were exposed, the monster under the couch might've grabbed them.

Those were simple days and simple nights and nothing much could harm you. Whether it was for a night or just a few hours or minutes, the world went away. The problem came with age and the ability to do the harm yourself. There were options you had, but didn't take. You came out from beneath the comforter and there it was, the real world.

More than 300 years ago, Thomas Hobbes wrote *Leviathan*, wherein he presented a dreaded state of nature, when the life of man would be *"solitary, poor, nasty, brutish, and short."* Social contracts were the only option, Hobbes argued, but there is no social contract that can protect against cruelty, and it is cruelty you grew too accustomed to, cruelty you learned to navigate far too often and far too well.

Since the womb is no longer an option, better to self-medicate with the rage you've become comfortable with. There's no opiate of the masses you understand better than to remain angry. You don't need Jesus or Allah or any other form of delusion. Better to keep the fire burning, Little Jesus. Better to live it through and without looking over your shoulder. Better to focus on what's ahead before the reflection in the mirror changes and the weight and length of the strong chain you bear is too great to ignore.

And make no mistake, it is a ponderous fucking chain.

Going Dutch ...

Your honeymoon is in the Netherlands where you learn enough about socialism to want to learn more. You do some research on your own, and the name George Bernard Shaw keeps appearing. You know of his work without knowing you know. Why? Because you're an idiot. You paid more attention to baseball and football rosters than what might be meaningful for far too long. You need to catch up. You make a note to read Shaw when you get home, but while you're in Holland, you and your bride take a trip to Paris and then drive into Germany. "What a beautiful land," you keep repeating. Everything you see is clean and pretty and you still can't get over the horrendous WWII history these places experienced. You visit war museums outside of Oosterbeek and spend the rest of the day trying to imagine the horrific battle of Arnhem.

A trip into Amsterdam is slightly uncomfortable once you're confronted with the red light district. This shit never interested you, Little Jesus. You understand the economics and why some women wind up in brothels, but the idea of gawking at them through picture windows is too much. You're the guy who can't walk into a porn store to look at magazines, although sometimes you wish you could.

You never make it through the red light district. You turn around instead.

A walk toward the Van Gogh Museum gives you some relief. Later, in the heart of the city, rather than gawking at the colorful buildings lining the canals and all the flowers, you're doing what you've always done— daydreaming. You're looking behind the windows and inside the bars at the lives of those living with universal healthcare and a retirement system that rewards those most vulnerable, its elderly, rather than punishing them.

And it all makes so much sense. The elderly are those who put in a lifetime of support to the government. Why shouldn't they reap the rewards?

Because you don't know the lives of the people behind the windows, you imagine the best. You see yourself living in one of those bright colored buildings, maybe in an apartment on the top floor overlooking one of the canals. You picture yourself sipping coffee while looking down from the window, your writing desk off to the side. The world is your oyster, you epic daydreaming motherfucker.

You make sure to pick up a few books before the flight back to the United States, but you're already sure you want to live in Europe someday. You read what you can during the flight, then again a few days later, after getting over your jet lag. After some research and reading, things you can't discuss with your wife because she's not interested, because it's starting to dawn on you, now that you've actually opened your world, that you made a mistake marrying a woman from fear of losing her. Your new obsession propels you back to school for a degree in Political Science. Why political science? Because you've always chased what you wanted and ignored the pragmatic.

President Stella?

"Eejit!" rings in your ears. You look, but can't find your friend, St. Patrick.

Going Home ...

Your window cleaning work lands you at the Harper & Row building on 10 East 53rd Street. It's a stick window building and hasn't been tended to very well. It's messy, in fact, but easy enough once you get the knack of it: leaning out the middle window that opens almost flat so you can clean the windows above and below with two broomsticks, one with a brushes and the other with a squeegee mounted on its end. Cleaning an entire floor takes you just over two hours, but before long you're knocking a floor out in less than 90 minutes.

You make friends with the people you need to be friends with, the day shift building manager and the night porter. One, Karl, is open to being greased with coin, a twenty or so every other week, and the other, Max, will take free coffee and Danish. Both will cover you when you need protection.

Most mornings you're at the building between three and four o'clock. You head straight up to whatever floor you're working on that day, for which a master key was left for you overnight. You start at the north end of the building and work your way east around to the south end. There are very few windows facing west. Once you're finished, you take the freight elevator down to the basement, wash up, and head to a coffee wagon on Madison Avenue. You buy a couple of coffees, Max's Danish, and a donut for yourself. You return to the building and shoot the shit with Max another half hour or so before you clean the lobby doors and glass.

Over time you and the night porter, Max, exchange conversations enough to become friends, although you each have reservations. Max tells you about the delicatessen he owned for more than thirty years and from which he made a lot of coin. The porter job gives him spending money, but more importantly, it provides him with the essential union benefits that preclude him from paying out of pocket health insurance. Max is in his late 60s and he distrusts both his wife and son, and it always has to do with money. He hides his from them, he tells you, and then he feels he has to prove it to you by showing you three different bankbooks with more than fifty grand in each. You know he's showing off, but you're not sure why.

He'll like you fine so long as you bring him free coffee and Danish. You want to like the guy, but his greed makes it hard. You also know it is his greed that keeps you in good stead in the building. There are rainy nights when you're exhausted from working a second job and can get away with sleeping in an empty office. Max will cover you. If you leave early, Max will cover you. If you want to take a night off without losing the time, Max will cover you, and all for the cost of a cup of coffee and Danish.

One night when you're cleaning the windows in a corner office up on the 30th floor, an opened envelope on the President of the company's desk catches your eye. You pick it up and some pictures spill out. It is a naked Hispanic woman tied and bound. Some pictures show her tied to a chair with ropes around her body and a rubber ball in her mouth.

"That's some sick shit," you say.

You go through the envelope and can't believe what you're seeing. You take one picture, put the rest back inside the envelope, and then head down to show Max. He's not as surprised as you, but he's clearly disgusted. He tells you about the bondage magazines he finds in the men's room on the same floor. You're still unfamiliar with the fetish, so you just assume somebody is a sick motherfucker.

Max is disgusted because he thinks the company is German-owned and he's still holding grudges over the Holocaust. Max is Jewish and thinks the building manager is also German. Max hates him, too.

You're intrigued about this sick shit you discovered, so you hang around in the lobby a few mornings to see if the woman in the picture shows up. The day she does, you feel as cheap as you should. You haven't told anyone else, not even your wife, but seeing her in the flesh, whether she was a willing participant to the role she played in those pictures or not, you know you had no business looking at them, never mind keeping one.

When you get to your car for the ride home, you reach into the glove compartment where you've hidden her picture. You look at it one last time, and then you rip it up and toss it out the window a few pieces at a time as you drive home.

The next few years on the job are easy enough. The 3-4 hours a day you have to put in offers you the opportunity to return to school nights and get your degree. You've been toying with becoming a lawyer of late, but first you'll need that Bachelor of Arts or Science. You're also still interested in history and socialism still rings true in your noggin.

You return to college in Brooklyn, taking a full-time night schedule so you can graduate in two years. You do well, earning a political science degree with honors, and then winning a political science award for a research paper you do for an International Law class on the Khmer Rouge.

Now that you're into it, education becomes something vitally important to your day-to-day existence. On nights when you don't have class, you grow frustrated trying to discuss things with your wife. She has little to no interest, but nights you do have class, there's a Hasidic woman you discuss politics and life in general with for an hour a night between and during classes. There's nothing more than mutual respect of opinions, and you find yourself disappointed when the semester ends. The final term paper had to do with current day Marxism, whether it had remained true to its foundations or had it become revisionist? She was conservative and wrote an essay arguing Marxism had remained true to its original intent. Your paper argued revisionism.

You both received A's, and for once opposite opinions do not frustrate you. There are indeed two sides to every story.

The more enlightened you feel, whether it's from doing research or discussions in and out of a classroom, you can feel the need for more in your life than the limits you've thus far set. Window cleaning for a living isn't a bad thing, but you're finding there's much more to life than an easy paycheck.

And one Friday, after working your way down from the 19th floor at the usual floor-a-day pace, you reach the setback floor where some of the Harper & Row big shot offices are located. It is an area of the office usually locked for the night, an area you can only clean during the day. You look at the books on the shelves and spot the hot one, Colleen McCullough's *The Thorn Birds*. You imagine the glory of being a best-selling author. You don't even care about the coin. It's the prestige you imagine comes with the status. You imagine what Ms. McCullough is doing at that very moment. Is she writing another bestseller? Is she reading reviews of her bestseller? Is she maybe tutoring another author?

It sets your epic daydreaming wild, because in the back of your head, you still want to be a writer more than a lawyer, a teacher, a politician or anything else. It's something Thomas Rocco and your sister would be forced to eat crow over, and that's what you're thinking that Friday morning when you're confronted with a note requesting the 15th floor setback offices be cleaned, the ones facing the south side of the building where there's no setback. They've even left you a key, which surprises you no end. The main office has French windows you haven't cleaned before. They require special attention, except you're not experienced enough to know what that special attention is. Instead of waiting for proper instructions, which would be to leave the windows alone, because they can only be cleaned from a scaffold, you step out on a ledge and try to do your job. You become the proverbial dumbass worker putting his job ahead of his life. In time you might learn such risks are nothing more than stupid, macho, dumb shit, but that morning, about 4:30 a.m. or so, you literally climbed out of a window with a 15 floor drop to a courtyard below. They were windows you'd never be able to reach.

Suddenly your hand slides along the edge of the window frame and is sliced open. The sudden flow of blood is a lubricant that causes you to lose your grip. You feel yourself slip away from the window down into the abyss of the courtyard 15 floors below. There is a thud you could hear but can't feel, a warm flow of liquid behind your head, and then darkness.

Is it a dream? If it was, it sure fucking hurt for a split second or two?

PART III

"For I know the plans I have for you, declares the Lord, plans
for welfare and not for evil, to give you a future and a hope."
Jeremiah 29:11

Voi sogno di Alan Rickman, Part Deux (la voce di Dio, II) ...

The last time he appeared to you, it was to present you with a
heavenly evaluation, a report card based on the Ten Commandments.
This time when the spirit resembling Alan Rickman intervenes in
your dream, he does so dressed like the character he played in the first
Die Hard movie, Hans Gruber. This time it's the future, your future.

And you're pretty sure *Jeremiah 29:11* got it all wrong.

It is Christmas Eve, 1987. You're somehow spending it at your sister's
home in Brooklyn. The two of you haven't spoken to one another since
she and her girlfriend called the cops on you two years ago, a call that
nearly resulted in you assaulting a police officer, the call you'll never
forgive her for making, not even on her deathbed twenty-one years later.
It was a good cop, bad cop situation, and you're lucky as fuck the good
cop listened to your wife's Uncle who was there to smooth things over
before you punched yourself into prison.

You'll never forget it was another man who was there for you and not
your father.

You're lying on a cot in the attic of your sister's home with a terrible
flu, despondent about where you are in life, and praying you'll die
before you have to head downstairs to play Santa for your kids, a role
you loved until this Christmas Eve. You've been chasing a Hispanic
woman, and are ready to leave your wife for her, but there's so much
involved in the process, you feel twice as trapped for being sick.

Your head is pounding. You cover your face with a pillow and somehow
fall asleep. You lose all track of time until you hear footsteps outside the
attic door and you pull the pillow from your face. When you look up,
there he is again, *la voce di Dio.*

He stands just inside the door, his weight shifted onto one leg. You smell
something fresh. Pine, you're thinking. An image of a snow-spotted
mountainside flush with pine trees comes to mind, a memory from a road
trip in college when the team bus passed through the Rocky Mountains

in Montana.

Suddenly there's a flash of light, and your headache is gone.

"Well?" Hans Gruber says.

"You look different," you say. "Not from Dogma this time."

"I wear what they give me."

Ten years ago the Voice of God told you some other things he claimed you'd forget as soon as he was gone, and you did, but suddenly you can recall the entire conversation, including the discussion you had about dying.

The Voice of God has read your thoughts. "Unless, of course, we take your prayer for an early death serious."

Your eyebrows furrow in an attempt to fool him.

"Little Jesus, do you really think I don't know what you're doing?" he says. "Your prayer not to wake up? Obvious as someone screaming in a church, except we frown on suicide."

"It was frustration," you say. "I didn't mean it. And I wouldn't do it now, not here, not with my kids downstairs waiting for Santa."

"Not to mention it's a mortal sin."

"Whatever, I'm not going to church, so you can forget that bullshit."

Hans Gruber frowns. "That's not what I was going to suggest."

You wait for more.

"I'm afraid you're in need of an intervention, Little Jesus," he says.

"Excuse me?"

"You're going to be visited."

"Huh?"

"By ... let's call them situations. Ghostly situations, if you will."

"Like a Christmas Carol?"

"More or less. More probably."

"You know I'm starting over, right? I think I found somebody I want to be with."

"Yes, we know."

"So?"

"Remember Slaughterhouse-Five*?"*

"Yeah."

"So it goes," he says.

"What ghosts?" you say. "I've had them all along."

"Well, they'll be back."

"Why can't you all leave me alone?"

"It's not what you want, to be left alone. That's some bullshit, yeah?"

"Wait a minute. You sound like St.—"

You stop when it's obvious he's gone. You're confused. You shake your head in frustration and are about to yell for someone to tell you what's going on when the footsteps you originally heard outside the attic door grow louder. Alan Rickman is gone, but your headache is back. The door opens and it's one of your cousins with the Santa outfit.

"Ready?" he says.

Children, my children, why have I forsaken you ...

Speaking of children, your children, you were lucky as all fuck because they were all three healthy and smart and raised by their mother and your mother way more than you. You managed to maintain some of that Neanderthal-like personality, and like it or not, some of Thomas Rocco's insistence on discipline.

Do you love them? Of course, but you're too young, too stupid, too selfish and too scared to do the right thing and spend quality time with them. Not only were you spoiled by a mother willing to walk over hot coals for you, you assume that's a mother's job when kids are around, so you leave it up to your wife. Instead of patience, you show impatience.

You'll deliver the coin necessary for their upbringing, to include toys, vacations, culture, room and board, but you won't show up to little league games or show your kids how to hold a bat and swing, and when you do try to show them anything, you lose patience because it came natural to you and they're probably too scared to act natural around you. You let them know with your booming voice and often uncontrollable temper that what you say goes, even if they shake when you lose it. On the upside, you're a lot more affectionate than Thomas Rocco ever was. You hold them and hug them and kiss them and remind them how much you love them, even if you're too often a raving lunatic.

Great way to confuse the shit out of children, by the way.

You are your father's son after all.

The daily reading and writing assignments you give them before and during school is something good, as are the daily phone calls you make to them because you don't want them to think for a second they're off your radar. As they age you take them to more than just the usual bullshit amusement parks and baseball games. You introduce them to theatre and opera and reading more than just sports pages. You do okay in those categories of parenthood, but it's not like you're around. You assign them readings and writings. You aren't there to help them, and there's no making up for the lost time, or the impatience and temper tantrums that often leave them wishing you'd just call them on the phone.

In later years of introspection, you wonder if like Thomas Rocco, you probably weren't meant to be a father. It is painful to admit, or to be told by your mother that you've made some of the same parental mistakes as Thomas Rocco, especially regarding patience and time spent with your kids, but is there any way to rectify past mistakes?

You're the son of your father and maybe the grandson of his father in more than name only, a stain on your soul you can never deny. It is against everything you wanted to be as a parent. It is against everything you ever wanted for yourself from Thomas Rocco. Anyone can be a provider, but it takes a real man to be a father. Your sons will prove that to be the case when they become fathers. They will be the real men.

You know you've been lucky most of your life. Whether it was heavenly interference from above, coincidence or pure luck, you've never suffered the consequences you deserve until you lose the faith of your children. Some of that loss is natural, when kids finally understand their fathers aren't supermen who never make mistakes, but much of that loss has to do with the deliberate actions you've taken that have no excuse other than self-serving justifications.

And there is no justification for not being there for them. There is no justification for missing a little league game or not reading a book to them, or not spending an afternoon, ten afternoons if it takes that long, to teach them how to swing a bat or throw a football, or anything else good fathers do with their kids.

More fortunate for your grandchildren is the fact that your sons will not make the same mistakes with their children. At least one generation of Stella will get it right.

The Beginning of the End ...

"The fuck are you lookin' at?" a tall dude at one end of the bar says.

He's been eyeballing you since you showed up to meet friends for a drink. You're in a bar in Queens, a hitter joint in Ozone Park. You've been powerlifting in the 220 class since college, and you recently recorded your personal best bench press, 420 pounds in a power meet. You're running five miles a day to maintain your weight. You're still in football shape under the leather jacket you're wearing, but the tall dude doesn't know that. He's had a few, and he doesn't like the attention you're getting from one of the women there.

"Hey!" he yells. "I'm talkin' to you."

The two friends you're with wave him off and tell you to ignore him, but you're in the mood for a fight. Earlier in the day, you found out Thomas Rocco's been hiring your cousins, his sister's kids, since he opened his stores in Downtown Brooklyn two years before he left you, your mother and sister behind. There had always been a grand scheme behind his bullshit. The entire time he was crying about the lawyer your mother hired for their divorce, he was making more than enough to pay the freight for his ex-wife and kids.

His nieces and nephews have also been working in the new store in New Rochelle your sister is managing. You've been working two jobs the last six months, both on the books. You never made the call your sister told you to make, and now you're resenting Thomas Rocco for it.

The bar smells of piss and beer and cheap perfume and cigarette smoke, the perfect atmosphere to exorcise some demons, but you ignore the tall dude until he stands up on the footrest, waves and yells, "Hey, asshole! Over here!"

It's then you flip him the bird. A few minutes later, after he's landed the first punch, one you took more than willingly, you drive him into a wall and land several hard punches into his solar plexus. His slow-motion fold at the waist, then slow-motion drop to his knees is picture of perfect revenge. Unfortunately for him, you're in a dark zone, a very dark zone. You grab his hair and lift him just high enough to run his face into the edge of the bar. His forehead opens like a cantaloupe and there's blood everywhere.

You're escorted out of the bar by your friends and three bouncers. Outside the bar, one of the bouncers whispers in your ear, "That asshole is around somebody. Watch your back."

Around somebody is street vernacular meaning the punk has been sponsored, he's a wannabe mobster, except now you've damaged his reputation in a big way. There's a good chance he'll come looking for you, and it won't take long for him to find you. One of your friends was wearing his old high school football jersey, Canarsie stitched across the front, his name across the back.

When he does find you, it's Anthony Sforza's misfortune that you see him first. You're on your way home from jogging when you spot him sitting in a car parked off the corner from where you live. It's a muggy spring afternoon, the air thick with the smell of the ocean. You spot the nightstick with a metal collar around one end on the passenger seat. You can see some of where his head has been stitched because his hair has been shaved.

"What are you doing here?" you say.

He looks up, sees it's you, and reaches for the nightstick, but you fire a hard right through the open window and connect with his jaw. The crack isn't loud, but it's a sure sign his jaw is broken, so when he slumps forward, out cold, you know you should take off. The problem is you don't. You keep hitting him, and he's nearly comatose when the police arrive.

A month later the mess is cleared because he really can't press charges, not if he wants to be a wiseguy someday. You, on the other hand, realize the shit you might be in with whomever sponsored him, so you agree to attend an uncommitted ROTC camp in Fort Knox. It's the first of two camps where the Army attempts to sell you officer training. You can attend the first camp in Fort Knox and decide later if you want to go through with training at Camp Lejeune the following year to become a Second Lieutenant. It's a better option than dealing with the wiseguy who was sponsoring Anthony Sforza.

You're in Tennessee for your daughter's first birthday, but not for long after. Your days of blind faith loyalty ended with football. You're too old to take orders and nearly get into it with an officer who demands you take your hands out of your pocket. You tell him to go fuck himself, and start a mini-war of your own. After going through a maze of high ranking officers who try and convince you to stay anyway, only because the draft was no more and the Army was desperate, you're on your way back home, the country still safe and secure without you.

And then you, Little Jesus, are back to riding your scaffold and cleaning windows.

Do The Math ...

"Your girlfriend called," Tammy says. She's literally shaking.

Your eyebrows furrow, your best Thomas Rocco impression. "What?"

"Helen? She wanted to know if you lived here."

Although you've been trying with the Hispanic woman, Helen is your first affair, and you've made all the mistakes necessary for a spouse looking to flee a marriage. You picked up a woman at a nightclub in Queens, drove her home, screwed her, then took a shower, but you were dumb enough to leave your wallet in your pants while you showered.

"I don't know any Helen," you say.

"Then why did she call here? Why'd she ask for you?"

Because she'd rifled through your wallet, you dumb shit.

"I have no idea," you say. "Maybe it's somebody playing a prank."

Yeah, right. Even you wouldn't believe that line of shit.

It doesn't take five years before the lyrics to your wedding song become a mockery. You've discovered you have eyes for many women besides Tammy, and in your warped mind, whether she's remained faithful or not after you were married, her pre-marital confessions were enough to justify a lifetime of paybacks.

You're already thinking two steps ahead of your wife, much the same way Thomas Rocco had played the long game.

You've earned your degree in Political Science, something Thomas Rocco and your sister had tried their best to convince you to avoid even attempting because it was out of your league. Yet you graduated with honors and were accepted into graduate school. You were still contemplating law school, and so you went to your father and sister for advice.

"Last time it was to become a writer," Thomas Rocco says. "Now you wanna be a lawyer? You've got a wife and kids. You have any idea what it takes to be a lawyer?"

"I won a political science award," you say.

"Yeah, how much they pay you for that?"

"A hundred bucks."

"And it cost you how much to get the degree?"

"About five thousand."

"And you're still washing windows."

"And working a second job off the books to pay my way. Why can't you congratulate me for that?"

"Do the math," he says. "Figure it out for yourself." Then he goes about stocking the shelves of his store as if you aren't there.

You move to the back of the store and confront your sister. "What do you have to say about it?"

She rolls her eyes. "About what? I'm busy back here."

"I was accepted to graduate school. I'm thinking of going to law school after that."

"Good, go. Just leave me alone, okay? I have work to do."

And that resounding question fills your head: *"Do you think you deserve to get hit?"*

You return home a much angrier man than before you left, but there's no chance for solace there either. You've grown apart from Tammy and hanging around her has made your oldest kid fear you. She's only three but she shakes when she sees the anger register on your face.

When you tell your mother about your plans to leave, she lays a guilt trip on you to rival the one she tried with Thomas Rocco.

"Don't leave your kids," she says. "Remember how you felt about your father? Don't leave her alone with them? It's not right. The baby, your son, he's only three months."

Could you be a worse human being? Maybe. You'll certainly give it a shot over the next twenty years, but you need out and you need satisfaction for what you're trying to achieve.

You tell your mother that you'll be a much better parent than Thomas Rocco. You'll certainly make the effort to stress education and support whatever it is your kids are into, and you'll always be a good provider. You promise a lot of things you'll never come close to delivering on, especially spending time with your kids, but your mother remains heartbroken. She loves your kids the way she loved you. Maybe more so.

It isn't long before you fall for the other woman, not Helen, and that becomes the catalyst for finally leaving you wife and kids in peace. A few months after falling for the other woman, you separate from your wife and take a basement apartment in Canarsie where you grew up. It's a shithole but it's cheap and you're a good tenant. You'll still spend a few nights a week with your first wife, but now you have a place of your own to call home.

Your Road To Perdition ...

A few years earlier, your mother suffered a stroke during an angiogram. She permanently lost her peripheral vision and could no longer see out of the right side of either eye. A lawsuit ensued, something both Thomas Rocco and your sister seemed to root against from the outset. When it finally came to court, it was in one of the two conservative boroughs in New York, Queens. You accompanied your mother through the four-day trial and had to bite your tongue as you watched the defense's expert testimony, doctors defending doctors, claim your mother could see perfectly fine out of both of her eyes. You had to clench your teeth as the insurance company's attorney waxed sarcastic in his cross examination of your mother, bringing you into his riff when he motioned over his shoulder, dangled one arm and said, "And that's your son leading you around by the arm?"

You wanted to break his face. You dreamed about it right there in the courtroom. You saw yourself rubbing his face over broken glass. Your epic daydreaming turned dark.

When she lost the case, your decision to abandon law school was an easy one. You could never put up with the theatrics of a courtroom. The sarcasm alone would trigger a reaction that would leap from your head to your fists and earn you disbarment along with an arrest for assault.

Maybe the law is the exact wrong way to go? Maybe Thomas Rocco, for all the wrong reasons, was right after all? Money is what it's all about, this life. Why put your faith in a court case or a lottery ticket?

Why kill yourself working two and three jobs? Why not go for the green? You've already learned how cash demands respect, and if you have enough, even Thomas Rocco has to accept your success.

Maybe even respect you.

You started off working two full-time legitimate jobs, cleaning windows in the early morning and working security nights, but your net take was more exhaustion than money due to tax brackets. Now that you've left, paying the freight on two households is expensive, and suddenly Thomas Rocco is coming up short on what he owes your mother. You have to find other ways to earn, especially since you've become intimate with that other woman, a woman ten years older than you. You'll need money and a lot of it to take care of your wife, kids, your Mom, and yourself.

"You can't take blood from a stone," Thomas Rocco tells you when you remind him he owes money to your mother.

And once again you think about her cousin Gazut, and how he'd handle that bullshit.

It's time to make some mean green, Little Jesus. It's time to cross into the darker shades of life.

Back in the day, Thomas Rocco taught you about loansharking, lending money at usurious rates. The start-up cash is all you'll need, because you already have the right look and a nuthouse reputation. So, how do you do that? Where do you get the coin?

Earning dirty money often requires borrowing dirty money. You're quickly schooled by a street rabbi connected with family how mob connected street financiers, a loanshark's loanshark, will lend out coin at 1% a week interest (a.k.a. vigorish or vig). If you can find yourself ten customers and lend coin to them at 3% a week, the profit is 2%. Ten thousand borrowed at 1% lent out at 3% will yield you two hundred cash free dollars. Twenty thousand will net you four hundred, and so on. But what if some of the thousands you lend out won't or can't make their payments? What if you have to collect? Do you make threats? Do you use violence?

Thomas Rocco taught you this illegal entrepreneurial wonder when he drove through a car wash and didn't have to pay. The poor bastards drying his car off owed him money, no more than ten or twenty dollars, and they performed their work for free.

"Twenty bucks," he told you. "If they take off or get fired, I'll never see them again, but I have the manager in my pocket for a hundred bucks. He vouches for the others and has to pick up the slack if they're gone one day. He's probably taking something from their paychecks anyway."

You don't understand then how long those particular loans can last, but over time the business is explained to you well enough. Just like the television commercials expressing how you too can become a computer engineer, you figure out that you too can become a money lending parasite.

At first it's too steep a mountain to attempt to climb, so you learn the ropes the old-fashioned way, by doing the collections for the street rabbi himself. He schools you up and down the process, warning you against the use of threats and/or violence. The shit you see in movies is more fiction than reality. There are assholes who get off being tough guys when collecting, but they're usually the ones who wind up arrested, fucked-up or killed. There's a method to the madness and you quickly learn after collecting from an array of borrowers, which ones to seek and which ones to avoid.

Collecting nets you some extra cash, but it's a bigger hassle than seems worth the effort, especially when dealing with gamblers and other streetwise individuals. You learn to avoid women at all costs, because nobody will back you when their loans go bad. You learn gamblers are bigger headaches than their worth, unless they own or operate a business. You learn the streetwise punks are often backed by other wiseguys looking to rip off neophyte money lenders or anybody else foolish enough to lend them a dime.

When you start your own loansharking business, the first customer comes from a friend who knows a guy in need of a few hundred bucks. It's a good loan and grows over time from eight hundred to two grand. The guy pays on time and never misses, so you expand the business little by little.

You want to be fair about it, so you don't encourage customers. You make them wait a full day after they hear the terms of the loans.

"You want a grand, it'll cost you thirty a week," you tell them. "That's three points a week, no exceptions. You do the right thing, we won't have a headache. You can pay me thirty a week for a year and still owe me a grand. You want to knock down the principal, you pay more than thirty, but it's always three points a week on the balance. Make sure you want this money before you take it. If you can get it someplace else, do it. If you think you're going to scam me, don't. Think about it over tonight, because once you take it, I'll expect what you owe every week."

Way more often than not they accept the terms of the loan and you hand them the thousand dollars or whatever the amount is the next day. You've now become every bit as dirty as Thomas Rocco was when he lent money to the poor bastards at the car wash, except you're doing it for a lot more money and profit.

Two years later, after paying off what you'd borrowed, you have ten grand on the street earning you three bills a week. The few times you're tested, you do a good enough job of convincing your slow pays to do the right thing. The most violent you ever have to be is to grab a guy by his shirt collar and growl in his face.

You've been reading *The Friends of Eddie Coyle* a few times a year, almost religiously. There's no other book that can get your creative juices flowing, and you still want to write, even while making money and living a fast life loaded with distractions. You try a few more plays and attempts at novels. You eventually let them go, but you know you'll be back to try again.

You're a rogue moneylender, because you haven't been officially spoken for by your street rabbi, because he's been looking out for you and you're too dumb to realize it. Eventually your action grabs the attention of another connected guy. It happens because one of his borrowers has also borrowed from you and there's a line forming for payment. You're asked to meet at a bar to settle the dispute. You're informed it's a sit down and that you need somebody to represent you. You reach out to family connections, and half an hour into your meeting you're connected too, like it or not.

And that's how it comes to fruition, your road to perdition. The same slow pay that brought you into a connected world tries to sucker you into a set-up loan that gets you arrested for an assault. It's your first visit to the Tombs and you quickly learn how this shit really isn't for you. When you're brought up for the arraignment, the guy you assaulted doesn't show, and the charges are dismissed.

A week later, you're tipped off about a fake routine a deadbeat gambler has been running on connected bookmaking offices he owes *a lot* of money. He has a guy hanging with him, his brother-in-law it turns out, playing undercover cop. The brother-in-law carries a fake badge and a gun, and the pair are backing down people looking to collect. You're told about it the day your sponsor sends you to collect for one of the bookies he also sponsors, he says, but you know it's also a test and you have no intentions of failing.

It's a calm summer night, and the deadbeat and his beard with the fake gun and badge are exactly where they agreed to meet you, at a crowded outdoor café on the Lower East Side, not far from where you were brought home after your first resurrection. You have a metal telescope club tucked into the waist of your pants. It is covered by the Jets oversized sweatshirt you're wearing over a white t-shirt. You sit across from the deadbeat and ignore the guy playing cop.

"You Larry?" you say.

"Larry for Junior," he says.

"You have what you owe?"

"I don't," he says.

"You sure?"

This time he smiles. "Fuckin' positive," he says, then looks to his brother-in-law and starts to say something else, but the telescope club shatters his jaw. He falls off the chair onto the sidewalk. He's spitting teeth as people who were seated at neighboring tables flee the area. The phony cop is stunned and doesn't move when you stare at him.

"You have what he owes?" you ask.

"Hey, I don't have anything to do with this," he says.

You shoot him a Thomas Rocco frown. "Tell your friend to find the money he owes."

You collapse the telescope club as you cross Second Avenue, walk one block north and grab a taxi heading west. You remove the Jets jersey in the cab and leave it there when you get out.

Two weeks later you're rewarded handsomely for your insanity. You never knew how much money the deadbeat actually owed, but the envelope you're given is thick with cash. You don't count it until you're home, but when you see it's almost a grand, you put it back out on the street in the form of street loans of your own.

You, Little Jesus, learn fast.

Schadenfreude ...

Between wives one and two, your sister and father have a tumultuous end to their relationship. You learned about it three weeks after the fact, how Thomas Rocco had watched his wife curse out your sister before demanding she be fired. He let his daughter walk, but not before he begged her not to tell you. His exact words: "Please don't tell your crazy brother."

Your mother, who knew within days, kept the secret as well.

The trouble had been brewing for weeks; your sister refusing to cow-tow to Gang Bang's nightly appearance at the store, during which she'd scold Thomas Rocco like the cuckold he was, yelling at him from the time she arrived until your sister left for the day. It was meant to reestablish a pecking order: Gang Bang first, everyone else second. At some point, whether it was a rare display of your sister's loyalty to her mother, or when she could no longer stand watching her father be made a fool of, or if it was jealousy for her father's attention, or because she was fed up with having to deal with the moronic Gang Bang at all, the store became a turf war in more ways than one.

It began with petty shit like Gang Bang pulling the eight-track tape your sister was listening to, usually Joni Mitchell or Carol King, out of the receiver to slap in one by Musique—the one song she'd play over and over, "In The Bush", the chorus of which was *"Push, Push, in the bush,"* the only lines Gang Bang seemed to know.

Other times it was Gang Bang telling Thomas Rocco to send his daughter across the mall for a cup of hot chocolate with marshmallows and extra whipped cream, usually ten minutes before the end of your sister's day, a last dig and reminder of who the real boss was.

The battle culminated after the funeral of Thomas Rocco's remaining sibling, his sister. Two of her five kids, the ones who had kept in touch with your mother post-Gang Bang, had invited your mother and sister to the funeral, and then later back to their house. Already incensed about your mother's appearance at the funeral, Gang Bang threw a fit.

Somebody had to pay.

The following workday, when your sister arrived at the store she'd been managing for Thomas Rocco, Gang Bang was waiting for her.

The Postermat was a 1970's head shop in a Westchester Mall. A store much deeper than it was wide, where the smell of strawberry incense permeated the space. Popular posters of the day lined the left wall, front to back, in two-sided racks. Along the right side of the store were a series of glass cases displaying the latest in drug paraphernalia—pipes, bongs, clips, scales, rolling paper, incense, incense holders, ashtrays, etc. In the back were display cases stacked with spiral albums filled with pages of transfers for T-shirts, two heat-transfer pressing machines, and a tiny bathroom.

Upon entering the store, your sister looked to her right and was surprised to see Gang Bang. She ignored the hard stare and headed to the back until Gang Bang yelled, "Hey!"

"Hey?" your sister said.

"You heard me."

Your sister waited for more.

"You and me need to get something straight," Gang Bang said.

"And what's that?"

"You can start by losing your attitude."

"Or else?"

"You're fired."

"Fuck you."

"Fine. You're fired."

"I work for my father, not you."

"And who do you think he works for, you fat, stupid, dyke?"

Somewhat shocked, your sister cocked her head to one side.

"You heard me," Gang Bang said.

Your sister went to the back to use the bathroom. When she came out, it was in time to see Thomas Rocco and how the color had drained from his face.

"Tell her," Gang Bang said.

"Tell me what?" your sister said as she moved out from behind the transfer cases.

"Please?" Thomas Rocco said to Gang Bang.

"Tell her so I don't have to look at her anymore, the disgusting pig."

"Please?" he repeated.

"He fucks you, lady," your sister told Gang Bang. "That's all he does."

"I swear I'll walk out and sue you for my half of the business," Gang Bang told Thomas Rocco.

A stare between father and daughter ensued before they spoke simultaneously.

"It's okay," your sister said.

"She's my wife," Thomas Rocco said.

Emotionally staggered, your sister said, "What?"

Thomas Rocco could have let things go, but he had to reassure Gang Bang. He shrugged and said, "She's my wife."

Your sister swallowed hard.

"Get out!" Gang Bang yelled.

"Please!" Thomas Rocco said.

"I want her out of here!"

A few minutes later, Thomas Rocco found his daughter in the parking lot. He tried to hand her five one-hundred dollar bills, but she turned away instead, an attempt to hide her tears. It was then he begged her not to tell you, her crazy brother.

The day you learn, you've already begun a life of crime without reservation. Your mother may not have chosen to use her Mob connections, but you'd had enough of being a sucker. That episode in the Queens courtroom where you watched your mother fall apart after a Queens jury found her doctor guilty of malpractice, but his guilt not the cause of her stroke and partial permanent blindness, that was the next to last straw. Seeing how glad your father and sister were that her malpractice case had been lost, that she'd have nothing yet again in her life, that bit of enthusiastic Schadenfreude sealed the deal. Revenge would be yours. Justice, at least your warped sense of it, had found a resourceful weapon—your rage.

You'd already been arrested for two assaults, but there were never trials, a direct benefit of having connections with the right people. Who in their right mind would show up to court and testify? Your ideals and faith in your fellow man, never mind family, had been beaten into a corner of your heart you wouldn't glance at for another dozen years.

Little Jesus had turned to ice.

What you managed to maintain, no matter how convoluted the form, was a sense of justice. You didn't like bullies anymore then than you ever liked them, and the justification you used to become one was a self-serving sense of vengeance.

The day your sister tells you what happened and begs you not to do anything, you're already getting into your car and firing up the engine. The drive to Long Island takes twenty-five minutes. You're there in fifteen, your mind blurred with vengeful adrenaline.

Your cousins, most of them, are seated around their kitchen table in the same house two of them had invited your mother and sister to visit after their mother's funeral. You walk in and want to know why your sister was fired from the store. The eldest, a woman used to running things, says, "We don't know anything about that."

"Bullshit," you say. "You invited my mother and sister here, Gang Bang threw a fit, and now my sister lost her job. Why'd you invite her here?"

No response.

"Nobody knows anything?" you say. "Are you kidding me?"

"We did that for Uncle Tommy," the boss lady says.

"You people have been feeding off Uncle Tommy for years, working at his stores when his kids didn't even know he had any. You think you took enough yet?"

"We don't know anything."

"Fuckin' leeches, every one you," you say, and then you shove a chair out of your way as you leave.

When you get to the store, Thomas Rocco tries his best to deflate your anger with an exaggerated bullshit story. Whether it's true or not, what he claims his niece told him over the phone is irrelevant. You were there. You know what happened.

"How could you turn over the table and throw chairs?" he says. "They just buried their mother."

The next few seconds require the most restraint you'll ever exercise. In your mind's eye you're watching his head split open off a corner of one of the display cases. It is what you want to do, but you don't. You smile instead. Then you proceed to kick out the glass in one of the cases. Thomas Rocco runs out from behind the counter to close and lock the front door.

The two of you face each other, five feet apart. "You want to hit me now?" he says.

"So bad I can taste it," you say. "You're a real piece of shit."

"Your sister wasn't innocent in this."

Another coward's trick, shift the attention to someone else, someone you don't get along with, maybe deflect some of your anger, so it isn't so focused. He assumes you're angry at Gang Bang, but he's clueless. You couldn't care less about Gang Bang.

You're grinding your teeth. You force a smirk and say, "Fuckin' *cornuto*."

"Don't say that," he says.

"Fuck you. You're gonna tell me what to say? You're gonna tell me anything anymore? Think about it, *cornuto*."

"I'm not a *cornuto*," he says. "Don't say that. You don't understand."

"Understand? What's to understand? A man lets his wife shit all over him, calls his daughter names to her face in front of him, fires her, that's not a cuckold, a fuckin' *cornuto*? That's exactly what you are. She let you watch when she fucks her boyfriends?"

His face turns red. You step closer, but he doesn't bite.

"To think we were afraid of you," you say. "Afraid of you and all your bullshit. You made us feel like shit. And all you are is a fuckin' coward."

"You don't understand."

"I don't, huh? You let some cunt fire your daughter. Some twat's been fucked by half of Brooklyn, you let her call your daughter names right in front of you. Me, I would've killed her, but I guess that's why you begged my sister not to tell her crazy brother."

He swallows hard.

"Where is the cunt tonight?" You say. "She fly out of here after my cousins called?"

"She carries a gun, Charlie. She knows how to use it. She shoots clusters in targets at the range."

You feel the hurt in your soul and have to bite your lip not to let it show. He's warning you: fuck with her and she'll kill you. Worse, he'd stand behind that as well, your death at her hands. What kind of a father says that to his son?

Answer: Abraham, the father who would slaughter his son to prove his love for his God.

In the Postermat, where it's just you and Thomas Rocco, his rejection hurts yet again, but you've learned a long time ago how to turn hurt into determination. What doesn't kill you indeed makes you stronger. In that instant, you climb half a dozen steps on the sociopathic street ladder.

You step chest to chest with Thomas Rocco and whisper in his right ear. "A range?" you say. "I'll be this close."

He steps back. Your eyes remain locked on his until he looks away. You turn and take one last kick at the shattered glass in the display case.

The crash is loud. You purposely brush shoulders with him on your way out, knocking him to the side. During your walk from the mall to the parking garage, you expect mall security to stop you. As soon as you're out of the garage, you're looking for New Rochelle police cars, but there aren't any. Instead of going home to your apartment that night, you drive to Tammy's apartment where you can cry like a baby in your first wife's arms and feel loved again.

Bless me Father …

It's a time of reflection for you, Little Jesus. You wonder where you've gone wrong, because no matter how much you try to deny it, Thomas Rocco remains the final arbiter when it comes to your successes or failures. It is an unfortunate fact of your life and it will take a few more years and many more distractions before you can reject his opinions, but even when you're most justified in your rage, you fail to see the folly in your methodology. Handling the burden all sons must bear with their fathers isn't unique to your over-sensitive self.

Writing for the 1st District Court of Appeals in the case of *Little Jesus v. Thomas Rocco, et al*, the court finds the following:

> "[T]he pressure brought to bear by Defendant on Plaintiff were so egregious as to fuck up his life for much longer than necessary. To Wit: the acts of defiance due to insecurities born of rejection; the acts of a coward born of rejection; the acts of philandering and/or philandering behavior with women due to insecurities born of rejection; the criminal acts born of same, etc."

It is horseshit and you know it. You got played like a fiddle, but all of the above opinion can be wiped clean with one simple counterpunch rejection of the perpetrator(s).

So, no, it isn't them. It's you. You're the fuckup, except for earning. Your loansharking operation grows to the point of silly money and you'll no longer need to clean windows. You're making more collecting cash than Thomas Rocco could ever dream. You're the big Kahuna now, except not really. You're a fool playing a game he knows can't last for long, but the lifestyle is too good to allow your conscience to get in the way.

As it turns out, you Little Jesus, were playing the short game.

Calling the Cuban ...

Between a few of the women you've been seeing on an off is an old reliable, a woman far more beautiful and sexy and great in bed than she is a conversationalist. She's Cuban and gorgeous and you can't believe how easy it was to get from first to home with her. And if there's ever been someone well experienced in the sack, it's her. She's the type who can get you in trouble if you're not careful, the kind other men have to stop to look at.

She's also a good person with a heart of gold, and as reliable as anyone has been in your life. Although you know she can't wait around for your phone call, whenever you do make contact, it's a done deal. It's the perfect tradeoff, incredible sex with a beautiful woman for a night out. When you're not depressed or reflecting on why you should be depressed about your superficial life thus far, you're the king of the world, able to juggle a few women and situations at a time. You're keeping Tammy happy by continuing to screw her when you visit the kids most weekends. Cheating on girlfriends doesn't count in your Little Jesus brain, so whichever woman you're with at the time, you've got the green light to be with someone else.

It's an ironic approach to your future relationships, doing unto others before they can do unto you, cheating before being cheated on. Whether you think you love the woman you're with or not, the most efficient way to maintain your new false confidence is to have a special someone in longtime reserve, a woman you can keep with just a few of the easy dollars you're earning as a criminal.

The fact she's Cuban, beautiful, and equally as uncommitted as you are is a huge bonus. Maritza is the go-to-girl for the next decade, outlasting a two-year relationship with the Hispanic woman you originally left your wife and kids for, and your next two wives. She's an armpiece for your newfound love of craps tables, where you'll blow much of the extra criminal money you're raking in.

She becomes an option you won't take out of play for a long time to come, so when the going gets tough, you call the Cuban. She's every cheating man's dream, and one night when you take her to Atlantic City, she's wearing a short, skin-tight, white, tube dress and stiletto heels, and she turns just about every head in the casino. They all want to look. Fortunately for you, you're with your criminal friends and nobody is going to say anything loud enough for you to hear. That night you can't get the image of her ass and legs in the tight white tube dress she's wearing out of your head. As she walked a few steps ahead of you to play a slot machine, you were in awe of her perfect body. The image is with you when you fuck later, and it significantly shortens your trip. Even more fortunately for you, Maritza can get you back up to speed like no other woman ever could, and you'll go three rounds before you collapse from sexual exhaustion.

Another time, after you put coin in her hands, "to take a vacation someplace," she snuggles up to you, nearly sucks your tongue from your mouth and says, "Sometime I think I love you."

"You don't have to give me that bullshit," you say, and it's mostly because you can't believe anyone could love you anymore.

"You don't love me?" she says.

"You're a ball breaker, Maritza. We'd kill each other if we spent more than a night together. Don't fuck up a good thing."

Maritza giggles. She knows it's the truth.

"So all I am to you is a piece of ass?"

"Think about it, you've seen my temper. You wanna be my wife?"

She saw it the night a drunken patron in a restaurant near where she lived made a comment about her perfect *culo* when she returned from the bathroom. You pushed his face into his bowl of ravioli.

"*Carajo,*" she says.

You set two fifties on her night table and say, "Merry Christmas."

"It's July," she says.

"Make believe."

Bootstrapping ...

Somewhere between cleaning windows and becoming a criminal, a woman you met where you washed windows suggested you teach yourself how to type. She supervised the third shift word processing department for the First Boston brokerage firm and said she'd teach you the WANG word processor once you could type. She knew you were working a second job standing in the same lobby wearing a security guard uniform nights, and that word processing paid a lot more than you were earning checking identifications.

She was doing you a favor. A big one.

One night she invited you up to her department during your break and pointed out the actors, musicians, singers and writers who worked there. She introduced you to a few and they told you how word processing had replaced waiting tables and tending bars, and especially how it replaced putting up with a lot of people bullshit, something you've been dealing with asking for identifications in the lobby. Word processing was where artists were flocking to because of the better working conditions, steady income, and health benefits most of them couldn't afford otherwise.

What they couldn't have known then was word processing would become the new big thing in employment because the technology permitted corporations, both financial and legal, to replace typing pools with more efficient methods of exploitation.

Before you could join the ranks of the cultured, you needed to learn how to type. You did so by purchasing an Apple IIe computer and a typing program that placed you in an on-screen spaceship amidst a galaxy of asteroids. You had to use your keyboard to fend off the letter/asteroids by typing them before they reached your spaceship and blew it up. It began a letter at a time, the easy ones on the home row first, then progressed to the other rows, then two and three letters at a time. From letters it formed short words, then more difficult, longer words. As your score and speed increased, the pace became faster and included short sentences. It was a game you became obsessed with, as was its intention, and you were typing 60 words per minute just in time for your first ever white collar interview.

You will eventually type 100 words per minute, but lose some speed and accuracy with age because of the fingers and knuckles you've afflicted with arthritis during your days of punching walls and doors while throwing moronic fits.

Rather than bother the woman who said she'd teach you word processing, you enrolled in a basic WANG word processing course. It started at ten o'clock in the morning and ran for two hours, four days a week. It cost $75.00, but was worth a lot more. You worked early in the morning cleaning windows, then headed from your job on 53rd Street to the classroom on 41st Street. After three days of class you decided the lessons were moving way too slow for your overanxious brain, so one day you stuck around after class and bribed the teacher to give you a copy of the classroom key. You wanted in early to race ahead in the instruction book and teach yourself. He asked for $25 and you were more than grateful to pay it. You would've given him $50.

You took learning the new skill seriously and were finished with the lessons long before the rest of the class. When you eventually took the test given by the temporary agency that ran the class, you were already typing close to 80 words per minute and finished an hour before anyone else. The agency was glad to send you out, because of the percentage of coin they earned off your back. The more temps an agency could send out, the more profit they enjoyed.

The owners of the means of production were never stupid people.

It was a time when word processors were being paid a premium, when temping paid anywhere from $17.00 to $25.00 an hour, depending on the shift. The hourly rate translation for temp agencies was a score. When a worker earned $25.00 an hour, the agency charged their clients $40-50.00 an hour, a $15-20 profit, which wasn't bad for sitting on one's ass and sending others out to do the actual work.

Your first actual job interview was a bust, because it was clear you didn't have a clue what to say and admitted to being a window cleaner the past several years. When you sought your sister's help, she shocked the shit out of you and said: "Just be yourself. People like you. Don't try to fake it. Let them talk. You listen. Ask questions, but don't trap yourself. You can tell them you worked for my accounting business. I'll write you up a resume."

Which she did, and although one interviewer made a sarcastic comment about your only experience being a job working for your sister, the next interviewer sent you to a brokerage firm for another test and you aced that one too. One temp job led to another, which led to gaining some advance knowledge and skills. After a few months temping at brokerage and legal firms, you were ready to try for a permanent position, which you did and were hired for a few dollars less than what you were earning flying a scaffold.

Bootstrapping your way to those legitimate incomes was not only a source of pride, it was also proof positive that you too could be a robot for the machine. Still, you expected more than that. You expected it would also earn you some extra points with Thomas Rocco, because you were not only working two fulltime jobs, you were earning two fulltime salaries.

At the least, you expected your bootstrapping efforts and rewards to preclude his and your sister's cracking jokes about which way you squeegeed the water off glass, left or right?

Six months later you were promoted and became the third-shift supervisor.

Any wise-ass questions about which fingers I use for which keys, Thomas Rocco?

Sorella?

The blessings that came from that job were more than financial. They were real blessings, those most important to your soul. You were exposed to people who didn't care about a Mets game, or a Jets game, or much of anything else you had centered your narrowly led life around. These new people provided a much wider world view, and while a few of them resented a former jock invading their turf, a philistine invading their space and one day becoming their boss, their diverse interests appealed to your curiosity.

You learned who Tom Waits was and gained hours of inspiration and pleasure from his lyrics and music. You engaged in discussions about communism and socialism, and the shrinking differences between the two major political parties in America. You engaged in book discussions and often attended theatre showcases where an actor or two you'd met on the job was performing, which in turn reestablished your love of playwriting. It was a new world and you fully embraced it.

Your workmates also introduced you to the opera your paternal Grandfather loved and that you would come to love and pass on to one of your children. Same goes for classical music and trying different foods from different cultures. None of those things would ever have happened had you remained a window cleaner. None of them.

The boost in confidence you received from conquering a world you never would have imagined possible was fuel for life.

Not to mention the money and how the more profitable end of the business came with the temping you could still do to earn extra coin, all of it legitimate. You could work 24/7 if you wanted, and sometimes you did by taking jobs on the weekends, or short afternoon shifts, or working vacation days you took from window cleaning. Those were the salad days of an industry you'd eventually retire from, when there was work wherever or whenever you wanted it.

Another bonus from learning to type and word process was how it facilitated writing, how you could transition from writing stories and notes on a pad to typing them on a screen. You could edit them over and over without having to decipher the chicken scratch your penmanship had become, and you would always have to edit them over and over.

Confidence is an essential character trait some seem born with while others have to work to achieve. Whenever yours took flight in the past, it was quickly knocked back down. Whether it was the voices in your head explaining away your accomplishments or the self-doubt born of those voices, there wasn't much room for your confidence to flourish.

When you hit long home runs playing in the little leagues, it was because you were a big kid. When you lifted heavy weights, it was because you wasted so much time trying, and what purpose did it serve anyway? When you achieved a football scholarship, what good did it do you? It wasn't as if you could earn a living playing football as a pro someday, nor were you ever really a student. When you earned an honors degree in Political Science and won a $100 award for a paper you wrote, it was still almost $5,000 less than what your degree cost. And weren't colleges and universities selling those degrees anyway? Was it really worth $5,000 to become a window cleaner? When you conquered the fear of hanging out a window to clean it, so could a monkey if they bothered to teach one. Big deal you taught yourself how to type and were promoted within six months and were making two fulltime incomes? You had to show up to those jobs and spend time there. Anybody could work two jobs if they weren't lazy. What did that prove? It proved you couldn't earn the same money working one job.

How the hell do you find some of the confidence you'll need to survive from working as a word processor?

The answer is obvious, by ignoring the knocks and moving forward, but you're not ready for that yet, Little Jesus.

That criminal shit pays beaucoup bucks.

The propaganda behind bootstrapping loses some credibility over time, but for where you were when you taught yourself how to type and word process, it was an undeniable plus that would not only bolster some much needed self-confidence, it would provide the healthcare you'd need for yourself and kids while living your other life as a criminal.

Deutschland über alles ...

Helen from the nightclub was the first, then it was the Cuban, but there were others. Most of them one-nighters you met on the job or in bars, but a few you remained involved with for more than a few weeks. When you fell for the Hispanic woman and left your wife and kids, it was the start of a hamster wheel leading to nowhere. Leaving your wife and kids marked the official beginning to the end of the family you wanted. This time you were to blame, the breakup had nothing to do with Thomas Rocco or your sister. It wasn't even Tammy's fault, and your excuse to use her past indiscretions was self-serving bullshit.

When the Hispanic woman did you a great favor by refusing your proposal to marry her, your next serious relationship is with the German.

She's also ten years your senior and beautiful, plus this one has the red hair, blue eyes, and the freckles St. Patrick had once prophesied. She's married, so she has to cheat on her husband. You're also cheating on someone new you met on a plane to Las Vegas, while the German was cheating on her husband and one of her boyfriends. She also has kids with her husband, so there's an extra potential headache with her. You're not looking forward to what you know has to become a mess at some point.

The first months are great. She doesn't question where you are nights you can't see her and she's always available when you want her. She comes to your place and you screw there, or you go to her place and you screw there. She's not a shy woman by any measure. She'll call you in the middle of the day and ask if you want to fuck. She shows up to your apartment in a mink coat over a blue lingerie outfit, an image that stays with you forever.

There are a couple of fights over the Hispanic woman who rejected your proposal and those fights become the first signs of jealousy.

Or maybe you don't want to see it, because it's always a good time with the German.

Still, it's an ideal situation until the German lets you know she loves you by leaving her husband. It's a perfect mix of passion and danger, right up your ally, except there's a problem. The German is not only exactly what you want, beautiful, with red hair and freckles, she's also successful, and that scares the shit out of you. How can an insecure motherfucker playing mobster maintain his manhood when the woman he's seeing earns one-hundred times what he can make on or off the street? You're still looking for love, but she may be looking for a good time with the riffraff.

Your first wife divorces you after growing tired of waiting for you to return. You're suddenly free to make another mistake.

You know you can't handle a wealthy woman who may be playing for the sake of having some extracurricular fun, so you break it off with the German after a few months, but then you see a magazine ad featuring a redhead with freckles, and you call her at work.

"What are you doing?" you ask.

"Working. You?"

"Wondering if the carpet still matches the curtains."

"Mr. Romance."

"Wanna go to Vegas this weekend?"

"Let me think a second. Yes."

Passion and lust turn into a romance neither of you can handle, but you fly back to Las Vegas a few months later and get married anyway. It isn't long before the insecurity any woman would have being married to a street guy rears its head. Now she does wonder where you might be when you aren't home nights. Sometimes it's legitimate why you're not home, because you're doing street shit she shouldn't know about anyway, and other times it's because you're banging someone else, most often the Cuban.

The kicker is that jealousy is contagious and before long you start to wonder about her business trips. You weren't her first affair, and she has the means to have one anytime, anywhere she wants. To your paranoid mind, money plus unfaithful can only equal leaving you looking like a fool. The ghost of Thomas Rocco having been a cuckold looms large, and it is a DNA you reject with extreme prejudice, especially after being played the fool by Tammy.

You need to set parameters, so you step up the fucking around.

"Don't make a fool of me, Charlie," the German says one day.

"The fuck are you talking about?"

"I know you have a girlfriend."

"You don't know shit."

"Bullshit. I had you followed."

"You what?"

"The Cuban bitch. I know you're still screwing her."

"You don't know shit."

"Look, I hate what you do for money, you know that, but I put up with it because you're still finding your way and don't realize what a good life we can have. You have to play your games, and I hate that. I try to understand, but I'm not willing to put up with a girlfriend. That's too much."

Her double dose of power is overwhelming. Aside from her money being a challenge to your manhood, the German's ability to maneuver requires someone remain on standby. The marriage came way too fast. The German takes a trip to Deutschland to visit family, but all you can think is she's going to see someone over there in retaliation for what she knew was going on over here.

The fate of the marriage is sealed when she admits to having contact with a former lover. Your passion nearly sends you looking for him, but he could be anywhere, and now you have an excuse to no longer feel guilty for fucking around. In your insecure mind, if she admitted to contact with the guy, it was the same as banging him, and if she was banging him, it disqualifies all the cheating you've done past, present and future.

You're a mess, and the fantasy you've created is way too much for your insecure brain to absorb. You remind yourself that a beautiful woman of means can do anything she wants with whomever she wants whenever she wants. Once again money proves the great equalizer. You see yourself as a toy husband, ten years younger and street enough for interesting conversation. The woman adores you, you moron, but you're too insecure to allow yourself to return the adoration. She was your salvation from the street and stupidity, but you couldn't handle it.

When you're arrested for another assault and have to spend the night in a Jersey City lockup, the German can no longer handle it. She wants you to stop what you're doing and become human. She manages to get you to stop gambling, no small project, but you're still too insecure to accept what could be a beautiful relationship if you weren't such an asshole.

Moron that you've become, you take her generosity as an insult. She'll do anything to keep you safe, but you equate her genuine love and concern with being a kept man. Instead of slowing down your street business, you expand it and go partners in a bookmaking office.

You're doing big numbers on the street and take your mother to Atlantic City to play her slots and a table game she's come to like called Let it Ride. Both Thomas Rocco and your sister aren't fans of your generosity with your mother, but fuck them. If your old man is jealous, that's even better. Hopefully his wife is foaming from the mouth.

He calls to talk to you out of the blue, but he doesn't have your home number and has to call your mother. When she tells you about his call, you say, "Fuck him."

Your marriage to the German eventually sours and it's your fault. Whether she's having affairs to compensate for the ones you have on her are irrelevant. You started the affair mess and you'll end it by forcing the German into depression. Your marriage unofficially ends the day she tells you she's thinking of committing suicide. You've become a piece of shit, but even you know you won't be able to handle being the cause of someone killing herself.

Princeton for Brown ...

The bookmaking business you've partnered up on is lucrative, but now you're a lot closer to mob heavyweights than you're comfortable with. Reporting to a Staten Island social club, you get to see just what a farce mob loyalty is. There are groups of men standing in circles, each group talking about one of the other groups. It wasn't so unlike the offices you've worked in or the blue collar jobs you've worked, everybody trying to get their noses as far up the boss's ass as fast as possible. Your partner is much further along the road to being straightened out, the mob parlance for becoming inducted into La Cosa Nostra, but you've already figured out it isn't a smart move.

First off, you're not good at taking orders, and criminal organizations are set up like the military, where those on top expect their boots to be licked. So, the first time you meet a wiseguy you're supposed to know, but have never been formally introduced to, you neglect kissing him on the check and just nod hello.

You can tell by the look on his face he's upset, but you manage to duck out of there before a stink is made, except stinks are always made when it comes to these guys, because it's all they have in this life, the fantasy that they're somehow special. The problem is, if you want to be one of them someday, you'll have to lick their boots.

And it takes less than 24 hours before the insult is communicated to you.

"Hey, you can't ignore these guys," your partner tells you.

You nod, but you can't believe that level of petty horseshit.

Maybe it has to do with the other mob parlance you're taught. Made guys are considered somebody. You and everybody else are considered nobody. That shit doesn't fly with your more socialist zeitgeist. Your honeymoon to Europe where you were first introduced to Dutch social democracy still haunts your psyche, and one night you decide to skip a night at the Staten Island social club.

And that too isn't missed. The biggest shot there, a genuine big shot, gives you a stern warning the following week. "Remember where you belong," he tells you on your way out, and he wasn't smiling when he said it.

He's keeping track. He's got eyes and ears everywhere, and you quickly learn how he has that ability the day your partner gets knocked down a peg because somebody he's considered a close friend gave him up to the boss for complaining about having to find the big shot's car one night. The big shot was too drunk to remember where he parked it.

That's the other thing nobody told you, nor have Hollywood movies portrayed it well enough, how some mob jobs are as mundane as picking up laundry or driving a made guy's wife, daughter or grandkids someplace. And those are considered perks, because it means your nose is further up someone's ass than the next guy's nose. Being a piss boy is part of the game, make no mistake.

One day the guy who gave up your partner to the boss has a brilliant idea to rob one of your bookmaking customers because someone spotted a ton of cash in his dashboard. Because of the size of the bets he makes when he calls in as Boston for Leo, Leo being the runner who brought your office his action, you and your partner know he's putting in bets for more than one person. Is he connected too? Probably, but associates looking to get made some day are always looking to impress. The guy who gave up your partner is a special kind of parasite, so the game plan is to rob Boston for Leo when your partner and the guy who gave him up go to pay him the 15 grand owed him for winning bets the week before.

It goes down smooth, except Boston for Leo was indeed connected and there's going to be a sit down to settle the dispute. Fortunately for you, your partner is good at this shit, but on the drive to the Bronx, he tells you, "We may not come out of this."

Great, you're thinking. It wasn't your idea to follow the parasite play, and now you may get whacked for it.

You aren't whacked. Neither is your partner. Turns out both sides are playing for the same team, so the settlement is a score. The two wiseguys who handled the sit down get a piece, which leaves you and your partner's office nine grand ahead of the game.

You're impressed with the power of the big shots at the table and start rethinking your long term play. Maybe getting made isn't such a bad idea after all?

"Eejit!"

You'll probably have to whack somebody sooner or later, but in the meantime, if you play the game and stay close to the power, you'll have the green to maintain the lifestyle you and your kids have grown accustomed to. You send them on vacations with their mother when you don't take them yourself. You give them whatever they want, including tickets to concerts, baseball and football games. Remember, you're a great provider, even if you're a terrible parent. But it's all about image, right?

"Eejit!"

You're admonished a second time by the big shot, but it's for shoving someone you were supposed to know was around somebody else, a guy like yourself, but spoken for by another made guy. You told in no uncertain terms it can't happen again. Those are the rules.

"Understand?" a big shot says.

"Yeah. Sorry about that."

He holds a hard stare to see if you look away. You don't, so he gives your face a light love tap and smiles.

"I can't stand that piece of shit you shoved anyway," he says. "Just don't let it happen again."

And you, moron that you've become, fall for the good cop, or good big shot, routine. You actually feel proud that he likes you, except he probably doesn't like you anymore than he likes the guy you shoved or anybody else. It's how they draw you in and they know it. You're a source of income for them. You and a few hundred other suckers who get to consider themselves associates, what the FBI calls idiots like yourself, the morons who do the grunt work and send the coin up the ladder to the big shots.

"Eejit!"

There really are rules in this organization. Aside from having to be the occasional piss boy, you can't have a mustache, and there's no casual clothing when meeting certain people. No touching another connected guy without permission, although you've already broken that rule once, so there won't be a second chance unless you're a big enough earner, and there are always exceptions for big earners. You're not supposed to go near drugs, but that's bullshit nobody bothers to talk about anymore. You already qualify on the Italian lineage bullshit, but if you really want to go all the way, you'll need to be married again.

Marrying for the Mob ...

You take a legitimate job out of the city and wind up in an affair with your next boss, the future number three, another woman in need of a white knight. She's a size two and an attractive executive, but not really what you're looking for or need. You want to screw her, but you know that'll lead to something more. Yet the flirting game takes on a pace of its own and before you know it, she's dressing to kill at work, and you're commenting on it.

"You might wanna hide those legs," you tell her the day she wears a short cocktail dress to work. "It's not easy walking around here with wood."

"Wood?" she says.

You smile until she gets it.

The same weekend you have something to do at the office and she shows up in tight shorts and a midriff top. The two of you roll around on the floor until you hear someone come in and have to scramble to get your clothes back on. You wind up at a local motel screwing the rest of the afternoon until it's time to leave, but by then she thinks she's fallen in love and you can't wait to get out of there.

It becomes a lot tougher at work where persistence eventually pays off, and the two of you wind up in that motel a few more times. The affair isn't as exciting as the one you had with the German, and there are times it leaves you feeling like shit for plotting and planning a night or two a week to screw around. Eventually, after you've put in enough time to cover your kids on the cheap with COBRA coverage, you leave the company and she gets wind that she's about to go too, except for her it would be unwillingly.

She finds a job in the city and escapes being terminated, but now she's closer to where you live in Manhattan. The hotels aren't as cheap there, and it's a lot more risky you'll get caught. You and the German have divorced, but you're still fucking one another when the opportunities arise.

And then one afternoon while you're lying in a hotel bed together after the fact, the future number three says, "I don't want to crowd you. I understand what you do is illegal."

"What I do is pay the freight for three households," you tell her. "And I'm not looking to get married or have any more kids. I don't do enough with my own as it is."

You're sure she isn't somebody you want long term. She's cheated on her husband with you and there's a vanity and selfishness about her you have little use for. She's also too clingy too fast, but once you're divorced, you let her move in with you, and then you can't get rid of her.

She's into fashion. Jimmy Choo shoes, expensive clothes, and getting her hair and nails done once a week is her religion. She can't walk past a mirror without looking at herself. She's attractive, but nothing near what she wants to believe about herself. She's also way too insecure around other women, especially other attractive women. The upside is her insecurity leaves her self-esteem in the toilet, so you can get away with more than usual with her. And you, having become a complete piece of shit, never ignore those opportunities. She's the answer to your marriage requirements with the mob should you follow that path.

Because she's from the country, Manhattan is a new world. Everybody in your neighborhood knows you, and it impresses her way more than it should when they schmooze her at local restaurants. She falls for the glitz as much as she thinks she's fallen for you. Just a few months into the relationship, she tells you she loves you.

"That was fast," you say.

"I can't help it. I do."

"I think it's too new for you to feel that way."

"No, I know. Is there a chance you'll want to get married again?"

"I don't know. I doubt it. Let's just leave it the way it is for now."

She'll do whatever you want, but you need to set parameters she'll understand. First about your relationship with your kids and mother, and then about your relationship with your second wife, the German, someone you'll continue to have several affairs with over the course of your relationship with number three.

First on your parameter setting list is a tattoo with the German's name, and you won't remove or cover it up until the year you marry number three. Second is the affair with the German. Third through whatever number it is before she finally agrees to a divorce are all the other affairs and one-nighters you'll have, because it's the lifestyle you've chosen and you have no intentions of ever playing the fool again.

You get too comfortable being an asshole and start to gain weight. You've developed shin splints and can no longer run long distances. You've even taking up smoking since you've become a wannabe, smoking two to three packs of Camel regulars, no filters, each and every day. Your body weight climbs from 225 to 255, but number three doesn't seem to notice.

You do the right thing and take her to the Caribbean and Vegas and California, and on a couple of cruises, but when you notice how selfish she can be, especially with coin, you realize whatever happens with this one, it isn't going to last. An incident with a cocaine dealer seals her fate as an inevitable divorce. A guy you lent ten grand to for his purchase of a brick of cocaine has gone bad. He's using his own product and fucking up big time. More important, he's not paying what he owes. When you find him, you take his brick of cocaine, what's left of it, and you bring it home and store it in your safe. This is during the Rockefeller drug laws in New York and what's left of that brick could put you away for twenty to thirty years. Unfortunately for your bride to be, she says the magic words you'll never forget.

"Too bad you can't sell it."

"What?" you respond.

"Think of how much money that's worth."

Fuck that shit, you're thinking. *Better, fuck you, honey.*

She's just sealed her fate with you. She's way too liberal with your life. Instead of entertaining her idea for a life in prison, you negotiate a deal and get some of the money back for the cocaine. A few weeks later you have to find the dealer again. This time you fuck him up and he rats you out to the law. You spend another weekend in lock-up and that kind of shit is what the people you're around like, because you keep your mouth shut, which is a badge of honor to a phony code.

In fact, it earns you a possible step up, because a few days later, you're told to go on a search for someone who needs to be taken out. It's the day you realize it's all for real, this mob bullshit. If you and your partner find the guy before other crews do, you'll have to kill him, and it doesn't make a difference which one of you does the dirty work. If you're together, you'll each have something to hold over the other one's head for the day the law finally catches up to either one of you. You already know from reading the papers, something not nearly enough wannabes do, that someone always flips first. One of you will cut a deal, that much is certain. You've heard way too many wannabes talk shit about snitches, calling them rat bastards and everything else under the sun, but one of the things life on the streets has taught you, Little Jesus, is that the talkers are the first to flip.

Fortunately, the guy everyone is looking for turns up with his own wiseguy to defend him and the search is called off. The fact you were willing to go on the search, whether it was ever genuine or just another test, is irrelevant. You assume your nose is closer to where most noses in that world are comfortable, around a big shot's ass. Certainly closer to that ass than it was a year ago, so you decided you'll get married again after all.

Before you tell number three about getting married, you reset the ground rules and fly the Cuban to Las Vegas on a separate flight when you visit Sin City with your partner in crime, your mother, and your kids. It is two months before you're Little Italy wedding when number three finds out, because she checked and the Cuban wasn't at work the same week you were in Las Vegas.

"I figure you had to get it out of your system," she tells you after throwing a thick brush at your head.

"I don't know what you're talking about."

"Don't lie to me!" she yells.

"Don't yell at me!" you yell, and that calms her ass down. She too has seen your temper.

"Do you really want to get married?" she asks.

"Yeah," you say, "if you're not gonna go crazy on me again."

The wedding takes place in a small enough joint to keep it low key. Her family attendance is small in number, just four people, none of them care for you, but that's mutual. They sit at a table with your Mom and kids. The rest of the crowd is made up of other wannabes and special friends. The mob big shot sends an envelope, because you're not yet worthy of his attendance, but what was inside the envelope he left will be returned a hundredfold and both he and you know it.

Your honeymoon is down in Florida where you have to visit someone for the big shot anyway. A week in Miami is more than enough. There's more talent down there than your new bride can handle. She's not the featured show she's used to being. Her close friends aren't nearly as attractive as she is and you're pretty sure she wouldn't have it any other way. It's not that you do anything to make it worse, but she's no competition for the model crowd strutting around topless or wearing thongs.

You report to the Cuban at the Plaza Hotel a few times over the course of your third marriage, because you're still a piece of shit when it comes to being a husband. It is an insane game you know will end badly, but after living together for four years and cheating on her with your second wife, the marriage lasts almost another four years, during which you've called the Cuban a number of times. You even introduce the Cuban to your kids as a proof of their importance over wife number three. Your kids will always come first.

You hear that Thomas Rocco?

Your Little Jesus mind has become so warped that you believe disrespecting number three is how to show you love your kids more. It's fucked-up and you know it. Number three doesn't deserve your shit. Nobody does. It was your mistake marrying her.

There's a big mob bust one day, and it's already all over the news that a couple of big shots have become cooperating witnesses. It's obvious they've taken notice of the deals the government is willing to make. Trading off Sammy Gravano's admission to nineteen murders for testimony against John Gotti didn't go unnoticed. The walls are closing in on the mob, but you still feel safe. You're still on the fringe and the only shit they can really nail you for is loansharking and bookmaking. The combination can put you away for a good amount of time, but you're too stupid to realize what that would mean to your mother and kids.

You know you really couldn't handle prison, not with the amount of shit you'd have to put up with, not with all the lunatics and gangs you'd want nothing to do with. You decide to put an end to your partnership in bookmaking. Leaving your partner the bulk of customers proves more than enough to keep him happy and you out of a race toward self-destruction. You won't be a wiseguy, but you're not ready to part with the money yet either.

You start a bookmaking sheet with another friend with another team and although it's small at first compared to the coin you make with street loans, eventually you build the sheet enough to where it's respectful. You've been given a fifty sheet, meaning you're responsible for fifty percent of whatever the office pays out. Should your sheet be in the red for ten thousand and everybody on it dies, you owe five thousand. The upside is obvious. When your sheet is clean and your players lose ten thousand, five grand is yours.

You may be a piece of shit, Little Jesus, but you're earning more coin than Thomas Rocco ever did.

"You Eejit!"

Call you Ahab ...

There's nothing quite like hooking a whale, and one night you do it while watching an executive outside a sports bar making a phone call on a payphone. He's writing numbers on piece of paper and you've already figured out he's shopping lines to make his bets. You sidle up to him when he's back in the bar and mention what you just witnessed. His eyes are glued to a baseball game on a television set over the bar, but he's paying attention. You give him the number of your friend's office, tell him your name, and make sure you pick up his tab before you leave.

The next week that little bit of detective work earns you five grand from the 10 he lost with your friend's office. The week after that it's another four grand, so you take your wife back down to Puerto Rico where she can parade around in an orange thong that highlights her cherry ass while you can play craps again for the first time in a long while. The upside is the craps tables makes you question your sanity and you cash out after two bad rolls, down six bills, but when you get back to New York, at the end of that betting week, you'll be handed another sixteen thousand dollars, compliments of your white whale.

While the whale is losing, it's a score for you. Fifty percent goes south into your pocket. And when your whale loses, he doesn't fuck around. There are weeks you'll pick up in excess of twenty thousand dollars, and more than a few times. It's when he goes on a winning streak, and every loser does, that he'll have you on the hook for more than 60 grand because he's over 120 grand in the green, putting you and your sheet in the deep red. You're a nervous wreck the few weeks that follow, at least until he manages to go cold again and you're back to earning.

Life at home isn't going well. You're pretty sure number three has figured out she doesn't need you in her life and probably prefers somebody else. You never intended for her to be in your life for long, but since you no longer have to report to Staten Island and play that game anymore, the money you're earning is making you more comfortable staying home and trying to do what you always wanted to anyway.

You spend some extra time attempting to write plays and novels and short stories. The writing bug is still at work on what is left of your Little Jesus brain. Your writing is inspired mostly by what you see in the theatre, and when you're not hanging out with other wannabe mobsters, you're going to a lot of theatre—Broadway, Off-Broadway, and Off-Off-Broadway.

Things are going good for Little Jesus. You're living two lives and have enough spare cash to do what you want. As it turns out, whatever you do, you do well.

So fuck you, Thomas Rocco.

Suddenly you can hear St. Patrick whispering in your ear.

"Proud of yourself, are ya, Eejit?"

"A little, yeah."

"Because you're a moron."

"And you're a potato head."

"Stayed up all night thinking of that one, eh?"

"Fuck off."

"How 'bout I tie a rope around my neck, secure it to an anvil and remind you of the ponderous chair you bear. You've labored on it, ya Eejit. It's one heavy fuckin' piece of bling."

"Fuck off, I said."

And just like that, St. Patrick exits, and you're thinking you've made it. Reinforcements to your delusion come in the form of cash, and lots of it. The extra scores from your whale provide you with extra coin to put out on the street, but now even collecting easy money is taking time from what you really want to do. It's the first time you start to think about putting some scratch away for a rainy day. You can always find another word processing job, and if you've got some backup coin, maybe you can start to back out of the street life you're no longer enamored with. You're pretty sure once you let number three know you want to retire from the street she'll want to retire from you.

Could that be a way out?

Maybe, but you're still too needy to attempt life solo. You derive little to no inspiration from number three and you doubt she's still enamored with you. She's become a lot less appealing because of the respect you've lost for her since her comment about the brick of cocaine. She's probably sick of you and your routine as well. Her greed and desires versus your lack of her greed and desires isn't a good match. She's a material girl and it's a giant turnoff, there's no working around it anymore. Aside from the total scumbag you've become, you're still a romantic at heart. You miss the German, but that bridge was burned when you made her too miserable to risk loving you again.

You screw one of the bartenders where you hang out and it's not a smart move. The day you and number two walk into the same bar one night, while you're talking with another loanshark about business, the bartender goes to your wife and whispers something in her ear. You can't see if you wife is smiling or if she's about to throw up, but you're completely paranoid the rest of the night. You don't dare ask your wife anything, nor do you ask the bartender. It was a one night stand and you never tried for it to be anything else.

Was she pissed off? Did she say something to number two? Do you always shit where you eat?

"Eejit!"

The next week your whale loses more than he can afford. It's his and your last big score. Close to thirty grand and you're gonna have to make him cough up at least fifteen or it's coming out of your pocket. He shows up with eight thousand and admits he's tapped.

"In other words you're fucking me," you say.

"Hey, I've got a problem," he tells you.

You want to smack him, but you know that's not the route to go, not yet. You've given the prick every opportunity to stop losing his life's savings, coaching him from time to time about gambling and the coin he was dropping. You even stopped his action once because you knew nobody could sustain the rate of loss he was taking, betting five to ten grand a night during the week and ten to fifteen grand on weekends. You even gave him a fifteen percent discount on your end of his action, but he did have a gambling problem he had no intention of addressing, except now it's your problem.

The bookie you're with likes you enough to give you an extra week to fork over the total. You give him ten, two out of your pocket you'll get back when and if your whale pays his end. He still owes you a ton of cash, and you can swing his balance with your guy the following week, but it pisses you off because your whale was showing all the signs of running out of cash the few weeks before he went bust, slow paying on amounts he usually had, or paying just enough to cover your end with the office, and owing you the rest.

His bill on your end is close to twenty-five grand. You meet him along the Southern State Parkway two nights before he's supposed to pay off the remaining seven, five of which you'll pass to the office to cover your end. Your youngest son is with you. He's learning the ropes about people, not the business, because he's not half as dumb as you are, nor will you ever allow him to be.

"I have it," the whale tells you, "but I won't have the rest for a while."

"How long's that?"

"A month or two."

"That's forever and you know it."

"I have to maneuver some money. Can't you make it a loan?"

"Yeah, right. That'll get you killed. I don't lend that much coin to anybody, never mind a degenerate gambler. If I made it point money, you'd owe me a buck-fifty a week, which is what you'd pay for a year before you couldn't pay that anymore, and you'd still owe me fifteen grand or so. That's crazy. I'll do this for you, though. I'll squash the fifteen down to ten, but you pay five a month until we're square. That should be enough fucking incentive to stay off the phones, but if it's not, if I find out you're betting with another office, betting at all, including the fucking scratch-offs, I'll forget I squashed anything and sell off the loan to somebody who'll take a fucking hammer to your face. I'll take fifty cents on the dollar and sell it overnight. You wanna go that route, be an asshole and keep betting."

"I can do that, what you said."

"Five hundred a month until it's paid off. No juice, but no missing either."

"I can do that."

"Okay."

"I appreciate it. Thanks."

You shake hands and say, "Do yourself a favor. What I told you a dozen fucking times already, before and after I cut you off. Get yourself help. You got a nice family. You don't need this shit and neither do they."

He nods, gets back into his Cadillac, and pulls away.

You return to your car and look at your son.

"What?" he says.

"You ever get involved in this shit, betting or taking bets, I'll break your face."

"I won't."

"Good."

"He pay you?"

"Yeah and no and yeah, but it's too depressing to explain. Let's just say I'm going to hell if there is one."

He smiles and says, "And if there isn't a hell?"

You shrug and say, "There should be."

Almost Dead ...

A big loan you went partners on a year or so ago starts to turn sour, but it's your responsibility to collect what's owed. The borrowers are two pieces of shit scamming any number of people in the garment district. Each has his own vice. The guy who funded them in the first place, unbeknownst to you, was a wiseguy with another team. The two pieces of shit owe the wiseguy 100 grand, their startup cash. They owe their suppliers another 20 grand. They also owe some friends and other investors, but you're not sure what those amounts are. All you and your partner know is there's a 50 grand bill owed to you two.

The other thing you know is that one of the two borrowers took the money from your apartment, so as far as you're concerned, he's the one who borrowed the money.

Like most con artist pieces of shit, they pay back less than half of what they owe before they run into trouble they can't avoid. One of the two is an inveterate gambler who prefers to lose your money at the blackjack tables at the Sands in Atlantic City. The other is your basic piece of shit who enjoys the high life, maybe some cocaine too, you're not sure. The problem for the basic piece of shit is that he's the one who took the money.

He calls you on the day of number three's birthday, and because he knows you're heading to Atlantic City to celebrate, he brings a leather jacket to your apartment for your wife. You take the jacket from him and throw it on the floor.

"You fucking serious?" you say.

"What?" he says. "That's a two thousand dollar jacket."

"You have the five grand you owe tonight?"

"I have some of it."

"How much is some? And don't think about adding that fucking jacket to the total."

"I have fifteen hundred."

"That's thirty-five short. Where's the rest?"

He goes about ratting out his partner, who he gives up rather than catch a beating, because he knows the kind of money still owed is worth a few beatings.

"He's in Atlantic City," the piece of shit says. "He has a gambling problem."

"No, you have a gambling problem," you say, reminding him how he was the one who picked up the money.

"I know, I know, but he's down there gambling. You might be able to get some of it back before he loses it all."

You take the piece of shit with you down to Atlantic City and you both go and find the other asshole at a $100 dollar minimum blackjack table. You almost pull him off his stool before he agrees to go to a bar in the Sands to talk it over.

Soon as he's sitting down, you put out your hand. He reaches into his jacket pocket and tries to feel which casino chips he's going to pull out. He comes up with three black and two purples, a total of seventeen hundred dollars. You make him empty his pockets, all of them, and find another four grand in purple five-hundred dollar chips.

"That's more than what we owe tonight," he has the balls to say.

"You want, I'll take your teeth too," you say. "How's that work for you?"

When you get back to your room, you call your partner and give him the bad news. He's glad you caught them, but he also knows the rest will be a big pain in the ass to collect. He does what you hate and reaches out to the big shot he's under, and within two days, you and your partner learn the real story. The wiseguy the two assholes owe the cost of their start-up cash was just put away for life and they thought they could pull it off again.

"Where'd they get the balls to even try this?" your partner says.

You shrug and say, "So, what happens now?"

"We squeeze them," he says. "Whatever it takes. We can't go back to their people or they'll tell us to get in line, but they can't go there either. We squeeze them."

Two days later it's you and your partner up to their offices in the garment district, but when you get there, so is a representative of a the other crime team. This cluster fuck is about as bad as it gets.

The piece of shit who picked up the money takes you on the side and says they have a truck on Staten Island loaded with goods worth a lot more than what they owe.

"You want to go check it out?"

You tell your partner what he said and your partner walks you outside the office.

"You're not going anywhere. He reached out to somebody and they're waiting at that truck. They clip you and get half of what he told them he owes and that's the end of that."

Whether it's true or not, it's your come to the *real Jesus* moment. You made a big mistake trying to reach too far and now you'll have to cut your losses, or at least come close enough not to do something more stupid than you've already done.

You follow your partner back into the office and he tells all three they'll be hearing from us by the end of the day. Like magic, because he made the right phone call, two days later the balance of what you and your partner were owed appears with the piece of shit at the bar you hang out at.

"He didn't have to threaten me," the piece of shit tells you.

"You mean he didn't have to warn you," you say. "Now get the fuck out of here and never let me see you again."

Your money secure, you decide you should give your partner a bigger cut because of the information he brought before you got yourself killed. You also know it's time to start thinking about an exit plan from this life because eventually everybody runs out of luck, and you're no exception.

When you return home and discuss your thoughts about leaving the business, number three wonders why?

"Because I was almost dead," you tell her.

"Oh," she says, but you can tell she's more disappointed in your frame of mind than upset you might've been whacked.

That night you can't even sleep alongside her and choose the couch instead.

White hat, Red hat ...

Not long before the end of your marriage to number three you take a temp job with an uptown Manhattan advertising company. Day two the supervisor of their department quits and you're asked to take over his slot. You have the experience and you're fast and efficient. The owner there is decent when you first start, but the honeymoon is quickly over once you get them out of the six week jam they were in.

During that time, however, you're taken to lunch by the office manager, a woman a few years older than you, still attractive, and a recovering alcoholic. Turns out she needed to vent to someone and you having the virgin ears to her story, were picked. She tells you about her affair with the owner the firm is named after, and how it had cost him his first marriage. She was still with him because he'd remarried and his new wife didn't know anything about her.

"You still with him?" you figure you'll ask since she's been so open.

"Once in a while," she says. "Let's just say I do him favors."

Is she giving you boundaries, showing her clout off, or just looking for someone steady? You hope it's not the latter, because you have zero interest in bedding alcoholics. You've been with one once and it was more than enough to never want to try that shit again. It was a one-night pick-up from a bar you frequented, but you didn't count on her lack of discretion. When a friendly bartender told you what the drunk told her, you assumed, correctly, it was the booze talking. Fortunately, for you, the drunk had a steady guy paying her freight so you told her to keep her trap shut about the one night shit fuck you both shared or her boyfriend with the cash would catch the beating, since you wouldn't hit a woman, drunk or otherwise.

The office manager is seriously big-chested, but all you can picture is her slurring her words and falling all over herself.

She spends the rest of lunch telling you her version of the office gossip, but she warns you about their boss, the guy she does favors for.

"He can be really mean sometimes," she said. "He likes being boss. He's fired a lot of people."

"If I'm supposed to be afraid, that won't do it," you say. "I'll do my job, but no more or less."

"Okay, cool," she says. "Just thought I'd let you know."

She insists on paying for lunch, but you've never been comfortable with that. You let her because she seems too determined and you don't want to piss her off. On the way back to the office, she grabs your hand at a light before crossing the street. You look at her and she smiles. She lets go before you reach the other side, but you're not sure what that was about.

She's a nice enough person, but that holding hands bit was discomforting.

You do the work they want, plus some more. Instead of 8 hour days, you pull as many as 16 hours, including weekends. You're a superstar to this firm, at least while you can help them, but you have a habit of reading during your downtime, including when you're on the throne in the men's room. Reading while taking a dump is something the owner doesn't like. One day he sees you exiting the men's room with a book in your hand and he says, "Have a good read?"

"Yeah, it's a good book," you say, completely naive he's pissed off.

The next day you have a new supervisor, a woman there you don't like very much. Nor does she like you. She's a schemer and sneak and a few days later one of your operators spots her hiding alongside a wall listening to your conversation. He tells you and you step outside the office and say, "If you want to hear what I'm saying come inside."

She huffs and heads for the owner's office.

The next day he calls you into his office to thank you for everything you've done, but he thinks it's time to end the relationship. He offers you a three thousand dollar bonus, but you turn it down.

Why do you turn it down?

Because you, little Jesus, have principal, except you also know you're going to screw with this owner one way or the other once you're gone. You ask him for your last check and he writes it out for you. You make a point of leaving the office key with the supervisor and that's the end of your employment there.

Two weeks later, you and your partner return. It's a Saturday night in the middle of a heat wave. The game plan is simple. You use one of your loan customers for transportation. Your partner has a friend come along as well. The driver will park outside the office and wait while you and your partner, wearing business suits, go in and rob the place of all its computer equipment. You'll take the stuff back down on a dolly and put it in the trunk of the Town Car as if you're both a couple of guys moving office equipment.

Your partner's friend will be stationed on the corner with two hats. One white, the other red. If he's wearing red, it means there's a squad car in the immediate area. If he's wearing white, it means the coast is clear.

By the time you get downstairs with the equipment, both you and your partner are pouring sweat. There's no air conditioning. You drop a screw driver and when you go to pick it up your pants split because they're clinging to you. To make things worse, it's a red hat you see your partner's friend wearing. Five minutes pass, but those few minutes feel like an hour. When the red hat is finally switched to white, you and your partner are out of there with the dolly and loading the trunk of the Town Car. Half an hour later, you're all four celebrating in Little Italy.

The computers are gifts to friends and relatives. Your driver gets a free month off his loan payments, because the feeling of victory is something you want to share. It's a euphoric feeling to trump an arrogant fuck like the guy who fired you. It was a Robin Hood moment, the one you like to convince yourself is what mobsters and their associates do to justify their criminality, take from the rich and give to the poor. It is pure and absolute bullshit and you know it, but fucking over that jerk-off owner at the advertising company makes it easy to ignore the truth.

When you get home you find the bedroom door is locked. There's a note taped to the refrigerator that reads: Go sleep at your girlfriend's place.

You don't even bother trying to explain and fall asleep on the couch.

In the morning she's pissed off, but calls in sick, something she never does. You decide to tell her what you did. You show her two of the computers.

"Can't they get a warrant for them?"

"Not without probable cause."

"I don't think you should keep them here."

"I'll get rid of them today. There's a guy around the corner said he wanted to get one for his daughter. I told him to hold off. I'll give him one."

"Can I take the other one?"

"Sure. Better now?"

"I guess."

"If we woke you up last night, it's because we were celebrating. It wasn't because we got laid."

"I know. I'm sorry."

"You going to work now?"

"No, I called in."

"Want to do something?"

"Okay."

"Can we start in the sack?"

"Of course."

Half an hour later, you're sleepy from sex, but you know you better do the right thing here. She took off from work and you need to be a decent human being, even if only for a few hours. What you do is take her for lunch at her favorite restaurant and during the walk back to the apartment, you pass a pet store and she falls in love with one of the dogs in the window. You take her inside, get her to hold the puppy and whip out the eleven hundred in cash it costs.

You'd intended to stop at a jewelry store, but the puppy was a ten thousand times better idea. It suggests you're going to stay together and maybe start a family of your own.

There really is no bottom to the depth of your deception when it comes to fucking with this woman's head, except the dog does form a better bond between you and number three, and you once again agree to her plea to have another child.

"Because I'll be alone once you're gone," she says. "You'll always have your kids, but I won't have anybody."

It's a prescient point she makes. How do you get around that? You ask her to give you another day to think it over and by morning you're back to selfish regarding bringing another kid into the world. It is simple math and it all has to do with the way you felt once you learned your stepmother was pregnant. You're not the greatest parent in the world, not even close, but there's no way you're putting your kids through that shit. Not in this life.

The next week the police summon you to a precinct near where you used to work. Your partner drives you there with a few of the computers in the trunk of his car. You speak to a detective in his office and he tries to scare you about special federal files that were on one of the hard drives you took. He mentions the FBI and you smile.

"Hey, I played cards all Saturday night," you tell him. "I never left Little Italy."

The cop smiles back, because he knows you're full of shit, but there's nothing he can do about it. Back in your partner's car, you tell him about the interrogation and he laughs. Later the same night the two of you celebrate over dinner at the *Grotto Azzurra* a block from where you live. You share antipasto and two orders of sautéed octopus with a side of rigatoni. You drink wine and hit a bar around the corner until it closes.

When you get home, the new member of the family is snuggled in your bed with number three, but he's happy you're home and proceeds to take a leak on your pillow. You can't help but laugh. You change the pillow case and flip it over to lay your head against. She's named the pup Keith because she's a Rolling Stones fan. You and Keith get along great, because underneath the psychotic you are, you're still a big softy.

In the morning you've discovered Keith has left another deposit on the bed, but this one stinks and it's wet. Number three calls in sick again to take care of Keith. You shower and get out of there with a bullshit story about doing a friend a favor, but where you go is to Brooklyn to visit your mother and vent about the latest mistake you've made.

"Why the hell'd you get a dog?" she says. "What are you crazy?"

"I know, I know. I love the thing too, but now she's gonna get all attached again. I think she was ready to bolt on me a couple of weeks ago."

"Moron."

"Yeah, I am."

"I warned you about her, Sonny. She's not good for you."

"I know."

"If you don't love her, get out of there. It's not fair to her either."

"I know."

"You know, you know, and you're still there, you stupid ass. And then you buy her a dog."

"Okay, *consiglieri*, I get it. Relax now, will you?"

"Hey, I'm trying to help here. Go shit in your hat."

On the drive back to the city, you're feeling guilty about everything, including buying the dog you've fallen in love with, but a thought pops into your head. Maybe, when you're ready to leave number three, at least she won't be alone.

The problem, of course, is you'll have to leave the dog, too.

Way to go, Little Jesus. You really are an Eejit.

PART IV

Blessed are the poor in spirit,
for theirs is the Kingdom of Heaven.
Matthew 5:3–12

Death of a Salesman (Part Deux) ...

Thomas Rocco dies six months before the end of your third marriage. You show up to the funeral parlor two hours before a private viewing for Gang Bang and your cousins. You kiss his cold forehead and leave, then cry in the car for a few minutes before your anger and rage take over and you punch the dashboard, hating yourself for giving a flying fuck.

He'd been sick for just over a year, the lung cancer discovered from x-rays taken after a car accident. He used to come to Little Italy to visit every few months with two to three weeks of the 20-25 weeks of money he owed your mother, the alimony you'd been covering for years. One visit, after lighting one of his Marlboros, he spit up blood into a handkerchief and you said, "Are you kidding me?"

"What?"

"You're bleeding."

"Go fuck yourself."

"Fine. You're probably dying from those cigarettes."

"The hell do you know?"

"Nothing. Want a few tissues for the ride home?"

He was pulling a macho routine, but you had to wonder if he was scared. Coughing up blood? Who wouldn't be?

A few months later you get the call, except number three answered the phone. When she was finished with the call, she said, "That was your father's wife. He's very sick."

"Yeah, and?"

"She thinks you should go see him. He doesn't have long."

You frown. You want to play the same macho game and wave her off, but you don't. You ask her if she'll take a ride with you.

"Of course," she says.

And you have to feel like shit all over again, because no matter how big a piece of shit you've been to her, she's been there for you.

You go there the next morning and he's barely able to speak. The cancer has spread and he's in and out of consciousness. He does manage to say something stupid, this time about his niece's husband and how he left her and took all their money, but it pisses you off.

In the car on the way home, you mention what he said about his niece's husband and how he'd done the same thing to your mother. Then you cry, because no matter how much you want to hate the son-of-a-bitch, he's your father.

The rest of the summer goes along pretty smooth, but closer to the holidays you overhear number three talking with her best friend, someone you hate, and she mentions so-and-so is gorgeous, and your defense mechanisms regarding relationships kicks in big time.

You call the Cuban.

You screw the Cuban.

You have an affair with a neighbor living in the same building. She's Chinese and married to a clueless American millionaire. She's kinky and likes the kind of sex that doesn't do it for you. You end it after a month of screwing in her apartment and quickly become friends with someone close to number three. It's a friendship you use to find out what number three is up to, but all you learn is she's being pursued by a guy with a reputation for screwing around.

"She going for it?" you ask.

"I don't think so, but she's enjoying the attention."

You remember the attention you gave her when you initially met her, attention that quickly turned into an affair. It's all you need to know. You've seen it with other women, how attention leads to the next step, an affair. It's also the perfect opportunity for both of you to get out of a marriage that has died.

Just like getting involved with mobsters, marrying for them was a bad idea.

A few weeks after you dump the friend of number three, you're confronted with an accusation. You assume the friend talked, but you're wrong. On the other hand, it seems as though number three is weighing her options.

"I want something from this marriage and you're not giving it to me."

"You feel that way, you should take off. You're still young enough. You don't need me to have a kid. You're an executive. You make more than enough money."

"That's a horrible thing to say to me."

"Neither one of us is getting what we want, right?"

"What's that mean?"

"How's the gorgeous guy at your office doing?"

"What?" she says, but she's blushing, the telltale sign you were looking for.

"You fuck him at work or a hotel someplace."

Her face is still red. "I'm not fucking anyone. What's this about?"

"Don't worry," you tell her, "it's not like I give a fuck."

She's burning now, but she has to measure what she says and she knows it. If she confesses, you're gone. If she tries to deny it, you'll continue to fuck around and she knows it. You've made it a no-win situation for her.

"Cat got your tongue?" you say.

She's a smart cookie and she manages to keep from saying anything. You follow her lead and keep quiet, but the staring gets intense. Finally, you see the tears in her eyes and then it comes.

"What the hell was I supposed to do?" she says. "You made a fool of me."

"What's his name?"

"I don't love him."

"What's his name?"

"It's not his fault."

"What's his fuckin' name?"

Now she's full blown crying as she clutches a couch pillow to her face. You give it another few seconds and leave.

She's still crying when you come home later and instead of telling you to fuck off, which even you know is what she should do, she apologizes.

"Not interested," you say. "Don't get me wrong. Part of me wants to break him in half, but that'd be playing into your hands. That isn't going to happen unless I feel it has to happen."

"I don't love him."

"Bullshit. You'll change that story soon as you're together, and that's fair enough. You're a clinger. You'll cling to him first chance you get. It's your pattern. Truth is, it's good timing. I need to get off the street. It's getting dangerous. The law is making deals with everybody they pinch. Deals nobody in their right mind could walk away from."

"Are you in trouble?" she asks.

"Not yet. Not that I know of."

"Maybe we can move."

"What?"

"Away from here, Little Italy."

"Why?"

"To get away from this. You said you want out of that life with the mob, right?"

"I'm not in the mob. I'm a schmuck on the fringes."

"But you want out, you said."

"Yeah, I do. And then what? How do I make money? You going to adjust to my income without the street? I'll be earning a word processing salary. That's a huge hit I'll be taking."

She doesn't even pause. "You can work two jobs."

You've also wanted to write again, but you don't even bother bringing that up. Her answer was all you needed.

This time instead of calling the Cuban, you take a midnight word processing job at a downtown law firm and your world changes once again, this time, finally, for the better.

The Kids aren't kids anymore ...

No they're not, and they're all doing fine with little thanks to you, Little Jesus. They've got minds of their own, jobs of their own, and lives of their own. They need neither your room and board, nor your counsel, nor your money or temper tantrums. Somehow they still love you, but you'll never be sure if it's from the obligatory guilt we're all born with for our parents, like yours for Thomas Rocco, or because even you deserve some form of kindness.

It is the result of your greatest fuck-up, leaving the kids wondering why you couldn't be a better father. It is a large part of the chain you'll want to hang yourself with, the same ponderous chain that continues to grow day-by-day.

Issues come up from time to time, silly shit that pits your stubbornness against your kids, and they quickly become classic versions of you tilting at windmills. A full year will pass with you not speaking to your daughter over a stupid meatball dispute. A discussion over confession will send one of your sons running for cover because you can't let an argument go and have to provide researched documentation over and over and over again to prove a point.

You eventually learn to ignore the windmills, but it takes you long enough.

Maybe too long.

When grandchildren are introduced almost 20 years down the road, you're humbled by the parents both your sons are. There is no way their kids will ever doubt their fathers' love. Neither will throw cash on the table and disappear for days at a time for selfish pursuits, and they will both be as much a partner in their marriages as they are devoted fathers. They set the example you were supposed to set. All three of your kids will bust your buttons with pride while you suffer the guilt you so much deserve for being so off the mark in so many parental instances.

Somehow they find it in their hearts to look beyond your shortcomings, at least you hope they do, and they are there for you when you regain some of the humanity you left at the altar of crime.

Once again your luck hasn't run out.

Reflections on reflections ...

Once you leave a criminal income behind, you'll be just another schnook. You won't be telling word processing supervisors to go fuck themselves the way you once did at Bear Stearns because a supervisor there wouldn't give you the Super Bowl night off. You can't rob employers because they might be arrogant pieces of shit. You can't walk off one job, not without another job already lined up. Where you're luckier than most is the fact you can always cover the gaps in your resume by temping as a word processor.

How? You worked as a temp for a few weeks or months at a time and could always stretch those jobs on a resume to years.

The bottom line is you're just another nobody with less options than you care to think about, but it's the thinking about it you can't stop.

The other thing starting to depress you is a weight gain that was inevitable. For a long time you kept in shape by running. You've run five miles without much effort. You've even run 12 miles on a dare, from Brooklyn to Manhattan before the start of window cleaning work one morning. The problem is you've developed shin splints and running is no longer an option, not at the weight you quickly put on. You've never stopped weightlifting, but now that's just an excuse to eat more. You can lift a lot of weight, but you've gained a lot of weight. The incline was steep and fast.

215, 225, 250, 265, 275, 290, 300, 310, and so on.

And when you look at yourself in a mirror, you can't believe what's happened. It probably doesn't help that St. Patrick is around to comment on it either.

"Way to go, Dago. You'll need a mirror to see your feet and another to find the wee Johnson, you keep it up."

So there you are, a 325 pound whale of a man with a future working for lawyers for about two hundred grand, tax free, a year less than what you were making as a criminal. Eating at The Palm will require scrounging some leftover coin. The occasional cruise will be out of the question. The extra coin for your daughter's wedding in a few years will be out of the question. The extra coin for all the extras you've spoiled yourself and everyone around you with will be out of the question.

Last but not least, the lifestyle number three has grown accustomed to will be out of the question.

The thought of a big sleep isn't as pronounced as it was when you had the flu, but you certainly believe in the option. It's not like anybody really needs you around anymore anyway. They're all self-sufficient, can read and write, they all have jobs and you still carry a hefty life insurance policy.

Buon giorno, Principessa!

Before you even think to take the easy way out, the lightning bolt strikes.

The first time you see her, it's at work. She's wearing glasses while studying for a test during downtime. You say, "Excuse me," to introduce yourself, and when she looks up from her book, you fall in love.

Later the same night, you follow her down to the lobby during a break and walk her to an all-night delicatessen. On the way, you say, "Your freckles, they're beautiful."

"Please, I hate them," she says.

"Why? I love freckles. Yours are gorgeous."

She rubs her arms with both hands. "I wish I could scratch them off."

"That would be a tragedy," you say. "I mean it, Ann. They're beautiful. And your eyes."

Her eyebrows furrow again, but this time the smile shows more suspicion than joy.

You say, "Don't get me wrong, I'm definitely trying to make some ground here, but that wasn't a line. I think you're beautiful."

"Thank you," she says, "but you're making me a little uncomfortable."

Over the next few weeks you're a persistent motherfucker and you get to know each other a little more each night you work together. You learn she's the sister of the woman you've helped, the one the young elitist wannabes in the department wanted fired. She thanks you for helping her sister more than a few times and you learn she's the next to the youngest of six kids, two boys and four girls. Her father was Italian, her mother Irish. She attended Catholic schools in Bay Ridge until earning a scholarship to NYU. She's been married twice and has a child from each husband. Her oldest is eighteen, her youngest ten. She's uncomfortable with her big chest and wishes it was smaller. That fact becomes clear the day she catches you looking at her cleavage.

"It's hard not to notice," you tell her.

"And it isn't polite to stare," she says.

"Maybe if we get it out of the way."

"Excuse me?"

You motion at her chest, shake your head and say, "What a rack."

Her eyes open wide and you're not sure if she's shocked or disgusted or both.

"Now it's out of the way," you say.

She can't suppress the smile she's fighting.

When you ask about her husband, you also mention you've been asking about her at work and have learned it's an unhappy marriage.

"You really listen to that gossip up there?"

"Only what I want to hear."

She tells you about the mess she's dealing with at home, a husband who won't work while claiming he'll commit suicide if she leaves him. You offer to get her a gun to see if her husband is serious, but it makes her nervous when she sees you aren't kidding.

"Sorry," you say. "What about school? What degree?"

"Science," she says, then explains how her pursuit of her degree has everything to do with her escape from the bad marriage. This one isn't looking to be saved.

"I blew my degree off while I had a scholarship to NYU," she tells you. "I was pre-med and it didn't cost me a dime, but then I got pregnant and lost the baby. I was devastated and wanted another one right away. Here I am twenty years later with two kids and I'm still chasing the degree."

You tell her your story, leaving off the criminal part for another night when you have more time, maybe over dinner, you suggest.

"Is this a date you're proposing?"

"Dinner it is," you say.

You take her to The Palm to impress her, one of your last few visits there, but you'll learn soon enough this woman doesn't need The Palm or any other form of glitz. She's interested in the hints you've dropped about yourself. You're committed to confessing, but not everything. You tell her about your kids, the dysfunctional family you come from, your prior marriages, a few of the affairs you've had, and that you're at the end of another marriage. The obvious look of concern registers on her face, but then you tell her the novels you've tried to write and those you're still playing with.

It is then she's impressed.

"So why don't you write?" she says, excited at the prospect. "My God, why wouldn't you? Can you get away from the other stuff?"

"Absolutely. I'm not a gangster. Any desire I had for that went out the window a long time ago. And walking away from my business, what I can't sell off, they'll be more than happy to take over. The problem is money. I haven't lived off a legitimate income in forever. I haven't even tried. The legitimate jobs, the word processing, is for health insurance for me and the kids."

"Well, if it's money, then you are crazy. You can always make money."

"I don't think you understand the kind of money I'm talking about. I take care of three households now. My old man went broke on my mother ten years before he croaked. I pay her way too."

"Then you scale back and make it work," she says. "And I'd love to read something of yours, if you don't mind. I really would."

That night, because you can't sleep, you start a crime novel about a word processor in a bad marriage leading a double life. It will eventually land you an agent and a publisher, but it only comes to fruition in your attempt to impress this woman you can't believe stepped into your life at exactly the right time.

The next weekend, after you and number three see the Roberto Benigni movie, *La vita è bella*, so does Ann Marie, except she sees it alone because her husband hates the movies, especially ones with subtitles.

At work her eyes fill with tears as she tells you how much she loved the movie. You also loved it, but number three was unimpressed, confirming your belief that she was all show and no soul, and that the two of you never really belonged together.

The next night when you see Ann Marie in the lobby at work, you shout, *"Buon giorno, Principessa!"* Her smile lets you know she's yours. In the elevator you tell her, "You don't have to say anything now, but I'm in love with you."

Meeting Ann Marie proved to be the luckiest break in your life, and you will continue to say your personal prayer in attempts to protect her from the bad you're sure you're still owed for having been such a shit and so guilty, yet so lucky, all your life.

The other thing you'll do every morning is send her an email, the subject line of which will read: *Buon giorno, Principessa!*

Big Charlie ...

A few nights later you hear Ann Marie curse from frustration dealing with an attorney over the phone and you say, "Tish, you spoke French." The Addams Family nostalgia sets her laughing hysterically and you can hear that laugh in your head through the night and well into your dreams.

So does St. Patrick hear it and he's there to give you the business.

"Took you long enough, Dago."

"I have to make a move."

"Yeah, no shit?"

"I hate what I've become."

"You should."

"But this is new. She's different. She can straighten me out. I mean, I want to straighten out, especially for her."

"About time, knuckle-dragger."

"Huh?"

"Nothing. Just keep moving forward. There's a chance for you yet."

The next night at work you send her an email. "Listen, I don't like to dick around, so I'm telling you now, we're going to wind up together. I know I'm not much to look at anymore, but I'm still a charming MFer when I want to be, and I've already written fifty pages to a novel I want you to read, but only if you agree to let me take you to dinner again."

You can hear her laughing from across the room. So does everybody else, but it takes her a few minutes before she can compose herself and send you a reply: "Okay, you drive a hard bargain, but I want you to bring what you wrote or I won't go."

At that dinner you confess about your criminal life. You tell her about the guy who still owes you money and that you'll have to hang on to that one, the whale, for what he still owes, especially if you're breaking clean. In the meantime you have to pick up a few envelopes before you drop her off at her car downtown.

"What envelopes?" she asks.

"Money," you say. "Guys owe me leave it in envelopes at a few bars in Murray Hill. I grease the bartenders there so I don't have to run all over the place."

"You what?"

"You'll see."

She waits in the car while you stop at several bars, run in, drop a ten or twenty on the bar, and then walk out with anywhere from three to six envelopes, all of them marked: Big Charlie.

By the last stop, when you come out of the bar carrying five envelopes, you notice she's slinking down in her car seat. You laugh when you get in the car. She is stunned by the entire process. You drive her downtown to where she's parked her car, trying to explain the ins and outs of your illegal life on the way.

"I can't believe this stuff goes on like that," she says.

"You sure you're not from Kansas?" you say.

"I'm shocked. Really. Do all bars do that?"

"Maybe not all, but most. There's another Charlie collects from the same bars for a different guy, that's why they write Big Charlie for me. It's got nothing to do with me being a big shot and everything to do with my size. This is nickels and dimes compared to the other Charlie. He's a made guy."

She's shaking her head.

"I do want you to see what I'm dealing with, though. The money I'm giving up."

"How much?"

"Unless they shorted me, there's about fifteen hundred in these envelopes. That's the street money end and I'm two envelopes short, another couple hundred. Bookmaking, that's another enchilada. Settle-up day is Thursdays for gambling. Long story short, I average about two hundred grand plus, tax free, over the course of a year. That's without a score or two that might come along."

"A score?"

You wave her question off. "It's irrelevant now."

"My God, that's still so much money. And you're doing this how long?"

"Don't get me wrong, because I'm not rich. Like most assholes on the street, I lived too fast a life. I did my share of gambling in the past. Craps tables mostly, before my second wife helped to cure me. Bookmaking did the rest. Gambling is a sucker's game. That said, I have street expenses too, besides places like The Palm and so on. I've never taken money serious. Truth is, I've never seen it do much good, outside of it being fuck-off money, but I've gotten more than used to it the last dozen years."

You hold the envelopes up. "It won't be easy going from this to a word processing check."

Ann Marie shakes her head. "This has to be dangerous, what you do. The people you deal with, they really are the Mob, aren't they?"

You smile and say, "When you lived in Bay Ridge, you ever come out of your house?"

This time she's not smiling. She's concerned, angry almost. "I'm serious," she says. "You have to give this up. How could anyone let you do this? Your wife, I mean."

"My second wife wanted me to walk, even after we split up. I fucked that marriage up. This one, she's more into the perks. She already told me I'd have to work two jobs to make up the scratch. That was the last straw for me, whether I walked into you or not."

"You really giving this up?"

"Everything."

"And you'll write?"

You reach under the front seat and pull out the fifty pages you've typed. "Only if you'll read."

When you finally drop her off, you exchange your first kiss and neither of you want to let the other go.

It takes another month, but eventually she asks her husband to move out. You leave number three and the new relationship is consummated on her fortieth birthday at a Sheraton hotel in New Jersey, where she not only proves she isn't into glitz, by not knowing anything about the brand of watch you bought her, a Rolex, she also proves it's all about the heart, because she cried like a baby when you remembered she'd once mentioned she loves strawberries. You brought a bunch for her. You set them at the base of two Waterford champagne flutes and a bottle of Dom Perignon, a champagne she called you crazy for buying because you probably could've bought a case of the Korbel she drinks instead. Cheap champagne is her favorite drink.

The two of you divorce your spouses and are married within a year. The wedding takes place under a beach gazebo in the Bahamas and she couldn't look more beautiful, except she will, she always will. You've lost 85 pounds to be presentable and although it's just you two and the Bahamian Justice of the Peace presiding, along with two witnesses you grabbed at the bar, it's the best wedding either of you ever experienced.

Pictures are taken and you are provided with your own special wedding cake. The photographer does his part and it's all a beautiful thing. You both drink cheap champagne afterward, get good and drunk, and then make love with all the passion each of you can muster.

It's the day after the wedding when you realize just how terrified you are of losing this woman. There's a snorkeling trip off the beach you take with several other vacationers. You're each given the equipment and told to stay near the boat. Not a problem for you because you weren't crazy about this shit to start with. You went because Ann Marie loves this kind of adventure. You do get to see a barracuda about ten yards from where you're swimming, but you start to swallow water and that's more than enough of this horseshit for you. You want to see the wonders of the tropics bad enough, you'll buy a National fucking Geographic video.

You're up in the boat with one other vacationer who isn't thrilled about being shark bait either, and it's a good half hour before the rest of the snorkeling fools climb aboard, except there's one still out there and you can't find her. The panic begins as you see the skipper of the boat is preparing to leave. You yell at him to wait and then she appears off the back of the boat. You want to yell at her but you can't because you're so grateful she's back, you hug and kiss her.

"Wasn't that beautiful?" she says.

"Not really, but you are," you tell her.

"Good answer," the wife of another vacationer says.

"Please never do that to me again."

She looks at you like you're nuts.

That night you can't stop touching the freckles on her back as you make love. It is making love again, the furthest thing in the world from fucking, and there's no substitute for that.

Taking a ride ...

You're out of the criminal business more than a year when your ex-partner calls and asks you to take a ride with him.

"Sure," you say.

"I'll pick you up in half an hour."

"No problem."

You tell Ann Marie you're taking a ride with your ex-partner somewhere, but she's a nervous wreck.

"Where? Why? What if something happens?"

You calm her down and kiss her goodbye, but it's clear she doesn't want you to go. As it turns out, it's a weird, but fun trip to a wealthy neighborhood. Your ex-partner is going to collect some coin from one of his customers, a guy whose family owns a moving company. The guy is a dick, but a wealthy one. Why he's borrowing from your ex-partner escapes you completely, but when you pull up to a mansion with an L-shaped garage with 12 separate doors for 12 separate cars, there are several beautiful topless woman running around a built-in pool. There's loud music and a ton of booze. You wait in the car to avoid any temptations.

When your ex-partner returns to the car half-an-hour later, the guy he collected from is following him with a box of cheap cosmetics. He offers you some for free, but you turn it down. Your partner takes the box, puts it in the back of the car, and then hugs his customer. The guy whispers something in your ex-partner's ear and then you're asked if you want a few minutes with one of the beautiful topless women. There are two waving from the driveway.

"No thanks," you say.

"You sure?" your ex-partner says. "The one in the blue gives great head."

"No, thanks," you say. "I should get back."

The drive back home is hilarious as your ex-partner tells you the story behind the moron borrowing money from him. Turns out the guy's brother works in the office while the knucklehead borrowing the money works one of the 25 moving trucks they own. He sells weed and other

shit off the truck and is always in need of extra cash for short periods
of time. They work a straight deal, five grand for 45 hundred over the
course of a month.

The family business is worth millions and the knucklehead is risking
it all to sell weed. You can't believe the stupidity of some people, but it's
also a good subject for a potential crime novel someday. You consider it
as your partner proceeds to tell you how he usually meets the guy in
the city, but since the knucklehead's family is in Europe on vacation, he's
turned the mansion they live in into a bordello.

"You think the ones at the pool were crazy?" he says. "Inside there were
two just as beautiful eating each other on the living room rug. And the
moron was getting a blow job while he counted the cash he was paying
me."

It's the kind of shit classified as stranger than fiction.

Two blocks from where you live, your ex-partner tries to give you a
hundred bucks, but you refuse it. It's an offer back into the life you want
nothing to do with. He thanks you for making the trip he really didn't
need extra muscle for and you tell him you're available anytime he
needs you, but not for money. You know he's too generous to ask again,
so that part of your life really is over.

When you return to the apartment, your wife is still a nervous wreck.
When you tell her what it was all about, you leave out the offer for a
blowjob, but tell her pretty much everything else, including your ex-
partner's offer. She's glad you said no and tells you straight out how
much she likes your ex-partner, but that she's glad that part of your life
is over. She couldn't handle another episode like you taking a ride.

"I thought they were going to kill you," she says.

"What?" you say.

"I thought they were pissed off at you for leaving."

"I told you that wasn't going to happen. I was a certified nobody,
certainly nobody to fear. Besides, they made money with my exit. Why
would they care?"

"I was still afraid," she says. "Please don't do it again."

"I won't have to, trust me. That's movie bullshit."

Her eyes water and her lips quiver and you know you could never
disappoint her returning to that part of your past again.

The Big Dodge ...

Two years after you're married on that beach in the Bahamas, and just six months after your first novel is published, most of the team you were under is swept up in a major bust. Half of them make deals with the government to testify against the other half. The big shot who spoke up for you also goes away, except he never gives up anybody and has to do ten years.

The dominoes keep dropping after the deals are cut and people you know are in the newspaper almost every week. Some of them you knew were full of shit when they used terms like "rat bastards" or "fuckin' rats." They were the first to flip. Others you weren't sure about surprised you and never flinched. They turned down the government deals and were sent to prisons, some for very long stretches.

You dodged a bullet because although you weren't anywhere near important enough to go after, there was always the chance your name might pop up. Some street guys unfamiliar with the penal system aren't as anxious to experience it as portrayed in the movies. They will say anything to cut a deal. The bottom line is once somebody goes down, nobody is safe. Two years out of the game, there's nothing anybody could say about you the law would care about. You've been one lucky motherfucker and nobody knows it more than you.

Your ex-partner escaped the mess, and when he invites you to his son's baptism party a month from the invitation, you forget to show up. Your wife reminds you about the missed party, but you're still thinking an envelope will solve the problem. As it turns out, it's a bigger offense than you realize. Your wife was right, you insulted your ex-partner and that's the end of that relationship. Even when you try to do the right thing and call to apologize, his wife picks up and says she'll give him the message, but there's never a return call.

A much smarter street rabbi tells you what you need to know. "Maybe he's doing you a favor. Maybe it's for the best."

All of those friendships and associations are in the rear view mirror and fading. There are one or two you maintain, because you truly love them for who they were and are. Your street rabbi, for one, who never steered you wrong and was more than generous with the fifty sheet he gave you. It came at a time when everybody else was running quarter sheets, but he liked you enough to make the running around worth your while.

And he's always been there for advice and for a dinner date. He'll call you from time to time, even when he's had a few, just to relive old times and to tell you he loves you. You tell him you love him back and mean it.

You'd still take a ride with your ex-partner if he ever called, but for whatever reason, maybe because you write novels that ultimately denounce the mob for what it is, he never makes the call. You understand the position he's in and let it go.

From time to time you wonder about the people you used to associate with and how they're surviving the long prison sentences. Do they regret the choices they made? Did they have choices? Some you know never did have a choice. They'd been brought up in the life, knew nothing different, and to do otherwise was to be disowned. Others went more than willingly, because it was the only ounce of respect they believed they could obtain in this life, the delusional respect that comes from fear.

Justice has avoided so much of your world, and you've certainly avoided it. When you consider the shit you've gotten away with, you often find it hypocritical to demand justice for others, except there are criminals who never seem to pay the price, especially those wearing suits. Whether they're corrupt politicians or corrupt business people, somehow they're immune from prosecutions.

There's a difference between simple street justice and the kind that is hoped and prayed for, the justice from a God that doesn't exist. You're not interested in the punishments a manmade God might deliver in some fantasy afterlife.

"They'll pay for it when they die," some say. "They'll have to answer to God someday. Jesus will be waiting for them."

You know it doesn't matter, not for the sense of justice you need to see. Or is it vengeance you seek?

The good you do will never outweigh the bad, not to your mind, no matter how hard you try for an atonement of your sins.

The big dodge will keep you honest the rest of your life. You will reach out to help others because the guilt you carry is more than deserved and requires a lot more than any hope for a heaven you know doesn't exist. It is all about doing the right thing. It's never too late to do the right thing. At the very least, you learned that much.

The Prosecution Rests ...

You and your wife are working two jobs each to save for a house. One afternoon, after working a double night shift at a law firm in Manhattan, you are exhausted and fall into a deep sleep. A series of

THE VOICES IN MY HEAD

anxiety dreams eventually lands you on a witness stand in a courtroom at 100 Centre Street in Manhattan. It's you alone on the stand and a judge whose face you can't make out. He or she is sitting behind the bench with a big pitcher of water and a glass you can see. He or she is wearing a robe and shuffling papers. You hear a gavel pounding and a court clerk, another person you can't make out, suddenly appears and says, "Stella vs. Stella. All rise."

You say, "Isn't that out of order? Aren't you supposed—"

"Shush," the judge says. The voice sounds masculine.

You know better than to fuck with a judge. Judges and cops you obey, not because you want to, because they have power they'd never have out of uniform, and they can make your life miserable. Much like the times you've had to deal with cops feeling their power and getting loud, when you wished you could slap them in the face, you didn't then and you don't now. You shut up.

The judge says, "You two, are you ready to proceed?"

Suddenly there's Justo and St. Patrick. They stand from behind the prosecution table.

"Si," Justo says.

"Yeah, yeah," St. Patrick says, very dismissively.

"And for the defense?" the judge says.

"The Eejit will be representing himself," St. Patrick says.

"Is that right?" the judge asks you.

"I guess so," you say.

He turns to the prosecution table. "Proceed," he says.

St. Patrick stands, faces you and says. "Money, the root of all evil. The belief that success comes from the accumulation of wealth."

"Capitalismo," Justo interjects.

"One at a time," the judge says.

St. Patrick continues. "Isn't it true, Eejit, that you've spent a good deal of your pathetic life not only believing that, but also pursuing money?"

You shrug.

"Answer the question," the judge says.

"I guess, yeah, but—"

"It's a yes or no question, knuckle-dragger. You don't get to blame your father or anybody else. Let me refresh your brain dead memory. 'Maybe Thomas Rocco, for all the wrong reasons, was right after all?' Remember thinking that?"

"Yeah."

"And now you expect us to believe you've learned your lesson. Is that it?"

You consider giving him some shit back but don't. "Yes," you say.

"Because you give to charities and whine on Facebook for the greater good, black lives matter, and everything else under a socialist umbrella."

"I do give to charities. Palestinians, Holocaust survivors, animal shelters. Go Fund Me pages for the sick. Yeah, I do."

"Go Fund Me pages for people with health conditions they can't afford? You think that absolves you, do you?"

"No, but—"

"Try and follow the program, moron. Yes or no?"

You want to throw something at him, but don't. "No."

"There's no absolution from some of what you've done, what you've been, is there?"

"I didn't kill anybody."

"Who asked you if you killed anybody, Eejit?"

"Never mind."

"Right, never mind. And how about forcing your kid to move back to Brooklyn before he was done with school?"

"I fucked up."

"Yeah, you did."

"I know."

"And?"

"I can't change it now."

"No, you can't. Nor can giving to charities help you. Or giving to animal shelters. Or forking coin over on Go Fund—"

"Okay," you say. "I know. I fucking know."

"And now that you're this reformed greater good socialist, do you intend to remain that way or fuck it up, as you're wont to do?"

You've had enough. "I'll tell you what I'm wont to do right now, Bogtrotter. I'm wanting to knock your teeth out about now."

St. Patrick turns to the Judge. "Permission to treat the Eejit as hostile, your honor?"

"Permission granted."

"Okay, you ignorant wop, have you made amends with your kids yet?"

"I've tried."

"No luck?"

"I can't speak for them."

"How about the wives you cheated on?"

"I'm sure they hate me."

"Have you made amends with them?"

"I don't see how I can."

"And your crime victims? What about them?"

You shake your head no.

"Speak up, you ignorant Dago. Yes or—"

"No!"

St. Patrick sits and Justo stands.

"Did you ever read the manifesto, pendejo?"

"Yes. More than once."

"Das Kapital?"

"That was some difficult shit, but I tried. I never finished it."

"Puta. Are you now or have you ever been a member of the communist party?"

"No."

"Why not?"

"I don't believe in joining political parties or any other groups."

"Like the Mafia?"

"Right, like them."

"Because?"

"Because it's bullshit. It's group think. Total bullshit."

"Yet you call yourself a socialist. Isn't that a political party?"

"Not for me. I didn't join the socialist party. I never paid dues or committed to them on paper. For me it's a concept. I believe in the concept of socialism."

"Concept how? What?"

You don't know how it comes out of your mouth, but it does.

"The beatitudes."

"Nice," St. Patrick says. "Have a clue what they are, Dago?"

You nod slowly, then say them: "Blessed are the poor in spirit, for theirs is the Kingdom of Heaven. Blessed are those who mourn, for they will be comforted. Blessed are the meek, for they will inherit the Earth. Blessed are those who hunger and thirst for righteousness, for they will be filled. Blessed are the merciful, for they will be shown mercy. Blessed are the pure in heart, for they will see God. Blessed are the peacemakers, for they will be called children of God. Blessed are those who are persecuted because of righteousness, for theirs is the Kingdom of Heaven. Blessed are you when people insult you, persecute you and falsely say all kinds of evil against you because of me. Rejoice and be glad, because great is your reward in heaven, for in the same way they persecuted the prophets who were before you."

"I'm impressed," St. Patrick says.

"Me too," the judge says.

Justo winks at you and says, "Like Jesus, no?"

"Like Jesus, yes."

"Like Che."

"Don't be an idiot," St. Patrick tells Justo.

"We done here?" the judge says.

"Si," Justo says. "The prosecution rests."

The judge turns to you. "Anything else, Eejit?"

You're surprised at the name calling, but don't think to look up and see St. Patrick holding the gavel. You're stuck in neutral knowing you don't have a defense. You're guilty and you know it. You have nothing but what you feel in your heart for all your indiscretions and the pain you've caused others.

You tell them, "I'm sorry."

The judge is back. He turns to the prosecution table where St. Patrick has rejoined Justo. The judge looks down as his papers, then turns to the clerk, and then back to the prosecution again.

"Case dismissed," he says.

The voice in your head ...

You're sitting in a nursing home awaiting your mother's last breath. She's close to the end of a death rattle that leaves you helpless. You want to talk with her one last time but that can't happen. The nursing home called you at work when she first went unconscious. You drove there as fast as you could, but were too late to tell her one more time how much you love her and how sorry you are for all the extra shit you've added to her life.

Several hours pass, during which you can't help but reflect on what this woman has gone through from the time she was married to Thomas Rocco. The good times were far outdone by the bad. The loss of love, her homes, at times her sanity and self-esteem. The loss of her parents and two sisters. The shit you put her through being a lunatic in desperate need of what she couldn't possibly provide because she wasn't your father. The loss of her daughter to cancer way too young. The estrangement between you with your youngest, the child she felt she needed to protect the way she needed to protect you. The last six years of a life spent in a bed because her legs no longer worked.

Your aunt, her only surviving sister arrives, and you hug and cry again. She sits on one side of the bed, you on the other. She tells you funny stories about their past growing up in Greenwich Village, the apartment where four sisters and their parents lived above a bakery, and how there was always food on the table, no matter how poor they were. She reminds you about the times your mother pushed the envelope by arguing with your grandfather, how their sister Vincenza once threatened a woman bully who had given their mother shit at her job and how the bully apologized and swore she'd never do it again. You remember your Aunt Vinny. She was the toughest of the four sisters.

Your aunt tells you a story you've heard dozens of times about the day your grandfather caught your mother on line to see Sinatra instead of going to school, and how she caught a beating for it. She reminds you about your mother and their oldest sister, Josephine, and how they played cards and always argued over the pennies they were playing for. And then she tells you how your mother admitted to finally going to bed with a man other than Thomas Rocco, the guy you disliked the most, the one who tried to tell you to not to walk around in your underwear.

"Really, ma?" you say, as if she can hear you. "That asshole?"

Her breathing is labored and every once in a while you stare at her the way you stared at your sister during her last few minutes of life. You don't want to see the light of this woman's eyes die after she takes her last breath, so you focus on her chest while holding her hand.

For all the fond memories your aunt has with her sister, memories only siblings can have, the weight of the guilt you feel is overwhelming. You could never atone for the lifetime of anguish she'd gone through, so much of which you feel directly responsible for.

Maybe if you had been a better son, someone Thomas Rocco could be proud of ...

Maybe if early on you weren't an epic day dreamer and had studied like your sister ...

Maybe ...

You know it's self-pity, yet you still hate yourself for shooting down the times she asked you if you thought Thomas Rocco was ever sorry for leaving.

"No," you used to say. "He knew exactly what he was doing. He was a selfish piece of shit."

How hard would it have been to lie and say, "Yeah, Ma, I think so. I think he still loved you in the end. I think he was sorry he left."

Or was it your own feeling of vulnerability you were protecting and couldn't lie about? Was it because you believed that you and your mother were the ones he couldn't love? Was it because you convinced yourself it was the only way to move on, to deny what you somehow knew was true, that he did love you, albeit in his way?

Your aunt is talking to you when you notice your mother has stopped breathing. You squeeze her hand and look to your aunt and say, "She's gone."

The two of you stand up and meet at the end of the bed. You hug and cry together. You each kiss your mother's forehead before spending a few more minutes alone with her. When you go out to the front desk to tell them she's passed, the nurse tells you she's very sorry, then leaves her station to attend to your mother.

You'd been in her room before, two and three times a week over the six year period she'd been there. Mostly you teased her about praying or sleeping, to make her curse and then laugh. You had a routine you're sure she enjoyed as much as you did.

"That bunt or steal?" you'd say when catching her making the sign of the cross while doing her rosary beads.

"Wake up, woman, I brought the donuts," you'd say to wake her.

You'd sit in the chair, lean over and hold up a hand and say, "Wait a second, Ma," before you farted and she called you a moron.

You'd tease her about any number of things to get her frustrated and to finally tell you to "Go shit in your hat, Sonny."

There were so many good times you shared together, but nothing could ever compare to the night of your sister's memorial when that picture of you and your sister was flashed on the screen and you lost it. For all the issues between you and your sibling, they disappeared in that instant. She was smiling in the picture, and it was what you had craved your entire life.

And when you lost it and turned to bury your head in your mother's lap, the crying she'd done for the loss of her child was mitigated by her instinct to care for you. You felt her hand on the back of your head and were comforted at a time when she was the one who should have been comforted. She'd always been your protector. She'd always put her children first.

The voice in your head becomes singular at your mother's side. It tells you everything will be okay. Everything will be fine.

"Don't cry, piccolo Gesù."

EPILOGUE

*"The soul takes flight to the world that is invisible but there
arriving she is sure of bliss and forever dwells in paradise."*
Plato

Dystopia Americano (Estados Unidos) ...

You once watched a documentary on the life of Pablo Escobar and liked
the Hispanic pronunciation of United States, so you've taken to
mimicking it when you remember to, and you seem to remember it most
when St. Patrick is around.

*"Hey, numb-nuts," he says, waking you in the midst of one of your couch
catnaps. "We've places to be."*

"Estados Unidos?" you say.

"Eejit," he says. "I'm serious. Get your ass up and follow me."

*You don't want to, you were happy dreaming again. You were walking
along the Jones Beach boardwalk, holding hands with Ann Marie and
stopping to breathe in her summer smell, a scent that will stay with you
forever. No flower in the world smells as good as your woman during a
summer day.*

You pressed your lips to her neck and breathe in deep as you kiss her.

*Unfortunately, St. Patrick's interruption takes you to a hell, and you
find yourself standing in the middle of what used to be Rockaway
Parkway, between Avenue N and Seaview Avenue, back in your home
town of Canarsie, Brooklyn. The sky is a blackish-grey, and there's a
putrid smell in the air you don't recognize as death. You do have to hold
your nose as you slowly turn around and take in a horrific vision. A
flattened wasteland of what used to be one and two family homes and
stores surrounds you. All of the former structures are rubble. The streets
are piled with it. Everything is charred from what must've been one hell
of a fire.*

*You head toward the Bayview Projects and Canarsie Pier to see if there
are signs of life there, but the projects are gone. What used to be a large
development of 23 eight-story apartment buildings has been turned
into 23 small mountains of blackened brick and twisted metal. Where
there was flat land there is blackened land, either ash from all the fires
that must've consumed the town, or the residue of long time dust*

accumulations. The stench of what has to be the dead fills the air.

You continue your walk toward the water to see if anything there has survived, all the while searching left and right for someone, anyone.

You wonder if this is the Twilight Zone episode where a voracious reader survives a nuclear war because he was in a bank vault, but then stepped on his own glasses once he was back outside on the steps of a library. You check to make sure your glasses are safe on your head. You nervously touch them to make sure.

By the time you reach what was the Canarsie Pier, you've figured out what you're observing is in fact the result of a nuclear war. The problem is you have no idea how much of the rest of the land is in the same shape, or if anyone else has survived.

"And what makes you think you survived, Eejit?"

You turn and look for him, but St. Patrick isn't showing himself. "I'm here," you say. "Ain't I, jerk-off?"

"You're long dead when this comes about, you ignorant wop, although it really isn't that long ago. Less than a hundred years from your fall."

"My fall?"

"Your death, moron."

"You know, sometimes I wish you were real again, just so I could knock one of your Mick teeth down your throat."

"Ha, Eejit," St. Patrick says. "You'd only feel like shit twenty seconds later. Get over yourself, you weren't meant to be the asshole you sometimes were."

"What the fuck happened here?"

"What's it look like, genius?"

"Nuclear war."

"Once again, how MENSA missed you is a fookin' mystery."

"So, who won? Who started it? When did it go down?"

"If I charged by the question, Dago, I'd be a wealthy ghost."

"Yeah, but you'd still be a potato head."

"Eejit. This is the year 2062, but there were other nuclear wars before this one. The big boys were playing a game of tag with nukes. They started on protectorates, if you will. Surrogates too. Puerto Rico, the Ukraine, the Middle East, but it escalated pretty fast after those."

"Who fired first?"

"First time it was America. First two times. Then it was Russia. Then Israel. Then Iran. Then North Korea. South Korea, believe it or not, but China was involved in that one too. Finally it was a free for all, Pakistan, India, everybody who had one. Smoke'm if you got'em."

"Why? Why would they do that?"

"Ha, as if you didn't know. Where else was mankind heading? One of

Israels did this. They had nukes in Eastern Africa where they'd been put along with the relocation of their Government. That strip of land they seized and turned into an open air jail went up with their mainland. Didn't take but three nukes to do it, too. When you think about it, we bombed ourselves. By the end it was allies be damned. Was all against all."

"It's crazy. Why? Why would this happen?"

"I have to say it again? Where else was man heading with his technology and fake nationalism and the tribal bullshit that has gone on forever? Suffice it to say, it was only a matter of time before the prophecy of a MAD theory came to be."

"Mutually assured destruction," you say.

"It sure was."

"Anybody survive? Anywhere, I mean."

"Sure, but it's a Cormac McCarthy novel now. Tribes are what're left, and they're all over the place. It's a race for survival and/or extinction now. You want nothing to do with this, boyo."

"So, I'm here why, to chat with you? You feel lonely, you donkey fuck?"

"Workin' on that one a long time, were you?"

"Come on, what's up? I was with my lady on the boardwalk at Jones Beach. I was taking in her summer smell, and then you brought me to this shit."

"The smell of death."

"Why'd you take me away from her?"

"You were dreaming, Eejit."

At that you huff.

"Hold your horses, Eejit. I can use a breather myself. This stink."

"Jesus fuckin'—"

"It's like The Hunger Games now, except there's nobody watching from up in some bubble. You didn't see the movie, so let's just say it's dog-eat-dog from here out."

"What movie?"

"Forget it. It's survival now. And if the race doesn't survive, the cockroaches take over, which they will, it's inevitable."

"If there are survivors, why wouldn't the race build back up?"

"Because man can't help himself, yeah? It's only a matter of time before whoever is left figures out it's good to be king. And when that happens, it'll be mini-wars to fuck all."

"Okay, so what am I doing here?"

"Getting a taste."

"A taste of what?"

"What you'd once wished for. Equal justice, eh?"

"*I don't understand.*"

"*Because you're an Eejit. You think the oligarchs running the world let themselves get caught in a nuclear holocaust? No, right. So what they did was find safe havens to survive, but where those are, there are others, the usual peasants. You're going to lead the peasants in a revolution against the oligarchs.*"

"*Seriously?*"

"*Not at all, ya moron Dago, but I just told you what happens to the oligarchs. Thought they were smart, wound up dinner for those in need of meat. Just rewards, eh?*"

"*Does it really end like this?*"

"*How'd you think it would end, knuckle-dragger? Big bombas, to use your newfound love of Hispanic pronunciation. It ended with big bombas, followed by sickness and viruses with nobody around to counteract them. The last poor bastard to go down? Guess what his last words are?*"

"*Fuck you?*"

"*Rosebud. Was all he could remember because he'd just watched the movie.*"

"*Huh?*"

St. Patrick shakes his head and leaves. You blink and are returned to your catnap, from which you feel something moist on your lips. Is it a puppy licking your face?

You touch your lips and come away with a spot of blood from your mouth. You remember the dream, the dystopia, and begin to mourn for lives that will be lost because there's no stopping the inevitability of human self-destruction.

Il sogno di Dio (In the Presence of the Lord, Part Deux) ...

You're close to your own end when you hear the mumblings of a conversation somewhere in the back of your mind. All those crevices you see in pictures of human brains that look like tightly packed intestines are really the caves and tunnels leading to the core, no bigger than a peanut, no matter what they tell you. It's a mini-sun, the spark from which energy flows to the various parts of the brain, the hemispheres and all its lobes of the cerebrum, its grey and white matter, the hidden cerebellum, and the brainstem leading to the spinal cord.

It is the core of life, not Jesus nor his father, and how that core came to be is irrelevant. The words of the conversation you can make out are those once attributed to Friedrich Nietzsche: "*Enjoy life. This is not a dress rehearsal.*"

Way back when you first started cleaning windows for a living, you stepped onto a ledge at 10 East 53rd Street to try and clean the outside of a corner office's French windows. As was already stated, you were the proverbial dumbass worker putting his job ahead of his life.

Remember?

In time you would learn such risks were nothing more than stupid, but that morning, about 4:30 a.m. or so, you literally climbed out of a window with a 15-floor drop to a courtyard below. They were windows you'd never be able to reach.

No one's past should ever be dismissed in its entirety, not according to the justice you want to believe in. Sooner or later, everybody has to pay. You've been guilty of way too much over the course of your life to be granted unfettered absolution, and finding Ann Marie at just the right time to keep you from going to jail has proved nothing short of a miracle you don't deserve. She's the priest who bought Valjean's soul for God and you will owe the rest of your life to doing the right thing because of her.

Because you're guilty of so much you haven't begun to pay for yet, you do what comes natural and panic about the wave of bad that has to happen to you sooner or later. Mostly it has to do with Ann Marie and your kids, and a nightmare scenario where one or more of them would be taken from you by some disease or tragedy before you get to die first. So you return to performing your nightly prayer, pleading for whatever bad that has to happen, happen only to you.

And one night after repeating your personal prayer ... *you dream something that couldn't be more real. A morning when you do slip from the same window ledge at 10 East 53rd Street and fall into the abyss of that courtyard 15 floors below. There is a thud you could hear but can't feel, a warm flow of liquid behind your head, and darkness that slowly turns to a very bright and blinding light. You swear you've passed into the beyond when a woman in white with long dark hair stands directly above you and smiles.*

You recognize her and say, "Alanis?"

The woman in white responds telepathically. The smile never leaves her face.

"It's okay."

"Am I dead?"

"Everyone is."

"Was it the fall?"

"It was."

You try to see beyond her but can't, the brightness remains blinding.

"You're really God? Not just in the movie?"

"For you."

You begin to sob until it becomes uncontrollable. You kneel at her feet, and she puts a reassuring hand on your head.

"I have so many questions."

"Everyone does."

"I don't know what to say, where to begin."

"No one does."

"I'm so sorry."

"Everyone is."

"For everything."

"I know."

"How do I ... what can I ...?"

"There was justice."

"When? How?"

"It happened."

"Was it a test? Our lives. Are they tests?"

"They were lives."

"Du allein weisst was es bedeutet," you say. "Am I speaking in tongues?"

She shakes her head. "That was a note Gustav Mahler left on his tenth symphony to his wife. It had to do with a funeral march, what he believed might be the end of his marriage and his life."

You're confused, but she calms you again by touching your head.

Suddenly there's a cloud alongside her and you can make out Alan Rickman, the Dogma version, St. Patrick and Justo.

"Hey," you say to Alan Rickman.

"Hey," he says.

You turn to St. Patrick. "Potato head," you say.

"Wop," he says.

"Pendejo," Justo says.

"Little Che," you say.

"You weren't kidding," you say to Alan Rickman.

"Never, Little Jesus."

"Is this it, though? Am I really dead?"

"Everyone is," Alanis says, still smiling as she fades away.

"I'll do the communicating from here in," Alan Rickman says.

You turn to him. "I can't believe it's Alanis Morrisette."

"To you. To someone else it could be B.B. King or Mozart, Steinbeck, Willie Mays, or Fitty Cent. The loving father of his children. To each his own."

"Is there a resurrection?"

"More or less."

"All at once, for everyone?"

"Each in their own way."
You pause a moment. *"What about my sister and father? Them too?"*
"More or less."
"And people like Hitler? Don't tell me that prick got a pass."
"He did love animals, his dog and so on. He was a vegetarian."
"That's some fucked-up shit."
Alan Rickman shrugs.
"Is there music?" you ask. *"I miss that. At least tell me there's music. And
can I pick my own?"*
"You already have."
The vibrato from Mahler's second symphony, The Resurrection, *begins.*

What You Wish For At The End ...

An epic daydream can last but a few seconds and cover a lifetime.

Floating, head to tail, diagonal in flight. Winter cool fills the soul, a
scent of pine, a freshly blown snow, an ocean mist. Blue before white
before blue; cool becomes warm becomes cool again. Soaring, breathing,
swooping left, swooping right, swooping down through pillows of cloud.
Shadows on pastoral turn to dots. The vertical pull gains strength
with distance, and the tiny lights ahead are silver sparklers.

Most left behind won't notice while some are left crying, heartfelt sobs
of longing for what was, what could have been, what should have been.
A force so sudden and great the sparklers of light make way, some falling
off the edge into oblivion, their judgment day.

And there's a soprano's voice reassuring a life not lived in vain.

O glaube: Du warst nicht umsonst geboren!
(O believe, You were not born for nothing!)

Hast nicht umsonst gelebt, gelitten!
(Have not for nothing, lived, suffered!)

The bells chime through drum rolls, between the horns and the
strings to the diminuendo ... and the tuba, restoring the life affirming
crescendo, your resurrection.